NIGHT MUSIC

Other books by Lilli Palmer

Change Lobsters and Dance
The Red Raven
A Time to Embrace

Lilli Palmer
Night Music

HARPER & ROW, PUBLISHERS, New York
Cambridge, Philadelphia, San Francisco,
1817 London, Mexico City, São Paulo, Sydney

FIRST U.S. EDITION

Library of Congress Cataloging in Publication Data

Palmer, Lilli.
  Night music.

  Translation of: Nachtmusik.
  I. Title.
PT2631.A36N313   1982   833'.914   82-48148
ISBN 0-06-015105-6

83 84 85 86 87 10 9 8 7 6 5 4 3 2 1

NIGHT MUSIC

PART ONE

Stilts

CHAPTER ONE

EARLY in the morning of 10 May 1977, Draza Rukovina, night porter at the Hotel Godice in Bled, was found dead in his little cubicle in the lobby. He was lying quite peacefully in his deckchair, an empty bottle of red wine beside him on a stool. He wasn't that old, seventy at the most, no one knew for sure, and he had no relatives. Consternation in the hotel. Now of all times, just when the season was beginning! The old man was irreplaceable; in all Yugoslavia you'd never find anyone who could speak the various Slav dialects plus fluent French and English. German was no problem; plenty of people had learned German during the war or brushed up what they remembered from their parents, for until World War 1 Bled had been called Veldes and belonged to Austria.

What now? For the time being two modern-language students from nearby Ljubljana were hired, but they spent the night asleep on the floor of the cubicle, stretched out side by side, no matter how severely they were reprimanded. The old man had always been awake, always available for long palavers or advice or reassurance. That's what you expected from a night porter: good manners and a certain international quality, not a Yugoslavian one. Above all you needed sympathy, more so than from a day porter, because the tourists' need for support began its upward curve around midnight and peaked at about three a.m. Father confessor, psychiatrist or pimp – that was old Draza. They had never really appreciated him and now there he was, dead.

But it was not only the nocturnal activities of the Hotel Godice that were transformed by the old man's death. It also had a decisive – though not immediate – impact on the life of a man named Kaspar Schulte, who lived three hundred miles away in West Germany and knew nothing about Bled except that it was said to be a beautiful place on a small lake somewhere in northern Yugoslavia.

Schulte did not learn the exact date of Draza's death, 10 May 1977, until much later, and then only by accident. He took it as evidence of a constellation of events designed for him alone.

For another event took place on that day, something not dissimilar, but this one disrupted Schulte's whole life instantaneously. You might say that Draza's death had been the first blow – even though he didn't know about it – and now came the second.

This one occurred in a lay-by off the Munich–Salzburg *autobahn*, just before the Tegernsee exit. A small Volkswagen was driven in rather jerkily and came to a stop beside an old Opel. From the half-open window of the Opel came the sound of music. The driver of the Volkswagen was a young fellow who had passed his driving test that very day and was making his first solo run on the *autobahn*. He wished somebody could have been watching as he applied the hand-brake and switched off the ignition like an old hand. But the Opel was the only other car in the lay-by and the woman leaning over the steering-wheel was listening to the music and paid no attention to him.

The young man disappeared into the bushes, returned and climbed back into his Volkswagen. From the other car came the *Rosenkavalier* waltz, and he leaned back to enjoy it for a moment before starting the engine. As he slowly reversed, he noticed that the woman was still in the same position, slumped over the steering-wheel. He stopped, rolled down his window and called out: 'Hello!'

The woman didn't move.

'Hello! Are you all right?'

Silence. He switched off the ignition, got out and walked over to the half-open window. 'Excuse me, do you need any help?' Now that he was standing close beside her, she seemed strangely inert. Cautiously he reached inside and touched her shoulder. 'I say . . .'

No reaction. He couldn't see her face, only the back of her head and her short brown hair. He hesitated for a few seconds, then opened the car door – and the woman's body uncoiled, slid out of the seat and collapsed at his feet.

'For God's sake!' he exclaimed, jumping backwards. He looked around. On the *autobahn* car after car went rushing by. There were people sitting in every one of them, but would they stop? He knelt beside the motionless heap of rumpled clothes and tried to turn the upper part of her body so that he could put his head against her chest. It was as warm as his own and he thought he could hear something beating, though he wasn't sure. At that moment a car pulled into the lay-by and came to an abrupt stop.

4

'Hey, you! What's going on?' called the driver, opening his door.

The young man looked up in a daze. 'This woman . . . I don't know . . . is she sick or . . .?'

The newcomer, a robust man of about forty in a loud checked jacket, got out, followed hesitantly by a plump little woman in a green hat. Suspicious and slightly disgusted they glanced at the figure on the ground.

'Do you know her?'

'No. She fell out of her car.'

'When?'

'Just now.'

'Have you done anything about it?'

'What – what should one do?'

'Call the police, man.'

'But where from? How . . .'

'Over there. The emergency phone. Oh, for God's sake! You stay here, I'll do it.' He walked over to the orange telephone stand at the entrance to the lay-by; the green hat trotted along behind him. As he slid back the cover of the telephone box, he muttered crossly: 'What the hell are you doing here? Get back over there and see if you can help. Go on.' But she wouldn't budge.

When they returned, the young man was holding the woman's head in his lap and stroking her hair from time to time.

'Is she just unconscious or . . .?'

'I don't know,' said the young man without looking up.

'Oh well. Anyhow the police are coming – and an ambulance. They won't be long. You stay here, right? You have to make a statement to the police, you're a witness. I've got the number of your car, see? You can't just run off.'

'I've no intention of running off,' said the young man.

'Well, you never know. Anyway, I've got your number. We must push off now, we're in a hurry. Sorry.'

'Sorry,' murmured the green hat. They walked quickly back to their car.

The first to arrive was a policeman on a motorcycle. The young man was still kneeling on the ground, holding the woman's head in his lap.

'I think she's dead,' he said and quickly stroked her hair again, as if to comfort her for this bald statement.

The policeman knelt beside her, put his ear to her chest and raised her eyelid. He nodded, glanced at his watch and took out his notebook: first the registration number, then the young man's detailed statement, given with extraordinary precision, as if the fellow had recorded it in his head. Next he looked for the woman's handbag and found it on the passenger seat, with her driver's licence in her wallet.

'What's her name?' asked the young man.

'What? Oh. . . .' The policeman opened the wallet again. 'Martha Schulte.'

'Married?'

'Driver's licence doesn't say,' said the policeman, keeping his eye on the *autobahn*. Here it came at last, the ambulance.

'How old is she?'

'Why do you want to know?'

'She looks to me quite young.'

'Oh, come on,' said the policeman, but he pulled the wallet out of his pocket again. 'Born 1935. That makes her forty-two.'

'Impossible,' said the young man firmly.

The ambulance siren drowned the policeman's reply. He went quickly over to the driver and gave some instructions.

'Quite young,' insisted the young man from his position on the ground, although no one was listening. 'And very beautiful really, Fräulein Martha. But you're probably Frau Martha, aren't you? Yes, there's your wedding ring. You're the first dead person I've ever seen. I'll never forget you, you can be sure of that. But you've got to go now. Here they come with the stretcher. I'm glad it's a nice soft padded one. Goodbye, Frau Martha.

'What was that?' asked the white-clad ambulanceman, slipping one arm under Martha's shoulder as the other attendant took hold of her feet.

'I was just saying goodbye.'

The policeman mounted his motorcycle and called out: 'Hey, you! Herr . . . er . . .'

'Wegmann, Harold Wegmann.'

'You follow me in, okay? They'll need a statement from you at the hospital. It'll probably take an hour or so.'

'I don't mind. I mean, I can't just go off and leave her, can I?'

The policeman watched as he rose awkwardly to his feet, his legs stiff from kneeling so long on the asphalt.

'Let's go then.'

The motorcycle roared off onto the main road, but the young man stayed where he was, watching Martha being put into the ambulance like a loaf of bread into a baker's oven. He didn't care for the policeman; he'd follow the ambulance.

Kaspar Schulte unlocked his apartment door at 36 Gellerstrasse, second floor left. Six o'clock. The hallway was dark: Martha wasn't home yet. He switched on the light and hung up his hat. He never wore an overcoat; he enjoyed seeing his tall, lean silhouette reflected in shop windows, always topped by a hat, although as yet he had nothing to hide, for his dark-brown hair was still thick.

In the living-room it was still light enough to read the paper, which she always left for him on the coffee-table, carefully folded to look untouched. She read it in the morning, because he didn't take it to the Institute, where he never had time to look at it, either during lunch with his colleagues or during the fifteen-minute break between classes. He spent his breaks in an armchair in the faculty common-room, inert with his eyes closed, listening to his breathing. Twice a week, on Wednesdays and Fridays, he gave private lessons and on those days he didn't get home until about six, pretty exhausted. The Serbs and Croats, or an occasional Pole, to whom he taught German wore him out. Most of them were young and working-class and didn't know the first thing about the structure of another language. All they wanted was to find a factory job – fast. He sometimes wondered how they raised the money for private lessons with a professor of Slavic languages. He was expensive: fifty marks an hour. Probably the word had got around that he could train students like performing seals to the point where they could fill out a standard application form and get through an interview.

Today was Wednesday. He flopped down on the soft sofa cushions, opened the newspaper, reached for the bottle of whisky and the glass that Martha always left beside the paper, took his first sip and began to read the leading article.

The telephone rang. Must be one of Martha's friends. Let her call back when Martha was home. After a while it stopped ringing.

Ten minutes later it rang again. Damn! He didn't feel like getting up; he'd stood at the black-board all day, his long, not very athletic legs were tired. But when, ten minutes later, it rang a third time, he looked up. Perhaps it was something important – Werner or Stefan?

He struggled to his feet, holding the newspaper and walked into the adjoining room to his desk in the library. He picked up the receiver and murmured 'Hello', his eyes on the unfinished sentence.

Later, he often thought back to that sentence. It concerned a session of the European Common Market. 'According to a well-informed Brussels source . . .' At that point he had stood leaning against the desk with the receiver wedged between his shoulder and ear, his life still normal.

Then a voice said: 'Professor Schulte?'

'Yes,' he had replied, reading on: '. . . imperative to level the butter mountain.'

That had been the turning point, exactly when the expression 'butter mountain' had made him visualize a hill of little yellow butter-pats and a number of men sinking their shovels into the soft mess, an image he found mildly funny – though only for a fraction of a second because the blow followed immediately.

'Holzkirchen Regional Hospital calling. Emergency room . . .'

On the way to Holzkirchen he kept thinking of the butter-pats, as though everything might have been different if that hadn't amused him. He steered the car slowly through heavy traffic. No hurry, he'd be there soon enough. Before he arrived at the hospital, he had to find out exactly what he was feeling; he wanted to wear a specific expression on his face for the doctor – and for the boys. Would they be there by now? Perhaps they had already seen Martha. That would make it easier for him; he dreaded the moment when he would have to look at her. He imagined her lying in a silent room, the air full of grief and tears; but if the boys had already gone in, the first pain-barrier would already have been broken, so to speak.

He forced himself to think of Martha, nothing else but Martha, she deserved that, and every thought ought to begin with 'never again'. Never again would she talk to him, never again sit opposite him at the supper-table, never again would she look at him . . .

As a matter of fact, though, she had only rarely looked at him for a long time now, at least two years. She usually stared at her plate or looked out of the window and this had always made him feel uncomfortable. And guilty. Not disconcertingly so, still – quite a bit. He swung out into the *autobahn* wishing he had felt even more guilty beneath her gaze.

Nonsense. Martha was a sensible woman, not at all sentimental, a marvellous woman, quite unusual. She would never have stipulated that he wasn't to sleep with anyone else, would never have expected it. After twenty-four years! Of course she'd known about Heidi, most likely from the very start, and that was – what? Five years ago already, good Lord! But what else could she expect? He and Martha had had nothing going for ages. Oh, once in a while maybe, but nothing worth talking about. And she certainly didn't miss it, perhaps she even preferred it that way.

Balls! His nose was no cleaner than the noses of other men who cheat on their wives. The only odd thing about it was that Martha had never said a word, never alluded to it, never even smiled when he said he had a meeting that evening. She would just nod in a friendly way and, when he finally got home, she would be asleep.

No, not an accident, the doctor had said, heart failure, and that he was sure she hadn't suffered. Thank God for that. Martha . . . far too young to die. Would he cry? Could he still cry? It would be a good thing if he did, for the benefit of the boys, make up for some of the harm he'd done through the Heidi business. They knew about that, naturally, although they never said anything. Martha's children, close as clams, especially the younger one.

But he must concentrate on Martha. On good times with Martha. Honeymoon in Verona in 1954. They had found a lot to laugh at and went everywhere arm in arm, the way you're supposed to on a honeymoon. The nights had been very nice too; yes, they had been very nice, absolutely – but he had to force himself to remember them. Martha was dead; reminiscences of that sort were in poor taste at the moment.

He would like to be thinking about something specific when he got to the hospital, but what? About the last time he'd seen her? That would have been this morning. Where? Where exactly, so that he could fix the scene in his mind. He slowed down and replayed his departure that morning in reverse. Front door – he'd been alone there. Putting on his hat – no, the entrance hall had been empty. Back to the breakfast table. Yes, there she was, of course, sitting opposite him, drinking her coffee and eating a piece of toast with marmalade. So that must have been the last time he saw her: in the breakfast nook in the kitchen, with the daisy pattern of the wallpaper behind her head. How did she look? He tried to recapture the picture. A bit pale – but then she was always pale. Brown hair combed back – he was quite sure of that, Martha never came to breakfast with her hair uncombed. What did she have on? Her dressing-gown? Or was she already dressed? A blank, no matter how hard he tried. He had no 'last memories', only over-all impressions from years gone by.

He was now driving so slowly that a truck passed him. Had he kissed her before getting up from the breakfast table? Of course. He had leaned over and kissed her, as he always did, just a quick peck on the cheek. And now at last he felt something, and not only did he feel it, it attacked and overwhelmed him: violent, gnawing remorse.

CHAPTER TWO

THE DOCTOR was rushed and made no bones about it. Two new emergencies had been admitted in the meantime, both still alive: a child who had been run over and a young man stabbed in a bar. Martha had already been taken care of; the sons knew all the details. Where were they? Upstairs on the fourth floor.

'With my wife?'

'I suppose so. Goodbye then, Professor. Matron will give you all the technical information.'

The long corridor on the fourth floor was deserted except for Werner, who was leaning against the wall beside one of the doors.

'Where's Stefan?'

The young man gestured with his head towards the door. Aha! Half way across the pain-barrier.

'Have you been in?'

'I was waiting for you.'

My son, he thought. We wait for each other, we don't push.

'The doctor says you know what happened.'

'There's a fellow downstairs who'll tell you about it. He was there. He says he won't leave until he's talked to you.'

'Why?' asked Kaspar, suspicion and anxiety in his voice.

'He says he has to tell you. Nobody else will do.'

They looked past each other without speaking. No use putting it off any longer: he opened the door. The room was in darkness, the window wide open, letting in the last of the twilight. The right atmosphere, he thought, looking around for Stefan. Perhaps he would sound the right note for him, like a tuning-fork.

Stefan was sitting in a corner, looking out of the window rather than at the bed where Martha lay. She was wearing a hospital gown; her hands were joined but not clasped. Behind him Werner burst into uncontrolled sobbing. Kaspar and Stefan acted as if they didn't hear him.

The ward Sister knocked tactfully at the door.

'Professor Schulte, there's a young man named Harold Wegmann waiting downstairs. He's been here over two hours.'

'I'll come down.'

The long corridors and the staircase had that deathly stillness of
hospitals at night-time, so that their steps seemed to ring far too
conspicuously on the freshly polished floor.

The nurse opened the door to the waiting-room.

'Herr Wegmann? But why are you sitting in the dark? Here's
Professor Schulte. I expect you'd like to be alone.'

The young man, sitting in the farthest corner, quickly stood up.

'Herr Wegmann, I'm extremely grateful to you. I understand it
was you who found my wife.'

'Are you her husband?'

'Why do you sound so surprised?'

'You look so . . . so relaxed.'

'It only looks that way.'

The young man stared at him, probably the way he himself
stared at his students during examinations. Kaspar turned and
walked slowly towards a chair; Wegmann took another one a little
distance away.

'Please – er – tell me about it. I suppose you waited so long to
inform me personally – very kind of you, by the way.'

'No, I wanted to see you. I was curious.'

'About me? Why?'

'I wanted to know what her husband was like. I'd already seen
her children. They fit.'

'And I don't?'

'Well – I expected somebody quite different – I hope you don't
mind my saying so.'

'Different in what way?'

'Not so – suave.'

'Suave? My suit is nine years old, shiny at the knees, as you can
see. The tie is a Christmas present from my students. A bit loud.'

'That's not what I meant.'

'What do you mean?'

The young man didn't answer and looked upset.

'My appearance is deceptive. Don't let that worry you. I don't
like it either. Do go on.'

'I've already given all the facts to the policeman and the doctor.
They've got it in writing. It isn't much, because she was already

dead when I found her. I just wanted you to know that I stayed with her the whole time so she wasn't alone, and I'm sure she knew it.'

'Knew what?'

'That she was lying with her head in my lap and that it was a tremendous experience for me . . . if you'll forgive me.' Since Kaspar didn't answer, he went on: 'I'm sure she was glad not to be alone. That must be the hardest time, those first few minutes immediately after you've died, don't you think so?'

Kaspar remained silent.

'She was quite warm, so there was still something left of her. I'm not religious, you know, I don't believe that she's somewhere up there now.' He pointed through the window to the evening sky. 'But there must be some kind of crossing over and I helped her with it.'

'How?'

'By concentrating on her. Do you understand?'

'Yes,' said Kaspar, envying the young man. After a short pause he added, 'Perhaps . . . perhaps you'd like to come over to our flat some time. We would like to thank you properly. Do you have our address?' He said 'we' and 'our flat' although the boys hadn't lived there for several years.

'It's in the book, I looked it up for the doctor. Yes, maybe I'll visit you some time if I have any more questions, though I think I know everything now. Goodbye.' He shook Kaspar's hand and left quickly, as if he were suddenly in a hurry.

Kaspar was still sitting in the chair when the boys came to join him. Werner had cried himself out; Stefan's face had a pinched look, as if someone had played a dirty trick on him. Kaspar got slowly to his feet. A paralysing silence enveloped them as though each were trying to give the others time to say something about Martha. Finally Werner asked him if he was ready to go home.

'Yes.'

Another pause. Kaspar looked at them standing side by side, their faces expressionless, and he knew exactly what they were thinking.

'No,' he said quickly, 'no, thank you. I'd rather be alone tonight. I would, really.'

When they'd first arrived at the hospital, Werner had parked carefully in the area reserved for motorcycles, behind the last row of cars. He had missed it twice, circling around, and Stefan had shouted, 'Stop, you idiot! What the hell does it matter? I'm getting off. Stop!' And when Werner rode on, still looking for the right place, he'd thumped him hard on the back of the head.

'Stop that,' Werner said mildly. 'It'll only take a few seconds. I have to . . .'

Stefan jumped off, fell, caught himself and rushed off across the car park towards the emergency entrance. Werner had followed him slowly, on purpose. By the time he found the doctor, his brother was already upstairs, in the room to which their mother had been taken.

Werner didn't mind, he wanted to concentrate and calm down before he saw her. There had been no time yet, things had been far too hectic: father's telephone call, getting his motorcycle from the basement, Stefan's arrival, inarticulate, his eyes popping out of his head, and then, suddenly, that raucous screaming of his – as if the roar of the engine had given him his cue – which he'd kept up throughout the whole long trip. Clutching him tightly around the waist, he had shouted loud enough to drown out the engine: his despair, his rage at his father, at Heidi, and at himself.

'I should have done something,' he had kept yelling.

'Done what?' Werner had called back over his shoulder.

'Never mind what. Something! Anything! Just to let her know.'

'Let her know what?'

'You know bloody well what I mean. Let *him* have it, and we should have beaten the hell out of Heidi.'

'You think Mother would have liked that?'

'Yes,' Stefan had gasped in his ear. 'Yes, she would. She'd have liked it. She'd have seen how we felt . . .'

'She knew that anyhow,' Werner had yelled back, throttling down to reduce the roar of the engine, but Stefan wouldn't let him.

'For Christ's sake, man, don't fall asleep. I can't stand this dawdling along. Get going!'

From then on there were no more exchanges, although behind him Stefan kept on ranting and raging. Just as well. By the time they met their father, he'd have got the worst out of his system.

In spite of the hair-raising speed, Werner had managed to check every car they passed to see whether it was his father's black BMW.

Then in the doctor's office, there had been that weird young fellow who had talked about Mother as though he'd known her all his life, a total stranger who had just happened . . . Stefan had apparently brushed him aside and rushed off, but he himself had listened to him and spoken to him about Mother. He had done so because the young man seemed compassionate rather than curious. But no one would let him express his compassion, as he was so obviously eager to do, not in a pushy way but as if he belonged to the family. Oh well, Father would get rid of him.

And then at last he was alone, upstairs on the fourth-floor corridor. No one asked him to do anything, no one shouted, and he could think about Mother in peace and quiet. There was no sound from inside the room. How was it possible that she could so suddenly . . .? She'd never been sick, she still went ice-skating twice a week. When he'd talked to her yesterday on the telephone, she'd told him she was making plans for her summer vacation, that the table was covered with brochures. He had said, 'Why don't we go somewhere together, just the two of us?' Thank God he had said that!

Then he had watched Father walking down the hall, and they had gone into the room together, and he had burst into tears and just held on to the thought that he had said to her: 'Why don't we go somewhere together? Just the two of us?' He couldn't remember what her answer had been, something like, 'Yes, why not?' The only thing that mattered was that she had heard him, heard the words 'just the two of us', from her son, if from no one else.

They had walked their father to his car in silence and then returned across the empty car park to Werner's motorbike, both walking slowly, even Stefan. He was still raging, though.

'He's not going home, you know. He's going straight to her.'

'I don't think so,' said Werner.

'Or he'll call her up and tell her. Maybe he's already done it. And they'll both say "What a tragedy!" and they're both glad.'

'I don't think so.'

Don't kid yourself, Werner. Now the coast's clear for them, everything's hunky-dory. Wait a few months for decency's sake and off to the registrar. Super! I'm going over there tomorrow to beat her up.'

'Don't talk balls.'

'It's all because of her, I tell you. She's responsible for Mother's death, and she's not going to forget it for the rest of her life. I'm going to remind her once a month.'

Werner sat astride the motorbike and started the engine. Stefan climbed up behind him and put his arms around Werner's waist. As the motorbike pulled out of the car park, neither of them noticed the young man sitting in his Volkswagen, staring through the open window at the fourth floor of the hospital.

Stefan started talking again, but in a different way this time, sobbing into Werner's ear. 'I'm telling you she died of grief. I know it for a fact. She talked to me about it once, a few months ago. She said she knew it showed in her face. "What shows?" I asked. "That it's getting to me," she said. "For the first few years I could handle it all right. I thought, well, one of these days he'll get tired of her, after all she wasn't the first one. But now I have a feeling I'll never get him back." "Oh, come on now," I said but she just . . .' He broke off, choking, and pressed his head hard against Werner's neck as they rode on in silence.

A few miles ahead of them Kaspar sat in his black BMW. He was driving even more slowly than on the way to the hospital, though he hoped his sons wouldn't overtake him. So far no motorbike. Perhaps they'd stopped for a drink somewhere. Should he do the same? And then get back in the car and somehow make his way to Gellerstrasse, climb the stairs, unlock the door, and go into the bedroom. Did he really have to do that? Was there no alternative? Of course there was! What were friends for? One called them up and said, 'I need you. Right now, tonight, in half an hour.' Somebody was sure to be home, somebody and his wife, and they'd gasp and say, 'Oh my God, Kaspar, how terrible! Come on over right away. Spend the night here. We were just going to bed but . . . we're so glad you called. What about the boys? Ah well, of course, young people . . . Come on over. We'll give you a bite to eat and a glass of wine . . .' Yes, that's what he could do. That's what he would do. Give his friends a chance to act like friends. A good role for friends: hold your hand, have a drink with you, find the right words, or just sit there with you in silence.

He drove on a few miles before he found an open filling-station. The Bannheimers, Alfred and Else, they were his best bet. And they had a guest-room. He dropped the coins into the call-box, hesitated – and then hastily dialled a different number. He let it ring a long time, after all it was pretty late, past nine.

At last a woman's voice answered, surprised at the late call.

'Hello?'

'Anya, it's me, Professor Schulte.'

'But the Master is . . .' in a heavy Danish accent.

'I know, Anya. I've got to talk to him.'

'But . . .'

'Don't wake him yet. I'll be over in half an hour.'

CHAPTER THREE

THE OLD man usually went to bed at eight o'clock. Or rather, he didn't actually go to bed, because he spent all his time there, even in the day-time, but he switched off the light. Unlike most old people, he needed more sleep each year; every six months or so he added another half an hour. Now, at eighty-eight, he slept for up to seventeen hours a day. No one knew whether he was really asleep, but he stayed in bed, under the covers, because he felt cold, winter and summer alike. When he was hungry or needed something, he'd ring the bell and Anya would appear if she considered it necessary. A few years ago he'd made her take a course in home nursing, but whether she had learned anything was another matter. She nursed him with authority, as she saw fit, and that suited him well enough.

When Kaspar rang the doorbell, she hadn't bothered to put on a dressing-gown, just a kitchen apron over her flowery woollen nightgown in case he wanted something to eat. But he didn't.

'My wife's dead,' he said, handing her his hat.

'What?' She looked at him dubiously. 'Why dead?'

'Heart failure.'

She stood aside to let him go down the hall to the old man's bedroom. He stopped for a moment at the door and glanced back. She was still leaning against the kitchen door at the other end of the hall, silently watching him.

But then what could she have said? After all she had worked for three weeks in his home, she knew the score. Martha had advertised for an *au pair* girl, but no one had applied; and then one evening she had said: 'I hired a Danish girl today. She's very beautiful, she won't stay long.' 'Why not?' he'd asked in surprise. 'The boys are still a bit young for . . .' 'I'm not talking about the boys,' Martha had said with a smile. That had been before Heidi's time, of course.

Next day Anya Södersen had come in with the breakfast tray.

'Good morning,' he'd murmured. Martha was right: a girl like that wasn't going to last. For the next few days he felt uneasy every time Anya entered the room, and the boys would stop talking altogether. She herself never looked at anyone, even when she was spoken to, merely nodding and muttering a word or two in unintelligible German. But sometimes, when he was passing the door to her room, he could hear her talking to her pet blackbird in a completely different tone and even laugh.

Once Alfred and Else happened to drop in for supper. When Anya entered the dining-room with the tray, Alfred, a professor of pathology, had broken off in mid-sentence, and his wife had stared at the girl, thunderstruck. As the door closed behind her, they both spoke at once. 'Who, for heaven's sake, is that?' demanded the Professor, while his wife said reproachfully to Martha: 'Why? If you'll forgive me asking.'

'She's only temporary. Just a stop-gap,' Martha had replied with a smile, and at that moment Kaspar had had an inspiration.

The next day had been a Saturday. No classes, Martha at the hairdresser, the boys playing football. Anya was sitting at the kitchen table, polishing the silver candlesticks with a chamois leather. He sat down facing her. She gave him a quick, suspicious glance and continued polishing vigorously.

'Anya, I've been thinking about you.' A misleading opening, and a grim Danish frown appeared between her extraordinarily arched eyebrows, but she didn't raise her eyes. 'You're going to have complications in any family you live with, with the master of the house or his sons or his friends.' 'Com-pli-ca-tions,' he repeated, hoping to dispel the misunderstanding and the frown.

After a brief pause, she answered in a low, husky voice, 'I know. Already one baby in Denmark. One is enough.'

'Why didn't you learn some kind of job?'

'Keeping house my job. In Copenhagen I work in department store. More men there, more complications.'

'How old are you?'

'Eighteen.'

'Would you work for a man who lives alone but would never bother you?'

'Is sick?'

'No, but he's eighty years old.'

'My grandfather eighty-two, in wheelchair, and hand up my skirt.' She hit grandfather over the knuckles with the chamois leather.

'You wouldn't have anything to worry about with my uncle. He's only this tall.' He held his hand less than four feet from the floor. 'He's a dwarf.'

She put down the candlestick and stared at him in surprise.

'In circus?' she asked hopefully.

'No, he lives here in Munich, in a flat, just like other people. Well, no, not like other people at all.'

'Okay,' she said, resuming her polishing. 'I go to him.'

Two weeks later he had pressed a bunch of flowers into her hand, carried her suitcase and bird-cage down to the car and driven her to the Kaiserplatz, where the dwarf lived. What he lived on was a mystery. His standard of living never varied, not luxurious, though ample enough to include a housekeeper. But he was so difficult to please that none of the housekeepers stayed. The last one had left a few months ago, cursing loudly, and since then he'd been making do with cleaning-women, whom he hated. He was forever pestering Kaspar to find him a good, sensible woman, preferably a large strapping 'wench'.

Kaspar had knocked at the bedroom door, pushing the girl with the flowers ahead of him. 'Here's your birthday present, Uncle Stilts. She comes from Copenhagen and her name's Anya.'

That had been eight years ago. Anya had no more complications and the little old man was in heaven.

He opened the bedroom door so that the light from the hall could shine in, and waited.

'What's up?' came a crotchety voice out of the darkness. 'Put out that light! Hear me?'

Kaspar groped his way forward and switched on the night-light, then closed the door. The faint red glow revealed the shadowy outlines of a magnificent four-poster bed and a dark little face against a pile of pillows. The dwarf was sitting rather than lying, looking tinier than ever against the vast expanse of white. Kaspar sat down at the foot of the bed, leaning against one of the velvet-covered bedposts.

'Oh, it's you. What's the matter, Inkworm? Anything wrong?' When Kaspar didn't answer at once, he went on: 'Had a rumpus with Martha? I don't want to know. Get lost.'

'Martha's dead, Uncle Stilts.'

The little head, thatched in snow-white, turned slowly towards him. The round eyes blinked and the mouth opened in a black grin.

'Done her in, have you? I'll be a pizzened wolf from Bitter Creek! How did you do it? Hold it!' He sat up, groped about on the bedside table for his spectacles, located the glass with his false teeth in it beside the lamp and fumbled about with them until they clicked into place. 'There. Now I can listen properly. Tell!'

'Heart failure.'

The dwarf heaved a disappointed sigh. Then he grinned again, a snow-white smile, radiant and almost child-like. 'Lucky devil!' Kaspar remained silent. 'I can't see you properly. Turn the big light on.'

'No.'

'Well, the floor lamp then.'

Kaspar was hunched against the bedpost, dark and motionless as a statue. The old man reached for the bell on the bedside table.

'She won't come now, Uncle Stilts.'

'But I want the light on,' yelled the dwarf, beating his tiny fists on the bedspread. 'I don't see well any more.'

'I can't stand the light right now.'

The old man clasped his hands and twiddled his thumbs. 'What are you doing here? What do you want? You know I never liked her. Expect me to be gloomy just because she's dead? Go see your girl-friend.' Kaspar shook his head. 'What did you have in mind? Want to sleep in Uncle's big bed with him? Want him to tell you a story?'

Kaspar thought for a while. 'Yes,' he said slowly. 'Yes, that's exactly what I want.'

The little man folded his arms and looked at him intently. 'Ah, something dawns on me,' he said. 'I was hoping you'd given up pestering me about that.'

Kaspar leaned his head back against the bedpost and closed his eyes. 'How much longer do you want to put it off? Twenty years ago you already promised you'd tell me the whole story some time. When is "some time"? Every few years you throw out a few crumbs, laurel wreaths and scandals, jails, St Petersburg and sleigh rides. Is any of it true? Well, today I want to know. So make up your mind: yes or no.'

'Brazen, bumptious bastard! Waking me up in the middle of the night and putting the screws on me. Why today of all days? Because she's dead? All upset, are you?'

'Don't ask me so many questions, Uncle Stilts. It's quite simple: I want to think about something else, I was hoping to get my mind off it. . . .' He fell silent.

'Speak up. Can't hear you.'

Kaspar sat up straight, carefully put his feet side by side on the floor, rubbed his hand across his forehead, stood up and walked to the door.

'Come back here,' croaked the voice from behind him. 'What d'you think I am, a tape-recorder? You think I've got it all neatly stacked in my top drawer, and all I have to do is reel it off? It all happened ages ago, buried God knows where. How do I know if I could dig it up again?'

'Bullshit,' said Kaspar evenly from the doorway. 'Whatever it is, it's right there in your head. You know it all backwards, you keep repeating it to yourself over and over again.'

'What the hell are you talking about? Who's repeating what?'

'Anya says sometimes when she comes in you're not asleep, you're just lying there cackling.'

'I. . . .'

'And she's seen you sitting up thrusting your hands out as if you were conducting. She's shown me how, looks very odd, I must say. What are you doing when you're flailing about like that?'

An ominous pause. 'You said it. Conducting.'

'Conducting what? An orchestra? And what's the cackling about?'

'Anya said I cackle? I'll kick her out.'

'That's the last thing you'll do.' Then more gently: 'Uncle Stilts, I'm tired. Either you tell me the story or. . . .'

'Lord help us!' muttered the old man. Then he began to scream in a falsetto voice: 'Blackmail! Help! Murder!'

Kaspar grasped the doorknob.

'Goddammit, Inkworm! Bring me my Napoleon brandy. Sideboard, bottom left. Never mind the glass. I drink it out of the bottle. None for you, you blackguard.'

Kaspar returned with a sofa cushion under his arm, set the bottle on the bedside table, swung his feet on to the bed, stuffed the cushion between his back and the bedpost, and faced the old man, who glowered at him.

'Comfy? Glad to hear it.' He reached for the bottle and cradled it in his arm like a baby. '1914, a good vintage. Not for dwarfs, though.
'Why? What happened to you?'
The little man fondled the bottle, but his voice remained surly: 'How much do you know? Do you know anything at all about – what happened?'
'Nothing. Father said he and Uncle Bernie swore, way back, never to talk about it. That's what he always said when your name came up.'
The dwarf gnawed at his upper lip with his false teeth. He always did that when something unexpected occurred to him, and it made him look like a midget gorilla. 'Dirty bastards!'
'Dirty bastards? Your own brothers?'
'A dwarf has no brothers. A wonder they didn't do me in, your father and Bernie. A fine pair they were! If anyone has the right to dig around in that old dirt, it's me. Me and nobody else.'
'But why all the secrecy? All Father ever said was that he didn't want me to think there was anything criminal involved.'
'He said that, did he, the old fox. I say it was a crime, and not just one either.' He fumbled impatiently with the cork and took a good swig. 'How do I know if I can remember? How am I to piece it all together, in the right order, so you can get the hang of it? Where am I supposed to begin?'
'Anywhere. As I say, I don't know the first thing about it. Whatever concerned you was taboo in my family.' The old man gave him a long look over the bottle. 'Why don't you start with Grandfather? I don't know anything about him either. But I do know a little something about Grandmother.'
'What do you know?' Almost threatening.
'I once found an old photograph. I never told anyone. In the background was some sort of travelling circus and in the foreground, right in the centre, was the entrance to a freak show. Above it was a sign: Anna Schulte, Managing Director. That was her name, wasn't it?'
The dwarf gnawed at his upper lip. He took another gulp, puffed out his cheeks and swished the cognac back and forth like mouthwash. He's playing for time, thought Kaspar, and felt guilty for blackmailing the old man with Martha's death.
'Your grandmother . . .' He broke off and fondled the bottle. Fresh start: 'Your grandmother – how can one describe her? I'll have

to go back first to *her* parents. Grandfather – *my* grandfather, don't muddle me up now – he sang in the church choir. He also worked in the post office. They had six children, a puny lot, all dead by the age of three. And then came my mother, the seventh one, and right from the start she was – something. By the time she was eight her mother was bedridden, TB I believe. The girl took over the household, dropped out of school, never learned to spell properly. If she mentioned me in a letter, she always wrote "duarf".'

He gnawed frantically at his upper lip. Kaspar opened his mouth to say something but it was too late, now.

'Shut up! Where was I? Well, there was Grandmother, lying in bed, coughing, while my mother cooked and sewed and took care of her. Except for the heavy work, she hired a man for that, all before her ninth birthday. And Grandfather? Every Sunday on his way to the sacristy he would walk past the six little graves, and then from the choir loft he'd praise the Lord – because the Lord had finally sent him my mother, as much as to say: "There now, we're quits. Here's a bonus for you." Grandfather understood that and let her do as she liked. Imagine, Kaspar, a child of eight! A child who never played, had her head full of other things: bills, medicines, groceries, watching the hired man to make sure he didn't rob her blind – just think of it! She can't have been any taller than I am.'

The little head covered with white bristles sank down over the bottle. Kaspar reached out, but the dwarf struck out at him with both hands.

'Sit still! You asked for it. Later on it gets funnier. So here was this girl, my mother – Anna was her name – and when people came over, she'd pour them a glass of wine and take one herself, and people forgot that it was just a child who said: "Your health, ladies and gentlemen." Of course the whole town knew about her and at first all the neighbours offered help and advice, but my grandmother would call out from the bedroom: "Leave my girl alone, she knows." And those were her last words when she died. Anna was ten then.'

A long pause. Another swig from the brandy bottle, then, almost inaudibly: 'Don't know what happened next. Wasn't there at the time. One thing led to another but I've forgotten how.'

'Led to what, Uncle Stilts?'

'Well, it's about time for my father to show up, isn't it? Where the devil did she pick *him* up?'

'How old was she?'

'Fifteen. Don't make that face, fifteen was old – for her.'

'What did he do for a living?'

'A living? Wait a bit – he had something to do with the circus – yes, that's it, of course, important for later – bears! He had a bear act – or he looked after them or something. Yes! Yes!' He screamed shrilly: 'That's it!' He sighed happily and tapped his forehead several times. 'Now it's all clicking into place. Old fool! Of course! That's how it happened.'

'What? Go on, Uncle Stilts.'

'That bear! My father had a pet bear. He took it to the post office in Landshut where the circus performed, the bear was all dressed up, of course, and had its hat on, and the two of 'em just went and stood in the line at the stamp counter. Suddenly somebody noticed them and everybody in the post office began to scream bloody murder, and Anna heard them because our house was next door to the post office, with just the garden in between, and she was doing a bit of weeding. She liked weeding, liked everything neat and tidy.' He stared fixedly at the bedspread for a while. 'She came rushing into the post office with a bunch of radishes in her hand and the bear sat up on its hind legs, begging for the radishes with its big clumsy paws.'

After a while Kaspar said softly, 'Yes?'

'Yes,' murmured the dwarf, lost in thought. 'Yes, yes. So she married my father and the bear, and it followed her everywhere she went. I've still got a photo of it, awful old monster, ugly as sin.'

'Do you remember it?'

The old man shook his head. 'I was the third boy, an afterthought. Came along eight years after your father. By that time the bear was all grey and skinny, with only one eye. But still shuffling along behind my mother. Maybe my father blamed it for me, for the freak; they say pregnant women should only look at beautiful things. All I know is my father shot the bear.'

He set the bottle down on the bedside table and sank back against the pillows, his arms folded behind his head.

'Well, there I was, not even seven inches long. At first my mother kept saying: "It's the wee ones grow faster," but I grew slowly and not all that much. Otherwise I was pretty, with blond curly hair. You probably know – at least you ought to know, Inkworm, up on your hind legs on your podium holding forth – there are several kinds of dwarfs. I went into all that later. The cause? Depends. Some of them are retarded too – and if you ask me they're the lucky ones. And then there are the nice-looking types, properly proportioned, like me. You could take a picture of me and enlarge it and you'd have a classical model. I mean you *would* have had, once, and I had a right handsome little head.'

Without looking, he fumbled for something behind the lamp, a hand mirror. 'I'm still not bad to look at.' He studied himself objectively, then put it back in its place. Kaspar reached for the tiny hand resting on the bedspread and pressed it before the old man had time to snatch it away.

'Let go, Inkworm, I can't stand being touched, you know that. Anyway, my mother had a gland somewhere at the back of her head that didn't work right. When the doctor explained it to her, she nearly went out of her mind. Flatly refused to believe him. The first two kids had been quite all right, over-size if anything. That Leopold, your father, was six feet two and the other one, your uncle Bernie, was a real giant, great lumpy louts, both of them. Of course I became my mother's pet. It was always me that got the tastiest bits of meat – "the little tyke needs it" – and the first strawberries. The others would watch me sitting in Mother's lap, being fed and fondled, and never say a word. So at first I didn't mind being so small. That was later. First came a time when I started hanging from ladders and doors until my fingers were numb. And then one day, it suddenly dawned on me. I don't know what it was that made everything click into place, but I suddenly knew – no, that's the wrong word, it hit me like a brickbat: ahead of me lay something terrible: my life. And it would go on for ever and my mother wouldn't always be there. Other children don't know what that means: their life. They romp through the day without a thought and look forward to what's still to come.'

He reflected for a moment and then began to giggle. 'It was funny, really, because it was so sudden. From one minute to the next, and I decided to drown myself in the millpond then and there. But when I looked down at the water, I thought: hold it! The millpond's not going to run away, you can jump in any old time. But how about making a virtue of this rotten deal? Or something of the sort – after all, I was only ten. I was pretty smart though, only I didn't know *how* smart. Well, as I knelt there looking at myself in the water, with all those blond curls against the blue sky, it suddenly came to me: okay, never mind if people stare at me – but I'll make them pay for it!

'I ran home and that very day I began to pester my mother to put me on show. In the circus. In an act called "Wonders of Nature" or whatever, I didn't mind how, together with a three-legged pig, for all I cared. But for the first time I came away with a flea in my ear. She'd rather see me dead, she said, and the tip of her nose turned dead white. At first, I thought she'd come around in time – she'd never yet refused me anything – but she stood firm. I did too, I wouldn't give up. I worked on my father, who was like putty where I was concerned, and finally on my brothers, but all three of them said: wait a bit, you're still too young. Although the boys would certainly have been glad to see the last of me. To them I was like a horsefly, buzzing around and stinging whenever it gets a chance. Mother wouldn't let me go to school for fear the other kids would torment me, so I was always getting in everybody's way. Hardly ever left the house. Mind you, I wasn't bored. Taught myself reading and writing and arithmetic without any trouble. Mother got me the books. You see, I had an absolutely stupendous memory . . . But there was something else in my life besides schoolbooks.' He broke off and pointed to a corner of the room, his owl-eyes strangely phosphorescent. 'Over there in my desk. First drawer on the left. The little carton. Bring it here.'

Kaspar laid the package, carefully tied with string, on the bedspread in front of the little man. He untied the knots, raised the lid and took out a wooden box which opened up into a miniature chessboard with a separate small pouch containing tiny, finely modelled chessmen. Silently he set them up, sticking each piece into a hole drilled in its square, until the two armies, white and black, were drawn up in battle array.

'This is how it began,' he murmured. 'A game – and the turning-point. Give a child a present, maybe a little fiddle, and it turns into a vocation. It happens. Somebody gave me this thing for my eighth birthday, along with an instruction booklet. From then on I played at least a dozen games a day, by myself or with my brothers. Mother forced them to play with me, to keep me happy. They didn't do badly but I could beat them easily. Before I was ten I'd beaten my father too, and the pastor. But best of all I liked to play alone in "my" corner of the living-room, behind Grandfather's huge armchair, where nobody could see me. *Nobody could see me*, Kaspar, and that's when I was at my best.

27

Remember that – for later! I was able to block myself off so completely that I could make a move without calculating the countermove.

'In the evenings the others would sit around under the big ceiling lamp with the pink shade, reading or doing handiwork – Mother would be sewing – and I'd be behind the big chair, giggling and chattering, because of course I talked to my imaginary opponent all the time, heckling him. "Aha! That caught you unawares, didn't it?" Or "Silly oaf, you fell right into the trap! Now I'm going to castle." All this went on on the floor, at Grandfather's feet. He was a bit muzzy in the head by that time and every few days he'd ask: "But where is he, the other one?"

'The family, sitting around the table, ignored me, all except that Leopold, your father, who wanted to be an engineer and would have liked a quiet place to study. I got on his nerves with my squawking and jumping around and he'd curse me and call me Rumpelstiltskin. Then that got shortened to Stilts.

'That's how it all began. Five-finger exercises for the imagination. You can train and expand your imagination, you know, just like a muscle. I had no need to see my opponent in the flesh, he was right there in front of me, old or young as the case might be, a cheat or a sport, a blockhead or a master. Oh yes, some of them *were* masters, and I often lost, although there really wasn't any "I". And during all the mad jumping back and forth – because naturally I changed sides, from black to white, for every move – during all that hustle and bustle, I thought I was just playing a game. Never dreamed I was in training.'

His breath came in short gasps, as though he had been running, and behind his glasses his eyes were as round and unblinking as an owl's. 'See what I'm getting at, Kaspar?'

'Not really, I'm afraid.'

'So you really don't know anything at all about it? To think that something of that sort could be wiped out without a trace!'

'I don't understand, Uncle Stilts, you *wanted* it all wiped out, your brothers were made to swear to it.'

A long pause, with violent chewing of the upper lip. 'All the same, I can't see how it could happen that the word never got out, outside the family, I mean. Oh well, maybe it was better that way. Anyhow, there I am sitting at Grandfather's feet in the living-room, playing, and it's Sunday morning and he's singing his chorales, though off key by now. It didn't bother me, I had no ear for music, but the rest of the family would always leave the room. And suddenly, right in the middle of a psalm, he stops singing. I kept on with my game – I'd just about mated my opponent – but a bit later, when they all came in to lunch, they began weeping and wailing because the old boy was dead. And I wailed too because somebody had stepped on my chessboard.

'That was the end of Grandfather. Too bad for me because behind his big chair I'd felt secure and invisible, but now they went and moved it, and suddenly the people sitting around the table could *see* me, hopping about and jabbering to myself, and I remember your father, that Leopold, saying: "Good Christ – he has a screw loose too!"

'Mother struck back fast. Up until then I'd slept in a recess next to my parents' room. From now on Grandfather's room was to be mine. And so I moved into my kingdom. I threw out all the furniture; all I wanted was Grandfather's bed, a table and two chairs. Your uncle Bernie – he was apprenticed to a cabinet-maker – had to saw ten inches off all the legs so I wouldn't have to climb up and down. And at Christmas, I found a full-size chessboard on my table, with pieces as tall as my fingers. From then on I never bothered anyone any more. I only appeared for meals, and then only for my mother's sake. A food bowl outside my door would have suited me fine. Suited my brothers too; they'd have liked to wall me up in my hide-out and feed me through a hole in the wall. I was an embarrassment to them. To Mother too, really, much as she loved me. They could never have company over. Even old friends would take a quick peep at my high chair, always with the same expression on their faces: "My, my, isn't the little fellow ever starting to grow?" As for new friends! Although, of course, they were coached beforehand, but I'd be watching out for furtive glances and when I caught them at it, I'd let them know. Let's see if I can still do it.' He rolled his eyes behind his thick glasses and bared his false teeth.

'Remarkable.'

'Shut your mouth. A freak has the right to defend himself. Or do you expect him to work on his beautiful soul? I really enjoyed being mean, I thought at the time it would be the only pleasure I'd ever get out of that miserable, godforsaken life of mine. I never dreamed that something extraordinary, something really wild, was in store for me – for me and nobody else.'

He stared into the distance while Kaspar waited patiently. After all, this was what he'd come for, and it was working even better than he had hoped: hours had gone by without his being conscious of Kaspar Schulte and his loss. Tomorrow morning he'd face it all. Break the news to his friends. Bury Martha. Decide: Heidi – yes or no. Stay at the apartment or move; if so, where to? Tomorrow. Until then: reprieve.

The old man suddenly reached for the hand mirror again and looked at himself intently. 'Not really much left,' he muttered. 'Too bad I always refused to have my picture taken. I had skin like a girl's, pink and white, and very large, dark-blue eyes. I used to wash myself several times a day and pester Mother for her cologne. I must have been really in love with myself, imagine! Instead of hating myself. Explain that if you can. Stubbornness or bravado? I know what you're thinking. You mean that at bottom I really did hate myself. Love – hate – I know all about that, Inkworm. *Now*, I do. At the time I only knew that I never stopped marvelling. Don't forget, there were two of me – me and myself, confronting each other and doing battle.'

He took a sip to restore himself.

'You're a good listener, Kaspar, you don't rush me. But I know I've got you and I enjoy that. Where were we now? Oh yes, I was reigning over my kingdom upstairs. I'd covered the walls with Toulouse-Lautrec posters – they'd just started printing them in Germany – my favourite painter, only an inch or two taller than me. And then – I don't remember exactly when – my father died. My mother in black, with her eyes all red from crying, then the funeral. I was looking forward to it – I'd missed all the fun at Grandfather's – but they wouldn't take me along this time either.

'And that day, Kaspar, the day of the funeral, that was *the day*! The doorbell rang downstairs. I was alone; they'd all gone to the cemetery. I went downstairs and called out: "Who is it?"

' "I'd like to see Frau Schulte." A man's voice.

' "She's gone to the funeral."

' "The funeral? Did . . ."

' "My father's dead." All this through the front door.

' "Oh, I'm sorry to hear that. And who are you? Why aren't you at the cemetery?"

' "I'm the dwarf," I said.

'A short pause. "Oh yes, of course, I've heard about you. Open the door, will you? Or can't you reach?" I stood on tiptoe and pulled back the bolt, opening the door a crack. There stood a robust gentleman, white at the temples, very elegant in light grey, with a top hat and cane and white kid gloves.

'"Ehrenreich," he said. "Don't you remember me?"

'"No."

'"May I come in? I was a friend of your father's." I hesitated – I was always suspicious. "I'm the managing director of the Sarasate Circus. Your father worked for me when we were both young men."

'I opened the door and took him into the living-room. Sarasate. That name rang a bell. The bears . . .

'He sat down on the sofa, I climbed into a chair and there we sat, stiffly facing one another. He rested the white kid gloves on the cane and looked at me. I looked at him.

'"We're performing in town right now," he began. I nodded; my brothers had been talking about it. "I heard that your father was sick so I came to see him."

'I didn't answer.

'"How old was he, do you know?"

'"All old people are the same age to me."

'He laughed, showing long yellow teeth, like a friendly horse.

'"What about you? How old are you?"

'"Older than you think."

'"Because you're a dwarf, you mean? I have three dwarfs in the show, but they're not a bit like you."

'"How do you mean?"

'"Come and see for yourself."

'"I can't spare the time."

'"Why, what do you do?"

'"I play chess."

'"All day long? Who with?"

'I tapped myself on the chest. He gave me a searching look, obviously wondering whether I was a bit daft. "And where do you play?"

'"In my room."

'"Could I have a look? I'd like to wait for your mother in any case. By the way, I play chess myself; I once won the North German championship."

'Without a word I led him upstairs. The chessboard was set up; I was halfway through a tough game. He bent down over it – it was of course far too low for him – and studied the positions. Then he looked up at me again, standing there with my arms folded, making it quite clear that I wished he'd go and wait for Mother downstairs.

'"Would you break off this game and play one with me? We could write down the positions."

'"No need to. I'll remember them."

'I cleared the board and set it up again and he managed to lower himself onto my chair. Of course I gave him white, in spite of his protests. It was over in seven minutes. "Checkmate," I murmured. Herr Ehrenreich was the first real opponent I'd had for years, and I was amazed how easily I beat him. He was, too. He stared and stared at the board, couldn't take it in. Finally he leaned back and gave me a strange look. But before he could say anything, there was a lot of noise downstairs and the funeral party came trooping into the living-room.

'From the landing upstairs Herr Ehrenreich and I watched them crowding in, one black hat after another. "I'd like to leave without anyone seeing me," he whispered. "You understand, don't you?" I showed him to the back stairs. He took my hand and looked intently into my eyes. "Tell your mother I'll come and see her tomorrow morning. Will you be home?"

'"I'm always home."

'He rumpled my hair, which I didn't much care for, and left.

'He was back first thing in the morning, embraced my mother and she had a few tears for him in memory of my father and of that old bear. Then he sat down in a peculiar way: instead of sitting on the chair, he straddled it, with his stomach resting against its back, looking us up and down in turn, as we sat there in a semi-circle around him, all in black, with him in the middle in light grey, wearing his kid gloves. Then he said quite cheerfully, not in a mournful tone at all: "What will you do now, Frau Schulte?"

'"Lord knows," said my mother. "They say my husband's shoe shop – God rest his soul – is in a bad way. If that's true, we'll sell the house, and the boys . . ." She broke off. My brothers suddenly pricked up their ears like two dogs that have heard a sound in the distance.

'"Yes?"

'She stared down at her hands without speaking. We knew what she meant: the boys would have to give up their apprenticeships and start earning, waiting on tables, construction, casual labour, something like that. "I can sew and clean and keep accounts," she said tonelessly.

'Herr Ehrenreich broke the silence. "I have another suggestion. It concerns *him*. What's his name, by the way?"

'"Stilts," said my brothers with one voice.

'"Not on your life," shrieked my mother. "Not on your life, let me tell you."

'Herr Ehrenreich shook his head gently. "Don't worry, Frau Schulte. I'd never put him in the dwarf act. That's what you were thinking, weren't you?"

'"Well, why not after all?" asked that Leopold, with his head on one side. "It's nothing to be ashamed of and people like to see that sort of thing!"

'"You'd be making money," said your uncle Bernie.

'"I'll kill you," whispered Mother, clenching her hands.

'"Have a think, Mother: what are we going to do with him when you're gone?"

'She looked from one to the other and took a deep breath. "You mean, you wouldn't raise a finger for him?"

'Leopold again: "We'd need money for that, wouldn't we?" A long pause. Then Herr Ehrenreich spoke up again. "I don't think you've quite understood me. I don't want to put him on show as a dwarf."

'"What else, then?" First my mother, flushed and suspicious, then my brothers: "What else?"

'"As a chess-player," said Herr Ehrenreich quietly. "I believe the little fellow is a quite remarkable player." And then, switching to a strictly business-like tone so that we could see he wasn't made only of honey: "Don't ask me now how I'll do it. I don't know myself yet."

'"I'll never let people gawk at him in a circus ring!" screamed Mother. I'd never seen her like that, quite demented. "I swear it. I swear it by the memory of my dear departed, God rest his soul. . . ."

'Herr Ehrenreich stopped her by getting up hastily. "You'll be hearing from me, this week, before we strike the tents." With that he left – he didn't even wait for someone to show him to the door.

'Three days later he was back. "I think I've got it," he said, straddling his chair again and letting us draw up in a semi-circle around him, the way he liked it. He looked everyone up and down again for a moment but from then on he spoke only to me. "You'll play chess against members of the audience. We'll get them to pick a challenger . . ."

'"Never!" shouted my mother. "I've told you once and for all that . . ."

'He interrupted her quite rudely. "Nobody will see him, he'll be sitting in a box."

'"A box!" exclaimed my mother, grasping his arm. "What kind of a box?"

'"A match-box," said that son of a bitch, your uncle Bernie.

'"Would you like that, Stilts?" asked Herr Ehrenreich.

'"Yes," I said.

'"Come to the main gate tomorrow then and ask for me."

'"We'll be there," said my mother firmly. She didn't like anything about the whole business. But I gave her a look so she said no more.'

The old man stopped speaking and closed his eyes for a moment. Kaspar held the bottle out to him but he shook his head. 'That'll get me more mixed up, there was so much going on at the same time, I've got to skip so many things, you'll just have to use your imagination.

'You see, Herr Ehrenreich's circus wasn't one of the big ones but it wasn't just one of those flea-bitten ones either, I'd say it was sort of medium-size. But to me, standing with my mother and the boys outside the fence for the first time, it looked a bloody marvel. Someone was waiting for us at the main gate: Herr Ehrenreich was expecting us in the workshop. He led us past the big tent, where the ring was, to another tent full of wooden workbenches, where they made everything a circus needs: cages, wagons, scenery, Lord knows what. It smelled good, of timber and sawdust.

'Herr Ehrenreich, minus hat and kid gloves, was talking to a small man with scars on his face and the tip of his nose missing. He had once been assistant to a lion-tamer, now he was the shop foreman. Andros was his name. Better remember that, he's important. He immediately grabbed hold of me with his large hard paws and stood me on a bench to measure me for the box, made me sit down and kneel and even crouch. "About twenty inches by twelve, that ought to give him enough room," he said. "Bring me four sheets of pine board, the thinnest you've got." "Don't forget the hole for his hand," said Herr Ehrenreich. "And the two slits for his eyes, as good as invisible. Knock it together while we walk around and take a look at the pets." He pulled on his kid gloves, so he could fondle the animals.

'My brothers were absolutely fascinated, but not me, I never really could stand them, bellowing, stinking creatures. He took us into the big tent – gigantic! Some clowns were in the ring, practising. I hated them on sight, and when they hit each other over the head with their pig bladders, I turned my back. But then came a magician – and they couldn't tear me away. I simply had to find out how the rabbits and the white dove got into the top hat. "That's his secret," said Herr Ehrenreich, baring those friendly yellow teeth. "That's what he gets paid for."

'By the time we got back to the workshop, I was getting quite excited. Andros was just filing the peepholes, and then they set the box on a table, lifted me into it and shut down the lid. I sat there quite comfortably in the dark and heard Herr Ehrenreich exclaim: "It's absolutely unbelievable! Stick your hand through the hole, Stilts." I did, wiggling my fingers about, but Ehrenreich immediately called out: "No, that ruins it. Pull your hand back in." My family said nothing at all. The lid was opened up and I scrambled out.

' "There's oceans of room," I said to Herr Ehrenreich. "You can make the box much smaller."

' "Why? There's no need for that . . ." he began – and then broke off as if something had struck him.

'And he wasn't the only one: your uncle Bernie suddenly piped up: "Herr Ehrenreich, wouldn't it work better if you couldn't see Stilts at all?"

' "What?" I yelled. "Not even my hand? Count me out, then. If nobody knows it's *me* in there – what's the point?"

' "Stilts," said Herr Ehrenreich, "you liked the magician, didn't you? Wouldn't you like to be one, too?"

'I couldn't make out what he was getting at, but Andros and your uncle Bernie had caught on.

' "A wooden hand!" exclaimed Andros.

' "No, an iron hook!" yelled Bernie.

'The old man paused, grinning. 'But who do you think came up with the solution? Your father, that Leopold, who hadn't said a word yet. At home he was the one always messing around with gadgets; he invented a special device for bottling fruit, and without even getting out of bed he could fiddle about with a couple of wires and press a button and the window would open. Well, he suddenly stepped forward and said: "Herr Ehrenreich, there mustn't be anything that could give the show away. The little cubbyhole's got to be so small that nobody would ever guess somebody is sitting inside it. There must be a way to move the chessmen about from inside – maybe with some kind of hook."

'"That's it!" shouted Bernie. "But the main thing is to have the chessboard fastened to the box. It's got to look all of a piece, like . . ."

'"Like a machine," said Herr Ehrenreich. "And that's what we'll call it in the programme: The Chess Machine." It was like a revelation; nobody said another word.'

He settled back into the pillows and closed his eyes. 'Now I'll have another drink, it can't muddle me up any more and I really need one, I'm all in.'

Kaspar handed him the bottle and the old man took a large gulp, his eyes closed.

'Is it nearly finished?' asked Kaspar.

'The brandy?'

'Your story, Uncle Stilts.'

'Why, are you tired.'

'No, I'm not, but you look tired.'

'Yes,' said the dwarf quietly, 'I am.'

'Is there much more to come?'

The eyes once more opened wide behind the spectacles. 'Inkworm! That's only the beginning.'

'It's midnight, Uncle Stilts. Shall I go now?'

'Yes. Come back when you need it. You *will* need it, you'll see. I'll need it too. Now that I've started, it's all got to come out.' One last tired grin. 'The best part's still to come – you ain't heard nothing yet.'

CHAPTER FOUR

H E COULDN'T complain. Hour after hour had gone by without the memory of Martha in that hospital gown eating away at him. It was still there, no doubt about it, gnawing and digging, deep down somewhere, but it never reached the surface. That had been taken over by the chess machine, with that crazy little fellow inside it. And to think that he hadn't even known that Uncle Stilts played chess! His father – 'that Leopold' – had apparently been a good player too, yet so far as he knew, they had never had a chessboard in the house. But what *did* he know? Making a mystery out of anything had been his father's favourite hobby.

He was already in bed, about to take his tranquillizer, when he suddenly realized that the thing he had been dreading – coming home to the empty flat – was well behind him without his having noticed it. No sooner had he become aware of this than Martha popped to the surface. Hastily he rummaged in his bedside table for a sleeping-pill to reinforce the tranquillizer. He found one and tried to swallow both tablets without water – Martha had always left him a fresh glass of water on his table. No glass there now. No glass! He didn't want to get up, couldn't get up. Trying to collect enough saliva in his mouth, he gulped and gulped . . . Martha!

The telephone woke him.

'Inkworm? Did you sleep?'

Kaspar muttered something.

'You slept all right. You're still fast asleep. Good. That's all I wanted to know.' Click.

He staggered into the kitchen and dug out the coffeemaker, and twenty seconds later with a loud snort the brown fluid began dripping down. Just watching it cheered him up. Two big cups and forward march to the telephone. What time was it? Barely eight. First the Institute, then Heidi. No, first Heidi: she left early for the lab. Maybe she'd have left already. Reprieved? He dialled, keeping his fingers crossed, but she answered.

'Heidi?'

'Darling! How are you?'

'Heidi . . .'

'What is it? You sound hoarse.'

'Martha's dead.'

Silence. Then, almost inaudibly: 'Oh, my God!'

'Yesterday. On the *autobahn*. Heart failure.'

'Oh, my God!'

'Heidi, right now I can't . . . You understand, don't you?'

'Of course. Call me whenever you need me.' She hung up. Thank God that was over; now for the Institute. Nothing to it, compared to calling Heidi.

'But that's terrible, Professor Schulte! . . . Oh no! What a terrible thing! . . .'

He hardly needed to say more than 'heart failure' and the words came pouring out: 'tragic', 'so sudden', 'still so young', and, over and over again, 'terrible'.

There! Half a dozen friends had been told and they would spread the news. He dialled again.

'Werner? Would you do something for me? Come over and answer the telephone.' Then, hesitantly, he dialled one last time. 'Heidi? Are you still there?'

'I thought I'd . . . go in a bit later today. Would you like me to . . . to . . .'

'Don't come to the funeral. Please!'

'Of course I won't, Kaspar.'

But she did come, although he didn't see her because she sat in the back. Stefan saw her, though; after all they worked in the same lab.

'Where are you going?' whispered Werner, trying to restrain his brother, who suddenly started to break away as the procession wound its way slowly out of the church towards the freshly dug grave, with the wreaths piled around it.

'Leave me alone.'

And he was gone to reappear beside Heidi at the tail end of the procession.

'What the hell are you doing here? Fuck off.'

Looking at him steadily and walking on, she said quietly: 'I wanted to see how your father looks.'

'You've got a nerve.'

'You've got it all wrong, I don't want anything. Nothing at all.
Now I can leave, now that I've seen him.' She turned and walked
quickly across the graveyard towards the gate.

'Are you crazy? What did you say to her?' whispered Werner
when his brother fell into place again beside him.

'Would you have liked to see her standing at Mother's grave?'

A little later everyone queued up in front of Kaspar and the boys,
and there was an endless line of hands to be shaken: Kaspar's
friends, Martha's friends, mutual friends, incredible how many
people one knew, all passing by in the same rhythm, each face set
and meaningful.

Among the last was one that Stefan didn't recognize, while
Werner racked his brain: the young man from the hospital! What
was his name again? To his amazement his father came out at once
with it: 'Herr Wegmann! Thank you for coming.'

Finally into the black, chauffeur-driven limousine and back to
the Gellerstrasse. Alfred and Else Bannheimer came along too.
That helped; they kept up a conversation, halting at first but later
almost normal.

Upstairs in the apartment Stefan drew his brother aside. 'When
do you think we can get lost?'

'You can get lost if you like. I'll stay as long as he wants me to.'

Biting his lower lip, Stefan hissed: 'I know it now: you never
really loved Mother.'

'Idiot!' said Werner and turned away.

By the time it was dark, everyone had left. Kaspar had finally sent
Werner away; he needed to study for his exam. Life must go on; a
commonplace but none the less – or perhaps for that very reason –
true. He stood by the window, looking down at the dark street.
Everything was busily functioning: the buses, the cars speeding
by, the bicycles, the people. What a hurry they all seemed to be in!
Hardly anyone walked slowly. They all knew where they were
heading for, and everyone post-haste. He waited, hoping to see
someone sauntering along or perhaps stopping to look around,
hesitating, unable to make up his mind . . . But they all kept
rushing, rushing by. It was only for him that everything had come
to a stop. He heard himself say to somebody: No, no, you're
wrong. It's not because I loved her so much that everything's
standing still. I *didn't* – hadn't for a long time now. Maybe I did love

her once but I'm not even quite sure of that. Probably I never really loved her 'passionately', Tristan-and-Isolde style. She never caused me any pain, and that's the test, isn't it? Is a person like Martha capable of driving anyone to the very limit? And what is my limit? Does everyone *have* a limit? Is it just that some people are never put to the test? I certainly have no idea what my limit may be. I liked that dark box of yours, Uncle Stilts, wouldn't mind sitting in one myself. With peepholes.

Slowly he went over to the telephone.

Anya answered. 'Again? No good, Professor. He much tired all day after you here, not eat anything, not my chicken with rice . . .'

'Go and ask if I may come over.'

She returned after a moment and shouted angrily into the telephone: 'He say yes but I say no. I'm nurse.'

'You're not the nurse, Anya, you're a silly cow.'

A little while later he rang the Kaiserplatz doorbell, rang and rang but no one came. Finally the door was flung open. Anya barred the way, broom in hand, cheeks flaming, long platinum blonde hair dishevelled, a Viking breathing fire.

'Out of my way,' said Kaspar, pushing her aside. He couldn't help laughing though – until the broom came crashing down on his shoulder. It took all his strength to hold on to it, let alone wrench it out of her grip. They stood there, face to face, panting, and suddenly he kissed her so hard on her open mouth that their teeth clanked together. Dropping the broom, she jumped backward, clapping both hands to her mouth.

Kaspar quickly grabbed the broom. 'Did I hurt you? Yes? Good.' He tossed the broom into her arms and walked off down the hall towards the old man's bedroom, then turned around, just as he had the last time, and saw her still standing there, the broom in one hand, the other still covering her mouth, like a schoolgirl. Well, well – so that's the way to handle her. Jesus! Here I am, making a mental note for 'later' – and at the same time I'm crushed by Martha's death! What am I? A psychotic or a piece of shit?

The little dwarf sat up and smiled, false white teeth shining, spectacles on his nose, at the ready, with the bottle beside him on the bedside table.

'Nothing to drink for me today, Kaspar, even if I ask for it. Gave me a splitting headache last time. I knew you'd show up tonight – bad day, eh? *You* have a drink. You look as if you could do with one.'

Correct. Why hadn't he thought of *that*, instead of pressing his nose against the windowpane, sobbing?

'Well, what's new? What's up with Heidi?'

Kaspar took a quick swallow and shook his head. 'Get on with the story, Uncle Stilts.'

'Don't be so sorry for yourself, Inkworm, and stop kidding yourself. You picked the wrong woman and you never felt anything. Lost your wife and never loved her, so now you feel guilty. Nothing new in that. You're a guilt addict, you wake up every morning hung over with guilt – and now it's a bit worse than usual. It'll pass. Mark my words, some day you'll wonder what all the fuss was about.'

Kaspar gave him a long, barren look.

'What do you know about it, Uncle Stilts? Go on, start now or I'll . . .'

'Don't threaten me again, goddammit, I've got to get up steam, I can't just jump into that box on cue. Why, the damn thing isn't even built yet. Have you any idea how long that took? Wait a minute – something important's just come back to me: that first morning in the workshop, when everything went wrong – remember? Herr Ehrenreich already had a hunch he was on to something extra special. And your father, that Leopold, he put it into words when he said: "There mustn't be anything that could give the show away." The little box and what was in it had to be kept a secret.

'Well, that very first morning Herr Ehrenreich set us all up in a semi-circle, the six carpenters and Andros and my family, and sat down straddling his chair. Then we had to swear on the Bible that we'd never breathe a word to anyone, even on our deathbeds. And then, Kaspar . . .' – the old man giggled and shook his bristly white head – 'then the sly old devil said: "There now! But I still don't trust you. *You'll* tell your wife, *you'll* tell your brother, and so on. So I'm going to offer a reward. If you all keep the secret for three years from today, let's say, each of you gets a hundred gold marks. Agreed?" He stood up and came over to each one of us in turn and we all had to shake hands and look him in the eye. "Good. That's under control. Now let's get going. Any suggestions?"

'So they all pitch in with their damn brainwaves, and I'm the one who has to bear the brunt of it because I have to keep kneeling down, squatting, ducking my head, bending over, until they were sure of all the things that would *not* work. After all, it was quite possible that I might have to sit for fifteen minutes in the same position, without moving, if I was playing against a first-class opponent. So far as I was concerned, though, I was counting on five or six minutes a game at the outside.

'Well, we didn't get very far that day or the next. It took weeks and weeks, Kaspar, for them to come up with the right solution: the chessboard was to rest, so to speak, on my "invisible" legs. The board was the length of my leg from arse to feet – about twice the size of a normal one, with chessmen to match. This board had a false bottom with room for my legs, stretched out flat as a pancake. I sat with the upper part of my body bolt upright, tightly enclosed in an oblong box about sixteen inches high and eight inches wide. The chessboard was fixed to the front of the box, which was gaudily painted and had a visible little hole in it. Out of this hole stuck a kind of steel hook, which I could manoeuvre in any direction, and within the painted design there were two tiny peepholes that I could peer out of.

'What gave me the most trouble was the hook. Hour after hour I practised until I could pick up a piece and set it down again in one movement. And you needn't think it was a picnic, cooped up in that little box; it was summertime and hot as hell in there. I hadn't even turned fifteen and I was pampered and temperamental. I stuck it out because of the money. There was going to be oodles of it, starting with my first performance.

'The worst problem, however, was my mother, though God knows she certainly needed the stuff. "Why do we have to go through all this?" she yelled. "My poor boy's being half crucified in there." And she flatly refused to take me to the circus for the rehearsals.

'So Herr Ehrenreich bought my brothers out of their apprentice-ships, paid them a decent wage and all of a sudden they were tagging along behind me and being so goddamn friendly and taking so much interest in the whole business that you'd think they'd already guessed they were going to make millions. Don't gawk at me, Inkworm. Millions, I tell you.'

'What happened to the millions? We never had a penny except for Father's salary in Yugoslavia.'

'War. Inflation. Ever heard of that? And you a teacher!'

'Only of Slavic languages, Uncle Stilts.'

'Do you teach Russian too?' He snapped his fingers and called out: '*Podajte sani! Skorej, Kutscher!*'

'What's that supposed to mean?'

'Bring my sleigh. Faster, driver!' St Petersburg, thought Kaspar to himself. 'But the sleigh'll have to wait a while; haven't given my first performance yet, have I? Well, the day came when Herr Ehrenreich said: "We're about ready. Now your mother can take a look."

'It was almost winter and freezing cold in the workshop tent, in spite of all the stoves. Everything was set up: a chair and a blanket for Mother, the chess machine on a table and Herr Ehrenreich himself sitting in front of it. The back panel of the box could be opened and I climbed in and pulled it shut behind me.

'"Yoohoo, Mother," I shouted. "I'm all warm and cosy in here."

'"No fooling around now," said Herr Ehrenreich severely. "Pretend we're on the stage. Curtain up!"

'We started to play, one of the games we'd played hundreds of times at rehearsals, just long enough to convince Mother that we were really having fun. Herr Ehrenreich opened with white and my hook darted out.

'"Jesus, Mary and Joseph!" exclaimed my mother.

'We went on playing. No one spoke. When I'd mated Herr Ehrenreich, the hook knocked three times on the table. Finis. I climbed out, beaming. "Well?"

'Mother was thinking hard but not saying a word.

'"Well?" added Herr Ehrenreich a bit impatiently.

'Slowly and haltingly Mother began to speak, as if she herself needed to sort out her impressions first. "Herr Ehrenreich – I don't rightly know . . . What if folks just don't understand what's going on and get bored, as I was, although I was fair flummoxed at first, I can tell you that. Here I am, sitting smack up against the thingummajig, right? Just think how it's going to be in the big ring! What about all those poor souls in the back seats? And all the dumb clucks like me, who don't know the first thing about chess?"

'Dead silence. It slowly dawned on us that we'd all been so submerged in the technical problems that we'd lost sight of the main one: our number wasn't a circus act; it was a wash-out.

'Herr Ehrenreich had been bending menacingly over Mother. Now he straightened up, walked silently back to his own chair and slumped into it as though his legs had suddenly given out. But

Mother kept right on thinking aloud and – get the irony of it, Kaspar! – *she*, the only one who had wanted no part of the whole enterprise, she was the one who found the answer. Just like she took over the household when she was a child, remember? Here she was again, faced with a practical problem that had to be solved somehow – and she completely forgot that she was really *against* the whole deal.

'"See here, Herr Ehrenreich, ain't there a freak show in your outfit? Well now, in my understanding a freak show only has a couple of dozen rows of seats, ain't that right? The people sit right up front by the stage. And maybe you ought to have a person, clever-like, to make all them moves clear and make it real exciting. 'Oh well done, Sir! That was a tough 'un for the machine!' or 'Bravo, Machine! Top-hole! A right genius! – or summat like that."

'"Summat like that!" exclaimed Herr Ehrenreich, jumping up. "*You're* a genius, Frau Schulte, a gold-mine of ideas, a real creative thinker!"

'"Good Lord," said my mother. "It's just plain common sense."

'Herr Ehrenreich bent low over her chair and said reverently: "Madam, that plain common sense of yours is exactly what we lack. Would you do me the honour of becoming managing director of the freak show?"

'My brothers and I just watched and kept mum. We knew, of course. While Grandfather was still alive, Mother had listened to that kind of chess-dialogue from me every day for years on end. It had stuck in her mind and now it came out again.

'"Managing director? Goodness me – if I live to be a hundred, I'd never manage that," she said, quite dismayed.

'But how she managed it! From one day to the next her entire life was turned inside out. No more cooking or cleaning house for her. Like in a fairy tale, practically overnight, Herr Ehrenreich had two rooms built on to our house and two big fat women moved in, for from that day on Mother worked full-time in the circus, lived in a caravan, went on the road with it, fired acts she didn't like, engaged new ones, "Nature's Wonders", one and all. My word, the things you could see patiently waiting in her outer office! But she drew the line at hideous freaks: the bearded lady with a bosom was as far as she'd go. And that one was no fake either, just as good as the one in Toledo painted by El Greco. One day an act showed up: a girl with two boa constrictors. I sneaked in while she gave an audition. There she was, writhing about on the floor, half naked, with the great fat snakes twining themselves around her in a sort of rhythm – oh my Lord! Really fascinating. But Mother would have nothing to do with that kind of thing. "We're running a Christian-like freak show," she used to say, and Herr Ehrenreich would nod severely and try to keep a straight face.

'I was to be the star turn. Over the entrance would be a sign in huge letters: THE CHESS MACHINE. THE EIGHTH WONDER OF THE WORLD. WHO WILL CHALLENGE IT? TEN GOLD MARKS TO THE WINNER.

'Of course we weren't sure whether the crowd strolling about among the sideshows would include any chess-players or whether enough people would drift into our tent anyway to see the other "Wonders": the two-headed calf, the orang-utan with three ears, the parrot that walked the tightrope holding a parasol in its beak and whistling "God save the King". Christian-like acts, one and all.

'15 December 1905 was the date of my first appearance, in Stuttgart. Herr Ehrenreich had had the entrance to our tent newly decorated. Mother found the lighting a bit gaudy but it certainly drew the crowds. We didn't have a fixed schedule – we'd begin whenever the house was full – and very soon it *was* full, shortly after the coloured letters outside started to blink.

'I was placed the last number before the intermission. Herr Ehrenreich hadn't found the right kind of commentator, so he'd decided to give it a try himself. He looked very impressive standing there in front of the curtain in white tie and tails, telling the audience how he'd spent a fortune on this machine with a built-in brain. Where had he found it? In America, where else? Yes, such were the miracles modern science could achieve with the help of magnets and electrical instruments – plus a secret process which for obvious reasons he couldn't reveal to them. "Ladies and gentlemen, if you think this is just some cheap trick, put it to the test! Pick someone from among you who plays chess – a *good* player if possible – let him play a game against the machine. If he can checkmate it, he gets ten gold marks. A fraud? Ladies and gentlemen, I invite you to come up here on stage and see for yourselves. Curtain up!"

'He clapped his hands; from the orchestra pit came a roll of drums, and the curtain rose, revealing an empty stage, an empty chair and a table and on the table a sort of box with a strut attached to it supporting the chessboard. The crowd laughed and applauded.

'"Well now," said Herr Ehrenreich, "the machine is about to start charging itself – I can reveal to you that it works on batteries – is there someone out there who plays chess?"

'Several men immediately stood up; then a couple more, maybe a dozen altogether.

'"Excellent, ladies and gentlemen! Plenty of experts to observe the machine in action; it is looking forward to it, I can tell. Please pick a worthy opponent for it."

'It was quite something: three of them began fighting for the privilege and finally they had to toss for it.

'"Ready? Bravo! A hand for the brave volunteer! Come up here, please, Sir, and tell us your name."

'I watched intently through my peepholes as a fat man of about forty climbed the steps to the stage, his face flushed, and sweating profusely. A Herr Kunstel, watch-maker by trade and a passionate chess-player. Ehrenreich shook hands with him. "Please walk around the table, Sir, and tell the audience if you see anything suspicious, wires, cables and the like. Nothing? Good! Please sit down so that the machine can plug into your electric wavelength. Oh yes, indeed, Herr Kunstel, you emit an electric wavelength. We all do. And now please count slowly up to ten." And to the audience, baring his teeth apologetically: "Patience, the mechanism's working. Well now, Herr Kunstel, the machine has offered you white, as you see." And, once more to the audience, "White always has the first move and therefore the advantage, you know. Please begin, Herr Kunstel."

'Kunstel opened with P–KB3. "A pawn! That leaves everything still open," sang out Herr Ehrenreich. My hook darted out – nervous giggling and exclamations of "Ah! Ah!" from the audience – and moved a black pawn, P–K4. But Herr Ehrenreich exclaimed: "Oh, oh!" and wrung his hands. "Oh, oh, Herr Kunstel, I'm afraid you've laid yourself open to Fool's Mate! Careful now! Careful! Think twice before you make your next move."

'My fat opponent breathed heavily and hesitated. Then he reached for another pawn and moved it two squares forward, P–KN4.

'Ehrenreich clapped his hand to his forehead and groaned. "What did I tell you? Oh my God, my God! Watch out for the black queen."

'I was so overcome by Herr Ehrenreich's acting talent that I almost forgot it was my move. Childishly simple: my hook shot out, seized my queen and neatly set it down beside Kunstel's second pawn, Q–KR5. Check! The white king was done for, poor devil. The hook knocked three times on the board, withdrew, and Herr Ehrenreich stepped forward and announced in a funereal voice: "Checkmate in two moves! Yes, ladies and gentlemen, it *can* be done! A slip-up. Probably the gentleman was nervous. Let's offer Herr Kunstel our sympathy and give him another chance. What do you say?"

'Applause and shouts of "Bravo!" Up on stage Herr Kunstel's head had sunk down on the chessboard. Ehrenreich patted him on the shoulder and said: "Agreed, Herr Kunstel?" Kunstel raised his head and nodded; his cheeks had turned a purplish red and words failed him.

'Quickly Herr Ehrenreich set up the board again. There must have been people in the audience who didn't know the first thing about chess but they didn't find it boring, as Mother had been afraid they would. The mysterious-looking box, the atmosphere of competition, Herr Ehrenreich's histrionics and Kunstel's genuine collapse were more than enough to satisfy them. Besides, money was at stake and that appeals to everybody.

'"*Da capo*," intoned Herr Ehrenreich unctuously. "Ready, Herr Kunstel? The machine is still plugged into your magnetic field. Once again it has offered you white. Yes, the machine is always generous. Ready? On your marks. Go."

'Again he opened with a pawn, P–K3. I countered with P–K4. Then his knight zigzagged over his pawn: K–KB3.

'"Aha, the Giuco Piano opening!" exclaimed Ehrenreich excitedly. "This is getting interesting!" My hook picked up my bishop, B–B4. 'Oh! What a cunning move, Machine!" cried Ehrenreich. "Reckless – but excellent."

'It wasn't reckless at all, of course, it was a standard move. Kunstel responded with his bishop . . .'

'Stop it, Uncle Stilts, I don't know anything about chess.'

'Inkworm! You're spoiling my fun. Oh, all right then, so we played the Giuco Piano – a gambit, Herr Professor, that goes back to the eighteenth century – and for about three minutes I gave Kunstel his head. From time to time Ehrenreich would warn him with old bromides like: "Anyone with any style keeps a bishop out of the file." Or "Don't be too greedy, Sir, the queen's not going to run away." And then it was as good as over because Kunstel fell into a perfectly simple trap . . .'

'Uncle Stilts!'

'Yes, yes, dammit, I keep forgetting that I'm talking to a moron. Anyway, after three minutes twelve seconds he was checkmate.'

'You can't possibly still remember that!'

'Why, Inkworm, you *never* forget a thing like that. Stop interrupting. Where was I?'

'Three minutes and twelve seconds.'

'Checkmate. I'd let him beat himself fair and square, and he got some applause as he tramped back down the stairs . . . But wait now, something else is coming back to me: yes, when my hook gave the three knocks and Ehrenreich called out: "Checkmate," poor Kunstel tried to shake hands with the hook! I quickly snatched it back and Herr Ehrenreich asked anxiously: "Did you get an electric shock?"

'"I – I don't know, maybe I did," said the poor man in confusion. They were all confused, Kaspar, everyone I played against. The machine threw them, they couldn't catch their breath. Later they'd say they'd felt groggy from the electric current and that's why they hadn't played their best.

'Instead of ringing down the curtain immediately, Ehrenreich let the audience take another look at the machine, standing up there on stage, so quiet and mysterious. This had a sensational effect, it never failed and never varied: first a second or two of awed silence, then thunderous applause for the solitary box – with me inside it.

'That first time I had pins and needles in my legs, my heart was thumping, tears were running down my cheeks. I heard the curtain come down and then I was carried off. Footsteps – doors slamming – then a knock on the back panel of my box. . . . But I had to take several deep breaths before I could open up. Ehrenreich lifted me up and kissed me on both cheeks. Then I caught sight of Mother and my brothers. We all burst into tears.'

He stopped speaking and gnawed his upper lip violently, then said suddenly: 'Doesn't it seem a bit strange to you that Ehrenreich should have been so set on this act? After all I was only one number in his little freak show. What brought him in the real money was the show in the big ring. Well, he was a strange bird all right, Herr

Ehrenreich. He had studied law and was about to join a law firm when his father died and he inherited the circus. He was fascinated by it, no doubt about that, but he never completely lost his liking for things intellectual, he'd lie awake at night in his caravan reading poetry and the classics. Chess sort of filled the gap. After all, it isn't just a game, it's a discipline. Not to mention the kick he got out of all the hocus-pocus. "The Chess Machine!" he used to say. "Nature's Wonders! The biggest wonder of them all is how keen everybody is to be bamboozled."

'I didn't like to hear him talk like that. I *was* a wonder, what else?'

CHAPTER FIVE

I T was still early, barely eleven o'clock, when Kaspar got home. Two hours at a time was all the old man could manage. In the end he had lapsed into muttering:'Good old box . . . my friend, that box . . . nothing could touch me in there.' But when Kaspar stood up to leave, he mumbled: 'You ain't heard nothing yet, Inkworm, just you wait . . . You'll be surprised . . . .'

Surprised – no, that wasn't quite the right word. He had listened, fascinated, to the old man in exactly the same way he used to listen to his father. Not to his mother: it was his father who would sit down by his bed and ask: 'Harun al-Rashid? Ulysses? Baron Münchhausen? What'll it be today?' Now it was Uncle Stilts's turn, incognito like Harun al-Rashid, tricky as Ulysses, outrageous as Münchhausen. The only difference was that Uncle Stilts's story was true. And yet Kaspar still found it hard to believe in the dwarf's physical reality, even when he was sitting right there facing him. Ever since his earliest childhood the little man had been for him an almost mythical character – he might as well have been a frog with golden eyes. He had listened, enthralled and entertained, yet never once had he thought: all this *has* happened – to my uncle, to my own flesh and blood, so to speak. Was that because of Martha? He had a weird feeling of being mildly anaesthetized. At the Institute they had offered him as much time off as he wanted but that would have been the worst possible thing. Tomorrow he'd go back, though he dreaded his students stammering their condolences. Maybe he'd pin up a notice on the bulletin board: CONDOLENCES FOR PROFESSOR SCHULTE IN SLAVIC LANGUAGES ONLY, PLEASE. Then he would be able to respond, grammatically correct.

He opened the flat's front door without turning the light on and drifted slowly from one dark room to another, including the kitchen. The sky was bright, the moon almost full. In every room he forced himself to stand quite still for a few minutes and look around. At last he returned to the living-room. Well here I am, he thought, I'm not expecting anyone, and no one will drop in. There's nothing else to be got out of this evening. Automatically he turned on the television, but the loud voices frightened him and he quickly switched it off again. The brilliant picture shuddered and faded out. Comforting silence.

He drifted into the bedroom and began to undress, obstinately refusing to turn on the light as a sort of challenge. He managed quite well, even the glass of water, and the tranquillizer too. In pitch darkness! Let someone else try that. He crawled into bed, folded his arms behind his head and waited. One could always rely on Valium. But that was about all one *could* rely on. Heidi or not Heidi, that was the question. And the answer? Not now. Definitely not now.

He woke without a headache but with no precise memory of the preceding evening; even Uncle Stilts's story had become fuzzy.

The telephone rang as he sat down to breakfast. A man's voice with a heavy accent, an unfamiliar name. Could he take private lessons with the Professor – but not at the Institute – beginning today? At five o'clock? Vairy goot. You've said it, thought Kaspar as he hung up the phone, vairy goot, I need to see a new face. And now for the Institute. For the time being things would be the way they'd always been. The mild anaesthesia made decisions impossible. 'It'll pass.' Yes, Uncle Stilts.

The man who showed up at five o'clock on the dot was not a student. Forty years old at least, high forehead, sparse black hair, stocky and muscular. The face seemed of an almost classical beauty, a sharply chiselled nose and dark, deep-set eyes, suspicious, yet melancholy too. Kaspar felt sure he was a Croat. Not a Yugoslav – that word was taboo – a Croat. Who was it the other day that had warned him to beware of Croat pupils? One of his colleagues at the university, no doubt. And he had secretly agreed, for ever since the strange disappearance of that young fellow Branco what's-his-name he had decided to try and refuse Croat pupils – though, undoubtedly, they were the most intelligent of the lot. Branco . . . About six months ago he had joined Kaspar's class, a thin young lad with oily black hair and blue eyes; he might have been Irish except for his olive-coloured skin. By far the brightest pupil, he never missed a lesson. And then he had suddenly dropped out of sight, and when Kaspar questioned the others they shrugged, and when he insisted he had faced a blank, impenetrable wall. Still he hadn't given up, had found out Branco's address and driven to the little boarding house outside Munich where he lived, to be told by the landlord that not only had the young man disappeared but his mother too, the very next day. A man had called on her, a stranger, and when he left, she had fled from the house in tears, leaving her few belongings behind, and never returned. Kaspar had gone into the small room where the two had lived. He had only stayed a minute or so, looking around the tidy, lifeless abode, and had experienced a suffocating feeling of anxiety and doom. None of my business, he had thought on the way home, steering his car through the Munich traffic and actually enjoying the throng that usually enervated him – but today it appeared downright protective. He was a Bavarian citizen, he belonged, nobody threatened him, life was unexciting but at least safe. Poor Branco, he had seemed such a quiet, industrious, decent lad – oh well, better not pry any further. And, above all, not get embroiled in those fanatic ethnic problems.

And now – this man. He was far too old for an immigrant labourer. What was he doing in Germany? Kaspar racked his brains but he couldn't think of an excuse not to start the lesson. What is more, the man impressed him. He wasn't the type to be shown the door without a very good reason. From the way he laid his notebook and pencil down on the table it was obvious that he was left-handed, though only recently so because he still had trouble handling the pencil with his left hand. On the right one he wore a black leather glove. His German was negligible, but after the first few minutes of initial awkwardness he turned out to be highly intelligent and even of a certain distinction, due to his eyes and his voice, which was very deep and, in spite of the kindergarten level of their conversation, full of authority. He learned more in the first lesson than most students learned in weeks. When he stood up, after exactly sixty minutes, he insisted on paying then and there, in cash.

Later Werner called to ask if he should come over. Or rather *might* come over. Might, yes. Should, no. In the end he did come, shyness all over his narrow, dark-complexioned face, which all of a sudden reminded Kaspar strongly of Martha. Eyes of the same nondescript colour – dishwater colour, she called it – the fine straight nose, the slightly hunched gait.

Frau Henning, the part-time help who had looked after them for the last five years, had bought cold cuts and cheese and arranged it on two big platters under a plastic wrap, like an illustration of gracious living in *The Kitchen and the New Woman*. Slices of salami formed a circle around a fat chunk of liverwurst garnished with radishes cut into rosebuds, and bouquets of parsley, which Kaspar detested, everywhere. Same with the cheese platter: slices of Edam and Swiss cheese rolled and arranged like a dahlia. Frau Henning had a marked preference for the finer things of life, as she herself was the first to admit. She also had definite ideas about how one communicated elegantly in writing, namely, in the third person. From time to time she would leave a note on the kitchen table: 'Frau Henning regrets that she can't come tomorrow. Yours truly, Frau Henning.' Or a postcard from her summer vacation: 'Frau Henning is revelling on Nature's bosom and reposes by the lake. Best regards, Frau Henning.'

Kaspar and Werner tacitly agreed to eat in the kitchen and not, as usual, in the living-room. Important: a downward trend in their social habits to accentuate the difference that Martha's death had made. They talked only of practical matters: Werner's approaching exam, Kaspar's new Croat student. In between, impossible to bridge, silence.

Pulling a packet of cigarettes from his pocket, Werner pushed his plate aside. 'I phoned you several times last night. The other night too.'

'When did you take up smoking?'

'You weren't home.'

'I *wasn't* at Heidi's.'

'Stefan's moved in with me, he's sleeping on the sofa. He's given up his room at the boarding house.'

'Why?'

'He can't sleep, he smokes all night. That's what got me started but I'll give it up again as soon as Stefan gets straightened out.'

'Is it because of Mother?'

'He sees Heidi in the cafeteria at the hospital. He always goes at different times but he can't help running into her occasionally.'

'And that upsets him?'

'He says she's to blame for Mother's death.'

'He may not be far wrong there.'

Werner opened his mouth but got no farther than a firm shake of the head.

'Yes, I mean it. Heidi *is* to blame. And yet it couldn't be helped. Do you understand?'

The young man nodded wordlessly, feeling like a traitor. Sitting beside Stefan's sofa at night, he 'understood' quite different things. The trouble with him was that he understood too damn much and too much of it was contradictory.

'We were friends, your mother and I. Don't underestimate that.'

'Are you in love with Heidi?'

'I don't think so.'

'You aren't sure?'

'No.'

'But, Father . . .'

'Why do you think I ought to be sure?'

'For God's sake, if you're not in love with her, why do you . . .'

'Why do I have an affair with her?'

'For so long, Father! It's not just a passing roll in the hay, it's been going on for years.'

'Five and a half. Seems long to you, doesn't it, a quarter of your life; to me it seems quite a short time. That's the difference between you and me – the only difference. Or does it seem unthinkable that you might one day cheat on your wife?'

After a short hesitation and without looking at his father: 'Not unthinkable, no.'

'But unthinkable to Stefan, I'm sure. He has no imagination.'

'I've tried to make him see things – well, the way they really are between two people. But he can think of nothing but Mother and how unhappy she was. He hates Heidi.'

'Does he know her?'

'No. It's like an obsession. He's waiting for you and Heidi to . . .'

'To get married?'

'Then he's going to let her have it. He won't say what.'

Kaspar was silent for a while. All of a sudden he noticed that he was gnawing at his upper lip just like Uncle Stilts, and he laughed aloud; he too probably looked like a gorilla.

'I don't think it's funny,' said Werner stiffly.

'I don't either. Do *you* know Heidi?'

'You once introduced us, don't you remember? At Toby's. I'd
come to pick you up after lunch.'
'But you've never talked to her?'
'No. Do you still meet there?'
'I haven't seen her since Mother's death. And you can tell that to
Stefan.'
'But – where *do* you spend your evenings then? I've called you at
the Bannheimers' too.'
'Are you worried about me? Relax, I'm at Uncle Stilts's.'
'What on earth do you do there?'
'He tells me stories and I listen. Don't ask me what stories, or
why; at this point I need him. More than I need Heidi. Besides –
and I know how unfair this is – I feel the same way Stefan does:
she *is* to blame.'
'But . . .'
'That doesn't mean that I'm not going to see her again.
Everything has its own time – and everything passes, even *my* guilt
feelings.'
Uncle Stilts again, he thought. I'm reduced to nothing but an
echo.
'*You* feel guilty? But you just said . . .'
'Heidi's guilty, I'm guilty, even your mother was guilty. Don't
jump down my throat, Werner, try to see what I'm getting at: your
mother was an extraordinary woman, I'm a very ordinary man.
Maybe she should have treated me in a very ordinary way. But she
didn't, she was generous and tolerant and – passive. Perhaps that
was a mistake. I don't know. But one thing I do know: nobody
intended to hurt anyone, including Heidi.'
Werner sighed like a tired old man. He felt like one too, with this
hide-and-seek father and a brother charged with dynamite. 'May I
ask what's going to happen now?'
'Nothing for the present. Tomorrow I'll go back to the Institute.
I'll eat whatever Frau Henning leaves for me; I have a new student
for private lessons. Go on home now and tell Stefan to return to his
old digs and start sleeping at night. If anything changes, he can
move back in with you and sharpen his knife.'

In her small flat Heidi had stayed home every night that
week but Kaspar didn't call. Of course not, after all she couldn't
expect him *now* to call her on his way home, just to say goodnight,

the way he used to. Equally impossible to meet him at Toby's for lunch, or for him just to ring her doorbell out of the blue . . .

When the doorbell did ring one evening, she turned so pale and breathless that her cousin, who had dropped in to borrow a picnic basket, was quite alarmed. No, no, she wasn't sick, just a bit overworked.

And worried. For days she had had the feeling that she was being followed. Walking down Leopoldstrasse in the evening, she thought she heard footsteps but she didn't want to appear afraid and glance back. But when she got to her front door and looked quickly around as she put the key into the lock, there was no one there.

On the ninth day after Martha's death she finally saw him. She had stopped suddenly outside a bookshop and there he was, right behind her. She could see his reflection in the shop window, a young man in jeans and windcheater. She turned around. He stood with his arms hanging loose and looked at her attentively, without embarrassment. Heidi took a step forward; after all they weren't alone on the Leopoldstrasse, a woman with a dog had just walked by between them.

'What do you want?' she asked quietly. 'Is there something I can do for you?'

'Yes, there is,' said the young man. 'Would you have a cup of coffee with me? There must be a café somewhere around here. Are you familiar with this neighbourhood?'

'There's one over there,' she said, taken aback by his easy manner. 'But why? Who are you?'

'My name's Harold Wegmann,' said the young man. 'I absolutely must talk to you.'

'I haven't time,' said Heidi. 'I work.'

'So do I,' said the young man. 'But this is more important.'

'What's more important?'

'I have to talk to you about Martha.'

'Martha?' she repeated tonelessly.

'Martha Schulte. Surely you can spare half an hour?'

Silently they walked side by side, crossed the street and entered a little café called Lottie's. The young man took her coat and led the way to a corner table as if he had been a steady customer for years. He sat down facing her and scrutinized her as impersonally as a passport control officer.

'Well?' she said, to put an end to the inspection.

'Excuse me, but I must look at you very carefully. I have to compare you . . .'

A waitress in a white apron approached. 'Two coffees, please,' he said, without taking his eyes off Heidi.

'I don't understand . . .'

'I have to compare you with Martha. I'm sure I don't have to tell you why.'

'Oh yes, you do,' said Heidi firmly. 'What do you want of me? Who are you, anyway?'

By the time the coffee came, he had explained. She listened stunned, unable to speak.

'Do you believe in chance?' he asked. 'I don't. Something *made* me pass my driver's test that Wednesday and turn off into that lay-by. Since then I've gone to the cemetery every day during my lunch hour. There's a bench not far from her grave and a few days ago I saw her younger son there. The father's never been yet.' He stopped but she said nothing. 'I talked to the son. His name's Stefan. Do you know him?'

'Not really.'

'He hates you.'

'I know.'

'He was in a very bad way, crying. I offered him a cigarette. He sat down beside me on the bench and smoked the whole packet. Then I said that I had been holding his mother's head in my lap. That's why he told me – about you.'

After a while Heidi said in a low voice: 'What do you want of me then?'

'I know it sounds crazy but somehow I feel part of it. I've already achieved a lot this week: Stefan's my friend now – and here I am sitting talking to you. That's very important. Important for you too, you'll see. Do you think it would be all right if I called the Professor sometime?'

'Try it,' said Heidi. 'Now I have to go.'

The young man brought her coat. As she was putting it on, he said suddenly: 'Here's my card. Don't throw it away. You may need it. It's quite possible that *you'll* want to talk to somebody who's part of it.'

'Thanks,' said Heidi, putting the card in her purse. 'Thank you for the coffee. You will stop following me now, won't you?'

'Of course. But I had to find out whether you fit in.'

'And do I?' she asked and wished she had sounded ironical rather than anxious.

'Oh yes,' said the young man. 'Everything's fine.'

CHAPTER SIX

PUNCTUALLY at five o'clock the Croat reappeared. His name was Ante Luburic. Besides memorizing all the vocabulary from the first lesson, he had learned several dozen words out of the dictionary, although his accent was atrocious. 'Struggle', 'freedom', 'independence', 'saucepan', 'spoon', things political and domestic, not just another case of quickly, quickly into a factory job. That would have been something of a problem anyway with only one hand.

He sat at the table, his face bent over his notebook, the powerful shoulders so hunched up in concentration that his head seemed to disappear into them. On one side the lifeless right hand in its black leather glove, on the other his huge left hand, clenched into a fist. From time to time he would bang on the table in a rage at his 'slow brain'.

'Take it easy,' said Kaspar, articulating every syllable. 'You're doing very well. *Prav dobro.*'

Luburic raised his massive sun-tanned forehead, moist with effort, and smiled for the first time, revealing teeth – his own – as white and even as Uncle Stilts's. On the dot of six he stood up, paid and shook Kaspar's hand in a painfully strong grip.

At the front door he lingered, hesitating before he took the plunge. Would the Professor also give lessons to a friend of his? Yes? Then his friend would come with him tomorrow. And could the Professor perhaps make it two for the price of one? – his friend had five children and no money.

Some nerve, thought Kaspar, but he nodded. They were taking advantage of him, yet the mild anaesthesia prevented him from getting angry. In any case, nothing could really upset him because tonight he was going to see Uncle Stilts again. He had woken up in the morning, strangely excited, his throat dry. He had dreamt that it was he who was sitting in the little box and it had been unbearably hot and at the same time rather enjoyable. He could hardly wait for the next instalment of the chess story. He had already checked with Anya, who hadn't even bothered to go and ask: the Master was expecting him.

She opened the door and stood there expectantly, her head raised. He kissed her quickly without really putting his mind to it. His mind was where it had been all day: in the box with the little old man.

The night-light was on. A small table had been placed beside the bedpost on 'his' side, with a bottle of whisky, soda water and ice, and a little heap of caviar on a plate, a spoon and a half a lemon.

'I'm not sure yet . . .' said the dwarf, who was sitting bolt upright in a dark velvet jacket with gold buttons over his pyjamas. 'We may be taking a trip to Russia today, Kaspar. But don't start on the caviar just yet.'

The sofa cushion was already propped against the bedpost. Kaspar swung his legs up and poured himself a glass of whisky. 'Let's go!' He leaned back and closed his eyes.

But the old man hesitated. He had clasped his hands and kept fidgeting with his fingers.

Kaspar opened his eyes. 'What is it, Uncle Stilts? Have you forgotten where we left off?'

'It gets very complicated from now on – and . . . er, embarrassing.'

'Embarrassing? Nothing embarrasses me. I don't know the feeling.'

'I'm going to have to talk about someone – a certain person – who comes into the story now. I can't leave her out, much as I'd like to. What I'd really like to do is . . .' He splayed his tiny fingers, then tightened them.

'Strangle her?'

The fingers relaxed on the bedspread, meekly clasped. I've never seen him like this, thought Kaspar, he's quite pitiful today, with his velvet jacket and gold buttons.

'You see, Ehrenreich had a niece, his younger brother's child, although he was long dead, the brother. Ehrenreich had raised her as if she were his daughter. He had daughters of his own but no one ever set eyes on them. They hated the circus and everything connected with it, and so did their mother. They all hung out somewhere on the Riviera; he never mentioned his family. It was one of the Trigolinis who told me about them. They worked on the high wire without a net, and one of them, Giorgio, was a friend of mine. But he had no idea, mind you, that I was the chess machine! In the evenings I used to hang around in the wings, but that was only natural because Mother was managing director of the freak show and my brothers did odd jobs all over the lot. Also, they all knew I was a personal friend of Herr Ehrenreich, so nobody paid any attention to the fact that just before the chess number I would quietly slip into his private offices, where the box was kept in a separate room with a big safe that he'd had specially made – the "safe room" – and that room was always carefully locked. I climbed into the box, Herr Ehrenreich rang a bell and one of "our" workmen, you know, one of the six who were in the know, carried the thing on stage. When the curtain came down again, he carried me off stage and back to the safe. Not a soul ever suspected anything.

'To start with: nobody knew I could play chess. If two people happened to be having a game, I would watch open-mouthed and mutter about how I wished I understood what was going on. Jesus – how badly they played! The more I watched the more it dawned on me what a wizard I was. And I needed to know that because – well, on account of that girl, Lisa was her name. She was initiated into our secret by Herr Ehrenreich in my presence, and, of course, solemnly sworn to secrecy. That was about a year after our first performance, I was fifteen or sixteen and we'd been on tour for months, not only in Germany, but in Switzerland and Italy too.

'By that time we all knew that Herr Ehrenreich's commentary and the way he carried on to build up the excitement was the heart and soul of the whole act. One time he lost his voice and couldn't appear – and it was a complete flop, I tell you, the audience didn't give a damn whether the machine won or lost, because they didn't understand what was going on! And in other countries – well, Herr Ehrenreich spoke pretty good Italian, but his French wasn't up to it. That's why he made his niece come, she'd been at boarding-school in Paris and he hoped that *she* might take over the number in France.

'One day I was called into his office – and there she was.

'"Ah, at last! That's him, that's our beloved Stilts," he exclaimed, or something of the sort, I can't remember; I was staring at the girl. Was she ever beautiful! I'd never seen anything like her in my life. Friendly, too, gave me a kiss right off. I went clean out of my mind.'

He stopped, gnawed frantically at his upper lip and stared at the bedspread. After a while Kaspar said: 'Uncle Stilts, you amaze me. Why is it embarrassing for you to tell me you fell in love with a girl?'

The old man gave him a long, dour look and stopped gnawing.

'What do you take me for, a bloody fool? A dwarf and a normal pretty girl – that's a laugh!'

'Why? Just because she was a head taller? She was probably two heads dumber too. She should have been proud! You were something quite unique, Uncle Stilts, didn't she know that?'

'She knew it.'

'Well then?'

'She was – unique, too. At least I thought so.'

'In what way?'

'She was quite – amoral.' He fell silent.

'Have a drink, Uncle Stilts.'

'You want to make it easy for me, Kaspar, but you don't fool me. I know you've been wondering what a freak like me got up to – in that department. Can't help it, it still shocks me and I feel – kind of humiliated to mention that sort of thing. Sure, I've had plenty of time to get used to the way people talk about it today like they talk about the weather, everybody putting in his pennyworth, and the children asking their parents when and where and how. It still – well, it upsets me, but I can't skip it, it belongs to the story. I was part of the circus by then, had been for over a year, and in a year of circus life, willy-nilly, you get to know all there is to know, from the animals to the circus folk – and, believe me, there isn't much difference. The way those trapeze-girls talked among themselves! And those phoney bigmouths, the muscle-boys! But the worst of all were the three dwarfs. Of course, looking back, I'm more of a mind to understand why they weren't exactly brimming over with brotherly love. I've met a few dwarfs in my time – in everyday life, not show business – who were intelligent and decent, but those three in the Sarasate Circus were lowdown, lecherous goats. Maybe the circus made them that way. They were forced to make a living out of the very thing that ruined their life.

'At the start they received me with open arms, naturally. They thought I was one of them, and in that respect they were quite right, only I refused to face it. Right away they invited me out for a beer and hamburgers. I couldn't think of an excuse so I went off with them to some favourite joint of theirs. They downed one beer after another and then they started to brag about their exploits and how they'd fallen upon the little daughter of our Indian mahout – six years old she was and no bigger than they – and all the fun they'd had with her. And no one knew, not even her father; she'd been too ashamed to tell. It made me want to puke, and I got up and left. After that we never exchanged another word, but sometimes, when I happened to pass by them, I could feel their eyes on me.

'The point is, after a couple of months in the circus there wasn't much left of my innocence except that in practice I hadn't . . . I mean . . . anyway: when Herr Ehrenreich told Lisa about the machine, she clapped her hands and couldn't believe it. Night after night she used to stand in the wings, watching, and when they carried me off stage and I climbed out of my box in the safe-room, there she'd be, and she'd kiss me – why, I really can't tell you. I'm inclined to think she regarded me as a sort of adopted child – people do sometimes get too much of a kick out of kissing children, don't they? – and she certainly wasn't short of – well, let's call it affection. Her father was long dead. Her mother had remarried and gone to live abroad. And at that boarding-school in Paris – God knows what went on there.'

'Naturally.'

'You call that natural? So much the better. Maybe I provided some kind of substitute for what she'd been up to with her girl-friends at school, quite harmless, sort of – don't you think, Kaspar?'

'Not necessarily, but it's not important.'

'Well, I'm convinced that what she did with me when I climbed out of the box – and let me tell you, I've given this a lot of thought – must have been some kind of sequel, only – well, more exciting because after all I was a boy.'

'Exactly.'

The dwarf continued in a much lower voice: 'You can imagine how exciting it was for *me*. There I sat in my box on the stage, focussing on that damned chessboard, but my thoughts kept running away to – to quite different things and I couldn't wait to checkmate the idiot playing against me. I'd take shortcuts and risks – Herr Ehrenreich was sometimes quite scared – but nothing ever went wrong. Applause and cheering and more applause, then a quick exit into the safe-room, open up the back panel – and there she was.'

He sank back into the pillow and stared at the ceiling. 'It's no use, Kaspar, you'll just have to let your imagination take over. But don't forget one thing: the safe-room was right next to Herr Ehrenreich's office and he was always going in and out, so don't let your imagination run riot, if you know what I mean . . .

'Well, this went on for quite a while. We were planning to go to France in the spring, and Herr Ehrenreich wanted Lisa to learn chess really well or she wouldn't be able to do the commentary. I was supposed to teach her. Who else? *He* had no time; running a circus there's always plenty of problems. For instance, two of his elephants had just died and the entire number was up the creek because now the other elephants messed up their polka by grabbing the wrong tails!

'I was supposed to give her lessons in our caravan, the one Mother and I shared, but she complained that there were too many disturbances, which was true enough, people always coming and going, never a dull moment with "Nature's Wonders". So she asked her uncle if we could work for an hour or two in *her* wagon, and he said of course we could. I remember how that "of course" rankled. Rankled and goaded me on.

'When I knocked on the door of her caravan for the first time, my chessboard under my arm – we put the chessboard aside for a while, after all we had two hours to spare . . . I taught her to play chess and she taught me something else. I was much quicker to catch on than she was.' He stopped. Kaspar's face was serious, he asked no questions. After a long pause the old man said, without looking at him: 'What I told you just now about the fun and games at the Paris boarding-school wasn't the whole story. There had been a piano teacher . . .'

'All the better.'

'You're right. But at the time, when I found out, I got into a terrible state. I picked up my chessboard, I wanted to get out, out of her caravan, out of the circus, I was going to drown myself in the millpond. Lisa burst out laughing, real nice, not nasty, she just opened her arms wide and said – I remember what she said, word by word: "Come, my sweetie, take it when you can get it. You're my little treasure. Come to Lisa."'

'Quite a girl, your Lisa.'

The old man looked at him for a long time. 'If only I'd had somebody to talk to! But I had to be so damn careful. For most people there was still something mediaeval about a dwarf – you know, cap and bells and hunchback-halfwit. I didn't even tell my friend Giorgio. I had tried him out once, pointed to one of the trapeze-girls, grinned the way the others did and said: "I wouldn't say no to that one!" He turned and gave me a look – half as if he felt sorry for me, half as if I'd stepped on his foot.

'Also, there was Mother. You know, mothers never think about what's going on at the time, they only think what will come of it. And what could possibly have come of it? I knew that perfectly well and I tried to keep my head, I really tried. I tried.'

He closed his eyes. Kaspar waited but there was nothing more. After a while he began to eat the caviar, taking his time, sitting on in the warm, comforting half-light and hoping that the little man would fall asleep. But Stilts lay awake with his eyes closed, his breathing rapid and fitful, and as if every breath hurt him.

CHAPTER SEVEN

ANTE LUBURIC arrived punctually accompanied by his friend, Ivan Martinac, about ten years younger, in his middle thirties. And five children already? By way of introduction he pulled out a photograph of a pretty young woman with five children under ten and stuck it under Kaspar's nose.

Martinac spoke much better German than Luburic: he had been in West Germany for several years. He did a lot of laughing but very little work. Throughout the lesson he leant back in his chair, until it teetered on its two back legs – apparently he didn't feel comfortable except in a precarious position – and kept up a steady flow of double talk, until Luburic flung down his pencil. But the young man was not to be stopped. Did the Professor know who they were?

'Foreign labourers,' said Kaspar.

'Revolutionaries,' whispered Martinac, recklessly rotating his chair, rolling his eyes and mysteriously raising his eyebrows.

Ante Luburic stood up and muttered a few words in a low, threatening voice, then sat down again, brandishing his pencil like a lance. Martinac, who was considerably taller than his friend, wobbled over to him on the hindlegs of his chair and gave him a loud, smacking kiss on his high bald forehead. 'Easy does it,' he laughed. 'Life's wonderful.'

Nothing much was achieved during the lesson and Luburic's face was grim as he laid his fifty marks on the table, though he said nothing and stared straight ahead when his friend placed both hands on Kaspar's shoulders and invited him to supper, very soon, please, Yugoslavian specialities – he kissed his fingertips. As for Ante, the Professor shouldn't take any notice of his sulks: he needed a woman. Could the Professor kindly enlighten him in *that* direction too?

Luburic wrenched open the door and ran downstairs with Martinac at his heels, laughing.

Kaspar decided to accept the invitation – and to hell with the 'Croat problem'. Right now he felt more comfortable with strangers than with his old friends who never let a day pass without asking if he wouldn't come over, and if not, why not? He was aware of a general attitude of respectful surprise that he was 'taking it so hard after all' – one had obviously misjudged him.

No, one hadn't. He had hit rock-bottom not because he was suffering from a broken heart but rather because his heart wasn't broken. He had always been firmly convinced that he couldn't live without Martha or didn't want to, which amounted to the same thing. He'd said as much to Heidi more than once. 'Martha's my partner, you understand?' Heidi understood. 'Partner' meant 'come what may'. Sex wasn't for ever, friendship cooled, but real partnership was something awe-inspiring. In her mind's eye she saw a heavy oak door with a sign saying: Kaspar & Martha Ltd. Keep Out.

And now the partner was dead and the firm out of business. This would have been the time to liquidate it, but instead there was business as usual, one partner still functioning, though mildly anaesthetized. He couldn't explain it to his friends, least of all to Heidi. Only Uncle Stilts had probably caught on long ago, or maybe he'd always known. That was why Kaspar felt so much at home with him. But Anya was right, he mustn't wear the old man out, once a week was enough. It took Stilts days to recover from the nocturnal memory-orgies.

So, off to the Martinacs. Ante Luburic would certainly be there too as watchdog. The three lessons Kaspar had given them had all followed the same pattern: Luburic with his notebook, angry, rigidly cemented in his seat, Martinac wobbling around on his chair, scatterbrained and cheerful. Kaspar couldn't make out what linked the two together, let alone why Luburic allowed the other man to share his lessons. They were both Croatian activists. Okay. *Their* business, nothing to do with him. About fifteen per cent of the Croatian 'workers' in the Federal Republic of Germany were actually working for a great goal of their own: the establishment of an autonomous Croatia, independent of the multinational state of Yugoslavia. In Germany they were active in underground cells, occasionally smuggled back into Yugoslavia on missions, hunted down by Tito's secret police, the UDBA, and caught and killed on German soil. Once or twice a month the papers reported various cases of violence; 'patriots' fighting for their country hundreds of miles away on foreign territory. The madness of it! As if they could expect vital results from their random murders or bomb explosions. It was downright silly of him to get personally involved with them even if it was only for the duration of a special Yugoslavian dinner. Still, it was something he'd never done before and that was exactly what he needed right now.

The Martinacs lived in Pasing, a Munich suburb, on the top floor of a small block of flats built after the Second World War – very soon after, judging by its quality. It didn't even have a balcony, though that may have been precisely the reason why they lived there. Balconies were risky for exiled Croatians.

By the lift was a cardboard sign saying in German and Serbo-Croat: 'OUT OF ORDER'. Below this somebody had scribbled 'SHIT', also in both languages. Kaspar climbed the three flights of stairs and wandered down a long hall. Thumb-tacked to the last door was a small hand-printed card with the name Martinac.

A dog barked furiously. Footsteps, then a woman's voice talking to the dog and apparently shutting it up in a room, where it continued to bark just as furiously.

The young woman, whom Kaspar recognized from the photograph, wrenched the door open with both hands, smiled shyly and murmured 'Howyouttoo' and then, using all her strength, pulled the door to behind him. The wood was obviously faced with metal. Martinac appeared, grinning happily, rapping on the wall as he went by and shouting: 'Easy does it,' at which the dog stopped barking. He hugged Kaspar and kissed him on both cheeks. His wife Vlada, he said, didn't speak any German except for 'Howyouttoo' but the children went to the shops with her and interpreted. Kids learn fast, without noticing it, don't they? Please come in.

The small entrance-hall was full of baby carriages and tricycles; coats of all sizes were piled on hooks on the wall. There was a not unpleasant smell of sauerkraut. *Sarma*, thought Kaspar, ground beef in sauerkraut, served with rice cooked with raisins; they had often had it for supper in Belgrade. The power of childhood smells! He felt nostalgic and momentarily vulnerable to the point of tears.

Ante Luburic was waiting in the living-room with the three eldest of the five children, standing with his back to the window, which was hung with a double set of curtains. The children, three boys dressed in jeans and plaid shirts, and all looking like their mother, lined up like soldiers and bowed. Since they didn't react to his outstretched hand, Kaspar tousled the three dark heads. 'Good evening, Herr Professor,' they said with one voice, in perfect German. Martinac beamed. For a moment Luburic remained by the window, looking thoughtfully at the children, then he came forward and shook hands with Kaspar in his powerful left-handed grip.

'Sit down, please.'

Kaspar took the only armchair. Martinac and the boys squeezed on to the narrow sofa. Vlada disappeared into the kitchen and Luburic returned to the window. A moment's expectant pause while Kaspar smiled cordially and looked around. There wasn't much to see: above the sofa a colour print of a Bible scene and an ivory fan in a glass case, a sideboard with a wedding photograph, a vase of pink plastic roses and a portable typewriter. In the centre of the room stood the table, already set for supper, and next to his armchair a huge television set. The assembled company followed every movement of his head and, feeling their eyes on him, he made several appreciative noises before he felt it safe to subside.

With the opening ritual out of the way, Martinac jumped to his feet and took a bottle of slivovitz from the sideboard along with three small curlicued glasses.

'*Nazdravje!* Cheers!'

'*Nazdravje!*' repeated Kaspar and Luburic.

'*Nazdravje!*' echoed the children whose eyes watched every drop that went down Kaspar's throat.

During supper they spoke German, which meant that the host was the only one who spoke, stopping only to bestow a kiss on his wife on his right or the child on his left. He informed Kaspar that he worked for a subsidiary of Siemens Electronics – in what capacity was not quite clear; that he had a new VW and that the children's report cards were the best in their class. By the time the *strudel* of puff pastry and nuts was passed around for the second time, he had reached the subject of his home town, Zagreb. All at once the mood changed, the children stopped laughing and Vlada for the first time raised her eyes from her plate and stopped eating. Luburic got up, apparently to refill his glass with red wine, but paused beside Martinac and whispered something that Kaspar didn't catch. The children understood, though. They slipped down from their chairs, as if synchronized, bowed to Kaspar and ran out of the room.

For a few seconds no one spoke. Luburic sat down again.

'Why shouldn't I talk about it?' asked Martinac in Croat. 'After all, he worked with Branco, he knows what's up.'

Luburic's left hand fidgeted with his glass. He looked at Kaspar. 'Ivan's forgotten that you understand our language.'

Martinac slammed his fist down on the table, and exclaimed with a loud laugh: 'You're right. You're quite right, I certainly had forgotten,' and kissed his wife on the cheek. She took no notice. The great black eyes under their heavy lids never left Kaspar's face. Suddenly she stood up, nodded to him and left the room with a curt 'Howyouttoo'.

'Hey,' her husband called after her. 'How about clearing the table?'

But she didn't come back. Martinac stacked the plates, waving Kaspar aside when he tried to help, Luburic collected the glasses, then they both disappeared into the kitchen. In a moment they were back, obviously angry.

'The Professor already knows, I tell you,' shouted Martinac. 'You know, don't you?'

'That you're exiled Croats?'

'That we're activists. You knew that, didn't you? Remember a pupil of yours called Branco? He was my friend.'

'Was? Is he dead?'

'A little accident. In Zagreb.' Kaspar looked from one to the other. 'He had . . . er, business there. Important business. Then there was an accident. The UDBA.'

Kaspar nodded.

'We're fighting against the UDBA.'

'Here on German soil?'

'Here or at home. Wherever it has to be.'

Kaspar stared straight ahead without speaking. On the white tablecloth opposite him lay two hands, one on top of the other, the upper one muscular and hairy over the black leather one.

'The UDBA did this,' Martinac cried gaily, trying to get the black leather glove out from under the hand that protected it. 'A little present in the letter box. But they only got one of them.'

With an abrupt movement of his forearm Luburic snatched back the artificial hand and quickly turned his head away to avoid his friend's conciliatory kiss. Martinac hurried over to the sideboard and brought back three more of the small corkscrew glasses.

'Now you must call me Ivan, yes? Let's have a drink on it. Okay? *Nazdravje!*'

He bent over Kaspar and kissed him on both cheeks. Kaspar offered no resistance, repeated '*Nazdravje!*' but did not ask to be called Kaspar.

Martinac scanned his face for a moment like a child trying to solve a puzzle, jumped up again and went back to the sideboard. This time he returned with the typewriter, placing it solemnly on the table in front of Kaspar.

'Now I'm going to show you something.' He glanced quickly at his friend, but Luburic said nothing, his face expressionless. Martinac opened the typewriter case. 'Do you notice anything, Professor?'

Kaspar briefly inspected the machine: an old Olivetti, a bit dusty. 'What is there to notice?'

'Easy does it. Can you type? Okay. Try it out. Here.' He inserted a sheet of paper. 'Type something – anything, a poem, a song, whatever you like.'

Kaspar hesitated for a second. Could the machine be booby-trapped? But why should these two want to kill him? He began to type: *Ich wei nicht, wa oll e bedeuten, da ich o traurig bin.*

'The "s" isn't striking,' he said, looking up. He glanced at Martinac's flushed face and Luburic's dark, impenetrable eyes. 'Does that mean anything?'

Martinac raised the cover and pointed to one of the black keys.

'See that? See the bullet?' Kaspar did see. The 's' key was bent completely out of position. 'The bullet wasn't meant for the typewriter,' he said proudly. 'It was meant for me. It came through the window. First it went through the cheek of the girl sitting next to me. She was writing a birthday letter to her mother . . .'

'Ivan!' muttered Luburic.

'The truth and nothing but the truth,' swore Martinac, raising his hand. 'Such is life. Went in here . . .' – he pointed to his right cheek bone, then to his left lower jaw – 'and came out here. And then it hit my typewriter with a crack. Easy does it, the girl's still alive. Nothing happened to me – except that I can't type an "s".' He burst out laughing and patted Kaspar on the shoulder. 'I can't get it fixed either. If I take it to a shop, they'll ask questions.' He assumed a resonant German bass voice: 'Herr Martinac, how did that bullet get into your typewriter?'

Kaspar smiled. 'And why are you showing this to me?'

'Just for fun.'

'Ivan!' said Luburic.

'And so that whenever you get a letter with the "s" missing, you'll know it's from me. Get it?'

A heavy thud came from the next room, as though someone had fallen. A quarter of a second of silence, then, without transition, a piercing scream. Martinac rushed out of the room. Luburic stared silently at the wall, from behind which Vlada's soft, comforting voice could be heard above the child's crying.

'My godchild,' said Luburic. 'He's always falling over. He's as wild as his father.'

'Why do you bring him along to your lessons? He speaks good German and he only distracts you.'

'I have to. He looks after me.'

'Your bodyguard?' asked Kaspar in amazement.

'He got bored waiting outside your flat.'

'Why do you need a bodyguard?'

Luburic raised his left hand. 'Got to hold on to this one. Now Ivan deals with my post. Keeps his eyes open. Dumps all packages in the river.'

'Do you live here, with the Martinacs?'

Luburic nodded. Kaspar didn't want to ask any more questions, so they faced each other in silence, listening to the sounds from the next room.

The crying died down and Martinac returned, obviously upset. He hastily filled their glasses with slivovitz.

'*Nazdravje!*' He downed his in one swallow. 'He almost put his eye out.'

Luburic grabbed his arm. 'What are you waiting for? Get a doctor. Quick.'

'Vlada says not to bother. He's asleep now.'

'Get a doctor.'

'Ante, you don't know anything about children. I don't want anyone noseying around here.'

Unobtrusively Kaspar stood up and left the room. Martinac followed him into the hall and opened the heavy door. 'Please excuse us, Professor . . .'

Vlada appeared on tiptoe, putting a warning finger to her lips.

Kaspar waved his hand to her and whispered: 'Thank your wife

for the supper for me. Goodbye, Herr Martinac.'
'Ivan! My name's Ivan, don't forget.'
'Goodbye, Ivan.'

When he got home, he found a note on his bedside table: 'Frau Henning wishes to inform you that a Herr Wegmann called. Sincerely Frau Henning.'
Wegmann – who could that be? A new student? Then he remembered: the young man at the hospital, the last person he needed now. But he couldn't just brush him off either; hadn't he even invited him to call?

Harold Wegmann sat in the living-room facing Kaspar, a glass of tomato juice in his hand. He's getting on my nerves, thought Kaspar, pushing his way in like this.
'You're thinking that I've pushed my way in here, aren't you?' said the young man. 'Please believe me when I say I don't do that – ordinarily.' Instead of helping him out, Kaspar stared straight ahead. 'I'm twenty-three years old and this is the first time in my life that something's happened to me that seems beyond my control. What I'm trying to say is: up to now everything I did, or got into, I did deliberately. I went to school – I *liked* school – but then I decided not to finish and dropped out. My parents didn't interfere. They let me do what I wanted.'
You don't have to tell me that, thought Kaspar, you look as if you've always made the right decisions; congratulations.
'I wanted to become a landscape gardener. I thought that was something I'd enjoy all my life. Do you know the old Chinese proverb: he who seeks everlasting enjoyment should make a garden? I'm working for a nursery, I'm head gardener now and I'm enjoying myself day in and day out. In winter I work in the greenhouses.'
A long pause, but Kaspar's stony silence did not disconcert him.
' It's the planning, you see. As a gardener you have to plan, you leave nothing to chance; you create. Sometimes you feel like a woman who's given birth to a child. It's a good combination, don't you agree? That must be what the Chinese meant by enjoyment.'
He smiled, swallowed some tomato juice and looked out of the window, watching the sunset. He had the air of someone listening to his favourite passage in a piece of music.

73

'You must be wondering why I'm telling you all this. I want to make sure that you won't misunderstand me: I don't need anything or anybody. I'm getting all I want out of life – or rather I *was*, until I encountered your wife in that lay-by. That showed me that things exist that I never dreamed of. Right now I'm acting under a kind of compulsion. That's something quite new for me, and the only explanation I can find is that it has something to do with your wife. Otherwise why would I have made friends with your son so quickly?'

'With – Stefan?' Obviously he couldn't mean Werner. 'You've made friends with Stefan?'

'Yes. And now with Heidi too.'

Kaspar stared at him in silence.

'But I haven't succeeded in getting them together yet,' the young man continued blithely. 'I'm quite sure they'll like each other though. I haven't met your other son yet – his name's Werner, isn't it? – but I don't really think he's important. That is . . . I mean, of course he's important, but he's not a decisive factor.'

Kaspar stood up and the young man followed suit. 'Herr Wegmann, you seem to know a great deal, so you'll appreciate that I don't want to ask you any questions . . .'

'Good,' said the young man and smiled with relief. 'I knew you'd understand without any trouble.'

'You're wrong. Your behaviour is incomprehensible to me – and unacceptable. I haven't the least desire to talk to you about my sons or about Fräulein Wennerstett, and I have to ask you to make your visit as short as possible.' He was keeping his voice low but he could feel his face burning with anger.

Harold Wegmann put his half empty glass of tomato juice slowly down on the table. 'I'm sorry to hear that. I would have liked to tell you everything. I didn't want to do anything behind your back . . .'

His sentence remained unfinished, and when Kaspar made no answer, he inclined his head slightly and left the room. Without seeing him to the door, Kaspar watched him leave the flat.

CHAPTER EIGHT

'ANYA? Go and ask if I may come over tonight.'
'The Master's expecting you.'
'Good. About eight then.'
'I tell him. Eight. But why you not come earlier? Seven?'
It took a few seconds before the penny dropped – he was really completely out of practice.
'See you at seven, Anya.'
His watch showed twenty past six. Harold Wegmann's visit had been short but not painless. Pain, yes, that was it, absolutely, he had felt a pain in the region of his stomach ever since the fellow had left. Should he risk a whisky? He wouldn't want to let Anya down, after all. Six thirty. Time to get going. Quickly he poured himself a drink and changed into a sports jacket. But why? An old sweater and jeans was what you wore to an encounter with the Viking.
He dug out an ancient pair of jeans, pulled them on and looked at himself in the mirror. He'd lost weight; they used to be tight, back in the days when he and Martha would take the boys on picnics to their favourite lake outside Munich or in the surrounding woods. Martha always used to spread out a white tablecloth, 'so you can see the bugs better.' Stefan – he must have been about four at the time – had once come trotting up with a round, black bug playing dead, and asked if it was a blackberry.
Stefan. What did he want with this fellow Wegmann, who'd only been in that lay-by purely by chance? After all, Martha was already dead by then – or not? Not quite? Was the chap keeping something back? Was it possible that she had still been alive and had said something – something to do with him or the boys or Heidi?
He was still standing in the middle of the room. Suddenly he came to himself and looked at his watch: ten to seven. Did he want to take Anya up on it or not? Odd question. But it *was* the question, which was even odder. Actually he didn't want to, would have preferred to climb straight into Uncle Stilts's box, but how was he

to bypass Anya? She might think he was past it. So what? It wasn't a question of proving himself to *her*.

'Very late,' she said in greeting. The flat's front door had been left slightly open so that he wouldn't have to ring; the dwarf always heard the bell. She was waiting in the hall and pointed silently to his bedroom door. He tiptoed past it and followed her through the kitchen into her room. She had drawn the curtains but left the kitchen door ajar to admit some light. Otherwise the room was in darkness and his eyes took a little time to get used to it. There was an indignant whistle and he recognized the faint gleam from the brass rods of the birdcage. The blackbird was still awake; Anya had forgotten to cover it up.

She was already undressing, piling her clothes neatly on the chest of drawers, item by item. Then she turned around so that he could look at her – and she was certainly something to look at, although he had a little trouble getting rid of the Viking image. He undressed without hurry, feeling quite confident. Just the sight of her had already disposed of any misgivings he might have had – misgivings attributable to the mild anaesthesia, naturally. In the nick of time he remembered that a strongman approach worked best with Anya, a purely technical reminder which happened to fit his state of mind, though. He pushed her firmly backward onto the bed, fully aware that what he was actually doing was raping two people: the Viking and Harold Wegmann. Anya fought – all the better, that was what he expected of her – while the blackbird protested at the top of its voice.

Perhaps it was over a bit too soon, but that was really all one could quibble about, for Anya demanded no show of affection, simply pointed to a door behind the birdcage, murmuring: 'Shower.' Then she turned over on her side and by the time Kaspar emerged from the bathroom, dressed, she was snoring gently. When the blackbird saw him, it sternly whistled again. He took the hint, covered its cage with the cloth beside it, and all was still.

He sat down and lit a cigarette. It was nice, sitting here in the dark, small room with the sleeping girl and the sleeping bird. He felt better, no doubt about it, the pain in his stomach had gone. He'd put Harold Wegmann in his place and re-established his own identity.

After a while he knocked on Uncle Stilts's door. The dwarf was lying flat on his pillows, his spectacles on his nose.

'What? I didn't hear you ring.'

Kaspar swung his legs up on to the bed and leaned back against his bedpost. Better not attempt to explain.

'No caviar today? Aren't we off to Russia?'

'Maybe. I don't know yet. Anyway, it's expensive, that stuff, I was a bit hasty last time. You can have some whisky, though. I don't know what the hell Anya is doing. I ring and ring . . .' He jabbed the bell several times. 'She let you in, didn't she? Whatever is the silly woman up to? Go and fetch her.'

'I don't want a drink, Uncle Stilts. I'd rather be off to Russia with you. Did Lisa go too?'

'Ehrenreich wouldn't let her. He said Russia was too far away and maybe dangerous for a young girl. She was furious with him, because he had told her she was now part of the show. By the way, that was a problem because Mother didn't like her. The more Lisa buttered her up, the less she liked her.'

'Did she know about you and Lisa?'

'Mother was always tight-mouthed, you know, and straight-laced, "Christian-like", she called it. My guess is she knew, though she never breathed a word and looked right through the girl as if she wasn't there.

'Ehrenreich's real reason for barring her was of course something else: he was a pro, and he knew by now that she simply wasn't up to it, although I was knocking myself out trying to teach her. In France, where *she* did the commentary, we didn't do nearly so well. But in all the other countries I was a smash hit, let me tell you, right from the start. Remember, there was no such thing as radio or television then – even phonographs were rare – so a *game*, a game that took some brains, meant much more to people than it does today. Whenever we got to a fair-size city, all the bigwigs would be after Herr Ehrenreich to give a performance at their private parties – and that's where we really made a packet!

'Our next landmark was the aristocracy. The Grand Duke of Hesse was the first. He was a sort of "patron of the arts", so when we appeared at his capital, Darmstadt, he invited us to the palace. My first real palace, Kaspar! As they carried me inside in my box, I kept my eyes glued to the peepholes, cursing because I couldn't see more. But what I *did* see was enough to give me a feeling . . . how can I describe it to you? On the one hand I was a dwarf – and on the other a giant; it almost tore me apart, all the way up those soft red carpets. I thought they'd be bound to hear my heart beating, the folks up in front. The Duke had rows of small gilt chairs set up for his guests, maybe fifty of them, the ladies all in décolleté and diamonds and the gentlemen in those uniforms, ablaze with colour and gold tassels and orders and decorations! Some sight, I tell you.'

The old man sat up straight, hands folded high above his head, rocking gently back and forth with his eyes closed.

'My first opponent was a Count Something, white hair and a cunning look. Herr Ehrenreich kept his eyes peeled because that count knew his onions, a first-class player, he was. I quickly developed my king-side and he moved straight into the Hungarian defence –'

'Uncle Stilts!'

'Goddammit to hell, Inkworm, don't keep spoiling my fun!'

'Did you win?'

The dwarf shot him a lethal glance. 'I was a genius. Can't you get that through your thick skull? Today I'd be world champion. And he asks me if I won! The first game didn't even take ten minutes. So then he insists on a revenge and just for a lark I decide to sacrifice my queen. You know, I may have been the first person ever to play that gambit! Queen-sacrifice – that takes some doing, and of course those people at the palace didn't catch on though he'd invited nobody but chess-players. Boneheads, all of 'em. They thought the machine had gone haywire or broken down, and they started to murmur and some even booed – but then Herr Ehrenreich calls out in a loud voice: "My goodness! Bravo, Machine! A stroke of genius – brilliant move!" and they shut up, quiet as mice – and three minutes later his lordship is checkmate. With a queen-sacrifice! What an uproar! And then the applause! The Duke presented an order to Herr Ehrenreich "for the machine" and they fastened it to the box.'

The old man took several deep breaths, then sank back on his pillows, murmuring: 'Takes it out of you, remembering things like that.' He lay staring into space for a while.

'Those medals! Mother kept every last one of them. . . .'

'Was she at the Grand Duke's too?'

'Mother was always there, wherever I performed. Herr Ehrenreich passed her off as his cousin and said she helped him clean the machine and keep the "mechanism" and the "instruments" in order. And that was no lie, she certainly kept *me* in order. Always. At the Grand Duke's she sat way in the back, and of course people tried to question her, but she kept her head, put on a grave face, and said: "Begging your pardon, ladies and gentlemen, that's secret information. There isn't but one thing I can tell you: it's right complicated."

'"Are there a lot of wires and magnets?"
'"Oh my goodness, yes. Dozens of 'em."
'"And you understand how they work?"
'"Uh-uh," she said, and opened her eyes wide. "I don't understand it, but I know where it all fits."
'"But how can you carry all that in your head? Did you study physics?"
'"I have a *diagram*," she said slowly, and the way she came out with the big word made them all shut up.

'Private parties like that were easy to organize: the box would be lifted into the court carriage with me already inside it, and as soon as the performance was over, it would be taken straight back to the carriage "because the machine had to be disconnected". The trouble came later, when we went to Russia – but for the time being no one was even thinking about Russia. After our success at the Grand Duke's, we were in such demand at all the princely houses that we could hardly find time for our freak show performances. I was riding high, I can tell you, didn't rub shoulders with anyone below the rank of count if I could help it. Partly because all this made such an impression on Lisa. I'd have loved to give her one of those gorgeous medals set with brilliants, but Mother kept them locked up. She'd sewn them one by one to a ribbon which was festooned over the front of the box during performances. It obstructed my view somewhat, but it was worth it because before the game began, Herr Ehrenreich would always "explain" the orders. The audience felt flattered by the long list of high-falutin' titles and my opponent would be in a muck sweat with awe before we even got started.'

Kaspar laughed and the old man looked at him reflectively. 'Did you know that the Tsar was a passionate chess-player? No? Now that so many books have been written about him, I thought perhaps one of them might have mentioned it. Well, he was. And he had heard of me.'

He raised himself up. 'Fix my pillows, I want to sit up. *He had heard of me*. In 1907 an invitation arrived from the Russian Embassy in Berlin: His Imperial Majesty the Tsar of all the Russias graciously announces his intention of inviting the Chess Machine, together with its retinue and maintenance team, to St Petersburg in order that it may demonstrate its new art to His Imperial Majesty.

'For me the news cut both ways: on the one hand I was bursting with pride, but at the same time it meant being away from Lisa. Our first parting. I was still giving her chess lessons in her caravan two or three times a week, even though she wasn't making much progress. Herr Ehrenreich was getting a bit impatient by now and from time to time Mother would drop remarks like: "There's a dud if ever there was one. Better give her up." But I didn't want to give her up. I wanted to marry her.'

CHAPTER NINE

'I WANTED to marry her.'
    After that, the old man had sunk back again and played dead, so Kaspar was forced to retreat. He strolled slowly through the dark streets. To be continued next week. Then finally they'd be on their way to Russia. Something special had happened in Russia, no doubt about it, something that had nothing to do with new honours and medals. What if he simply dropped in tomorrow evening? The old man could only be flattered by his thirst for the next instalment – on the other hand, the Viking would be there to block his way, either with her broom or with her expectant mouth. Funny thing, he thought as he unlocked the door to the flat, such a splendid specimen, good in bed too, but I have no need of her. Who do I have a need for? Martha. Not available. Heidi. Well then . . .
    Heidi was asleep when the telephone rang, and even before she lifted the receiver she knew it was Kaspar. The conversation was short: lunch tomorrow, at Toby's. She hung up, but couldn't go back to sleep for a long time trying to recapture his voice, and decide whether it had sounded only distant – or coldly distant.
    It was the same next day at Toby's. Sitting opposite her, Kaspar still sounded distant, occasionally distantly friendly – or was it really just plain distant, without any overtones at all? She had never seen him like that before; he talked as if he were somewhere else, glancing at her now and then as if by accident. Well – this first meeting was bound to be a difficult one, she had been prepared for that, it was only proper. Naturally they must both avoid saying anything personal or asking any questions. But did it have to be so lifeless?
    By the time the coffee arrived, Heidi had learned only that Kaspar was still living at Gellerstrasse, that Frau Henning was taking care of him, that Werner came over occasionally and Stefan never, and that he was spending one evening a week with Uncle

Stilts. When he told her about that, his eyes suddenly showed a spark of life. Odd. . . .

And then she suddenly remembered the beautiful Danish girl he had mentioned once or twice before. Glancing at her watch, she said in a low voice that she must be getting back to the lab . . . She'd forgotten . . . one of the girls was sick . . . she'd promised . . . 'Excuse me, please. . . .'

Kaspar looked at her in surprise, and noticed that something – he couldn't imagine what – was preventing her from drinking the coffee she usually enjoyed so much. Suddenly she seemed very pale and he said so, but she brushed it off, stammered a confused mixture of goodbyes, excuses and thanks, and hurriedly left the restaurant. He sat on, bewildered, watching through the window as she rushed across the street in the rain, without her coat. She'd left it behind – there it was, he could see it hanging in the cloakroom.

He paid and left, retrieving Heidi's raincoat.

Sitting in his car in the car park, he tore out a page from his pocket diary and scribbled a few words, then left the raincoat together with the note for Heidi at the main entrance to the hospital, Paediatric Clinic, Lab.

When Heidi's supervisor, Dr Vera Lamprecht, came to her work-bench looking for her, she wasn't there. She was back from lunch, they said, but she hadn't been feeling well. Dr Lamprecht went to the rest-room, heard violent retching and a faint groaning sound coming from one of the cubicles, and waited until Heidi came out and washed her face.

'Here,' said the doctor, handing her the note. Four words: 'I'll be over tonight.' No signature.

'Feeling better?'

'Yes, thank you, Doctor.'

Better, but by no means good, because it was quite clear to her that he had slept with the beautiful Danish girl. Since Martha's death, too.

He didn't deny it. Yes, he had, but . . . What did he mean – 'but'?

But that wasn't the reason why he'd gone over to Uncle Stilts's house. He said this so quietly, so without emphasis, that she immediately believed him.

They were sitting side by side on the sofa in her room. They still hadn't touched one another, not even when they said hello. Yet it wasn't quite so awkward any more. He was talking about Uncle Stilts, and although he didn't say a word about the chess machine, it already gave him pleasure to evoke the dim, red room, the huge bed, the silence, the little man with his glasses on his nose, and the tiny, ageless hands. Yes, of course she could understand why he liked to go there. The question remained: 'why Anya?' but it was left unasked. She knew the answer: because, like Mount Everest, Anya was *there*.

Suddenly the houseman on the third floor flashed into her mind: he was *there*, too, yet it had never occurred to her to join him for lunch in the cafeteria as he was pestering her to do. And why not? What did it matter, one way or the other? Ah, but for her it did and always would. In all other respects she felt she was completely 'liberated'; she had her work, her independence – financially. Her only blind alley was this wretched constancy. Quite puzzling, really, for it wasn't as if Kaspar had been her first man; he was her third, actually. Her first love, though.

She noticed that Kaspar had stopped talking. Had she missed something? Had he perhaps been talking about Martha? No, not yet. But now he began leading up to it via the touchy subject of Harold Wegmann. Heidi soon set him straight on that score and he nodded, reassured. You could rely on Heidi's word. She should stay away from that fellow, he said in conclusion, he was a bit unhinged.

Then, at last, he started to talk about Martha's death. In exactly the way she had expected, without sparing himself. No, no, no, he had no intention of taking the easy way out: it was entirely possible that grieving about him and Heidi . . . although his friend Bannheimer had assured him that it was more than unlikely, the medical evidence pointed to a purely pathological, purely clinical, cause of death: coronary insufficiency. All the same Bannheimer couldn't deny that marginal cases did occur for which medical science offered no definitive explanation – not absolutely definitive. . . .

He stopped and stared at the carpet. Heidi, next to him, did the same. They sat in silence for a long time. Finally Kaspar stood up and went to get his hat. She followed him, her eyes still downcast.

'Wait for me,' he said in the doorway, one foot already outside.

She nodded. He gave one swift stroke to the dark blonde hair that hid her face, and left.

Fully dressed, she stretched out on the bed and stared at the ceiling. 'Wait for me.' He hadn't said: 'Wait for me for I'll be coming to you.' That would have been a down-payment which might have strained his reserves, and Kaspar wasn't the man to live beyond his means.

CHAPTER TEN

WHEN STEFAN announced that he was leaving 'right away', his brother was taken by surprise. Not that he minded, but why so suddenly?

'I'm moving in with a friend.'

'Who?'

'Do you have to know?'

Werner shrugged his shoulders, pulled Stefan's suitcase down from the top of the wardrobe and watched his brother pack his few belongings.

'Do you think Mother would have been pleased – us splitting up so soon after her death?'

'I'm moving in with a friend. Someone you know: Harold Wegmann, the fellow who found Mother. He has a spare room in his bungalow out in Grünwald, and I can share the kitchen. Here's his phone number.'

'And you'll commute to the hospital?'

'He's going to lend me his motorbike.'

'Sounds all right.'

'Harold is a great guy. I've never met anyone like him. He's so – solid about everything, and when one talks to him it all makes sense.'

'What does he do?'

'He's a gardener, head gardener or whatever they call it, at a big nursery out there. Tremendous greenhouses, half a mile long. He showed me the whole set-up. Absolutely fantastic. Five thousand fuchsias, twenty thousand carnations, God knows how many chrysanthemums . . .'

'You know what a chrysanthemum is?'

'I do now. Harold's explained it all to me. Makes sense. A great job, I tell you.'

'Are you going to switch?'

Over the top of his suitcase Stefan gave his brother a weary look. 'What if I did?'

'Might be a lot more interesting than running those endless lab tests.'

'You mean – you wouldn't mind?'

'What if I did? Why should you give a shit?'

Stefan shook his head silently and slammed down the lid of the suitcase. Werner took his raincoat out of the wardrobe, about to accompany his brother outside, but Stefan hesitated and remained standing by the sofa, drumming his fingers on the suitcase lid.

'Father's only seen her once since . . . At least she always eats lunch in the cafeteria. And he never goes out at night except now and then to the dwarf's.'

'How do you know?'

'Remember the Coca-Cola Bar opposite our house? I go there every night with my books and watch his light go off. One time he did go over to her place, but only for half an hour, so it didn't seem worth going up and making a fuss. Maybe he went to tell her it's all over.'

'Stefan! And I thought you'd spent the evenings with some girl! Jesus, I'm glad you're moving out to Grünwald! Only . . .'

'Only what?'

'I only hope that Wegmann fellow isn't going to make more trouble between you and Heidi and Father.'

'He's no troublemaker. And certainly not with her. He likes her.'

'How come? He doesn't know her, does he?'

Stefan went on as if he hadn't heard: 'But I have a feeling he's not that keen on Father. Of course he'd never say so, he's a great guy, I tell you. Call me if there's anything new. *Ciao*, Werner.'

CHAPTER ELEVEN

A NYA telephoned before the week was out: the Master was
expecting him. And – how about coming an hour earlier?
No, unfortunately he couldn't, he had to give a private lesson
– late.

Even so she was waiting for him in the hall, just as he had feared,
so that he wouldn't have to ring the bell. He was prepared for
dialogue or for wordless gestures but not for her peremptory tone:
'Must talk to you. Important.'

She led the way to the kitchen, pointed to the chair and perched
herself on the table in a pair of jeans and a shapeless old sweater.
Her hair was pulled straight back and fastened with a rubber band,
like a Palomino tail. Far from detracting from her beauty, the
severity accentuated the perfection of her face. Holding her head
high, as if facing into a strong wind, she spoke, while carefully
avoiding looking at him. 'I been thinking: why we not get married?
I make you good wife. What you say?'

He stared at her, racking his brain for an answer, while it struck
him that the fearless Nordic features had a classical, almost Greek
cast. Perhaps the one neutralized the other. He felt like gazing at
that face and at that body from all angles, like the Venus de Milo,
but he didn't actually long to possess it. Neither had he ever gone
in for 'angel-raping'.

'Anya . . .'

But the pause had already lasted too long. Slowly lowering her
head, she looked him in the face, her extraordinary dark blue eyes
full of tears.

'Not necessary for more words. I have understood.' She jumped
down, ran into her room and closed the door.

He remained sitting on the kitchen chair and lit a cigarette. Then
he pulled out his notebook and wrote: 'Anya, I would make a poor
husband for a splendid girl like you. I think you know it too. Yours,
K.S.'

He slid the note under her door and left the kitchen.

The dwarf gave him a suspicious look as he entered the bedroom.

'How the devil do you get in nowadays? Is there something going on between you and Anya?'

'No, Uncle Stilts, you can take my word for it.'

But the old man was still eyeing him doubtfully. 'You won't hear any more stories from me if you're up to any monkey business. I'll kick you out – but pronto!' He gnawed his upper lip.

'Why don't you ask Anya? Shall I call her?'

'No. I don't hold with questioning women. But something's got into the girl. She's always after me for spending too much money on my brandy, and then today she comes bouncing in with this bottle of vodka, the real stuff, imported, expensive as hell, to go with *your* caviar, so help me.'

'Would you rather I left, Uncle Stilts? They'll take the vodka back.'

'And what am I supposed to do with the caviar? I don't like it – ate too much of it back then – and Anya doesn't like it either. So sit down and hang on till we're aboard the train, then you can have a go at it. Won't be long now. I know exactly where we left off: with me wanting to marry Lisa, right? We were in Baden-Baden at the time and I'd just been awarded another order – or rather the chess machine had, but from now on I don't have to keep setting you right about that, do I? That was one order Mother didn't get her hands on, though. A chimpanzee had tripped her up and she didn't want to appear at court with her arm in a sling. So that evening I happened to be playing against the Duke's chamberlain, a breezy young fellow, and the Duke was standing behind him, consulting with him before every move. I set up the Noah's Ark Trap for them – it's called that because it's that old – and they walked right into it. Shut up, Inkworm, you don't have to tell me! I'm not going to give you the details, don't worry, but Jees', it was a hell of a romp! Even the Duke had to laugh when he found himself so nicely caught in the trap. He was a decent old party and with his own hands he pinned a great flashy order alongside the others on the chess machine's ribbon. Quite a bauble, I can tell you. Blue enamel, with a couple of diamonds in the centre, real ones, of course. I swiped the thing later – Ehrenreich saw me, but he said I'd earned it fair and square.

'That night, when Lisa and I were sitting on a bench in that famous park around the hotel I pinned the order on her dress and asked her if she too would give me a medal by becoming my wife. I was very serious and so was she – very serious. At last she said: "Not just yet, Stiltskin, you're only seventeen. But if you're still in love with me by the time you're twenty, we'll talk about it again. All right?" Those were her very words, and then she lay down in the grass and . . . and . . .'

He stopped, chewing his upper lip hard.

'Okay, get going with your vodka, because that week we began getting our act together for the Russian trip. It was already spring with us, but the letter from the Russian Ambassador in Berlin said there was still snow on the ground in St Petersburg and we should bring warm clothing, fur-lined hats and shoes, and above all a woollen cover for the chess machine "so that the electrical system wouldn't freeze". Herr Ehrenreich had a fox-fur wrap made for it, good enough for Anna Karenina.

'Then we ordered our tickets, first-class of course for Herr Ehrenreich and the machine and for Mother and me – and then all of a sudden it struck Ehrenreich like a ton of bricks: the people in St Petersburg were bound to ask: "What's the dwarf doing there? A dwarf – along with that machine?" We sat up half the night in Herr Ehrenreich's caravan with my brothers and Andros but this time even Mother couldn't see a way out. Or maybe she did see one, the only possible one, but she didn't want to be the first to suggest it.

'In the end Ehrenreich had to say it: "The only solution is for the entire freak show to go to St Petersburg – not just the chess machine – and Stilts will have to appear as a regular member of the dwarf act, as if he'd always been part of it. And somehow or other we'll get him into the box without being seen. That's the only way, anything else is too risky. I'd rather cancel the whole thing."

'He didn't have to say another word. All eyes were on me. I thought I'd explode with anger and shame. *Me*, the phenomenon, the genius! To put *me* in a song and dance act with those scruffy freaks!

'"You're not obliged to do it, Stilts," said Herr Ehrenreich quietly. "No one's forcing you. If you can think of another way, say so. Tomorrow I must write to the Russian embassy. If you agree, I'll make it clear to them that I can't single out the chess machine act or the rest of the company will quit. If you refuse, it's perfectly simple: I'll decline the invitation on the grounds that the climate might be too much for the delicate mechanism, even with the fur cover. So make up your mind."

'Mother didn't say a word, just stared straight ahead. Why didn't she shout "Not on your life!"? Was it easier for her to accept the disgrace just because it would take place thousands of miles away, before a lot of heathen barbarians? And what about me? Was I supposed to swallow it for the same reason?

'Herr Ehrenreich gave me time. Finally he said softly: "Well, Stilts?"

'I nodded, unable to utter a single word. Same with the others. Mother bent low over the table so one couldn't see her face. And then Ehrenreich spoke, quite normal and brisk: "You know the dwarf number, don't you, Stilts? It won't matter if you get all mixed up during the dance or sing off-key. The main thing is that you travel with the other dwarfs, preferably by a later train." And that was like being stabbed in the heart once again. In the same train as those three bastards! Maybe I'd even have to eat with them . . .

'I spent most of the next few days by myself; didn't even want to see Lisa – I felt too ashamed. Mother and I didn't speak to each other and went around as if we'd been poisoned.

'A week later Herr Ehrenreich burst in waving a reply from the Russian embassy. He sat down astride his chair, holding the letter, sealed with the black Russian eagle, high in the air in his white kid gloves.

' "It's all going to be much easier than I thought. The Tsar has approved the freak show but he himself doesn't want to see it, he says he has no taste for marvels such as three-eared orang-utans. However, his friend, old Prince Yussupoff, has a special weakness for that kind of thing and is placing his palace on the Moika at our disposal for the performance.

' "And now listen, all of you: there's a real theatre inside, with dressing-rooms, and a gallery leading to a private drawing-room, and in this room the Tsar and a few of his friends can enjoy the game while the rest of the court will be in the theatre to see the freak show. What do you say to that, Stiltskin? Dressing-rooms! That's the one thing that really interests me. Look, he's even sent along a plan of the Moika Palace, as if he knew about our problem, bless his heart. We'll change the running order, we open with the dwarf number, and then you'll slip away and sneak into the room with the chess machine. From then on it's child's play."

'Child's play it wasn't, as you'll find out, but it was just as well I believed him because it scared me to death even to think of that journey.

'Herr Ehrenreich and Andros went ahead in an earlier train to make all the preparations – my brothers stayed behind to look after the circus – and two days later Mother and I and the entire freak show company assembled on the railway platform in Berlin, in front of the second-class coaches. Wonders of Nature don't travel first-class. What we didn't know, though, was that there were separate sleeping-cars for male and female passengers, Mother and son couldn't travel in the same car. We watched amazed as passengers separated and said goodbye to each other, and as we were standing there staring, a conductor came and simply led me away. In spite of my protests he insisted on taking me way down to another car and when I kicked him in the shin, he picked me up by the collar, lifted me up the steps, dragged me along the narrow passage, opened a door and shoved me inside – into the compartment with the three dwarfs! They'd been lying in wait for me, but they acted as if I'd attacked *them* and immediately began to fight back.

'I didn't have a chance. In the first place it was three to one, and secondly – and this was much more important – I couldn't afford to get my fingers damaged on account of the machine, couldn't risk busting them on their thick skulls. I was yelling as loud as I could because the train was still standing in the station, and the people in the next compartment, three Polish labourers, started banging on our door and forced the conductor to open it. My face was pretty bloody by then, and the biggest one of the dwarfs, Max, his name was, a nasty piece of work with great bulging muscles, quickly dropped a handful of my hair that he'd pulled out. But all three of them swore like one man that I'd started it, gone mad and attacked them, and the conductor put in his pennyworth about me kicking him in the shin. The Poles shrugged their shoulders, went back to their compartment – and the train pulled out.

'It's no use . . . I can't tell you what they did to me that night. I just – can't. There were three berths in our compartment, one above the other, so two of us had to bunk together. Well – the three of them took turns with me, and nobody could hear me screaming. They were absolutely beside themselves; for once they had the upper hand and they went completely berserk trying to make the most of it. They lashed themselves into such a mad rampage, they finally wore themselves out and let go. By that time I was lying on the bare floor, moaning, although they did try to drag me into the bottom berth – friendly as the devil all of a sudden, swearing I could sleep there all by myself, no one would touch me any more.

'I suppose they'd come to their senses and were scared shitless of Herr Ehrenreich. I could hear them whispering to each other. Finally the big brute, Max, said: "Aah, what the hell! The little stinker isn't that chummy with the boss any more or he wouldn't have been dumped off into our number, right?" Another of them said something about Mother, that maybe *she*'d fire them all, but Max said: "All we have to do is swear that *he* started it. The conductor will back us up. The little bastard can say what he likes . . ."

'I was half paralysed with shame and the terrible pain. I didn't close an eye all night, just kept thinking how I'd throw myself off the train as soon as someone opened the door. When it finally did open, in the early morning, and the three of them sat up in their berths, still half asleep, there stood the conductor – and right next to him, like the Archangel Gabriel, was Mother. "Holy Mother of God!" she whispered when she saw me on the floor, naked, smeared with blood, and my face black with bruises. The conductor didn't dare to say a word, just stood there in dumb silence. Without so much as a glance at the others, Mother knelt down beside me on the floor.

'"Think you can stand up, laddie?" she whispered, and then she set about getting me dressed, in spite of all the moaning and groaning I was doing, and then, with her supporting me and the conductor lending a hand, we staggered down the long passage – he had to carry me in the end – and through a door and down other endless passages – I think I passed out on the way. All I know is I woke up in a berth in the first class, next to Mother's.

'I noticed that the train had slowed down – we were about to arrive in Warsaw. The conductor, without even being told, ran off to find the station doctor. I suppose Mother's face put the fear of God into him. The doctor bandaged me up and gave me a sleeping-tablet and something for the pain. Finally I fell asleep, with Mother at my bedside, and later I woke up, with Mother still at my bedside.

'It was a good thing the journey to St Petersburg took so long, almost four days. I had time to recover a bit and the bruises were beginning to fade, but I had sticking-plasters all over my face to cover the deep scratches.

'We didn't have much to say to each other, Mother and I. I don't know if she was exactly aware of what had happened to me. One thing's for sure: she knew "Christian-like" wasn't the word for it.'

The old man stopped for a moment and slowly shook his head. 'That was some woman! You know, Kaspar, I think she knew everything that went on, every goddamn thing, but she never allowed it all to get through to her – she had a pretty good idea of how much she could take. Then the last night before we arrived in St Petersburg she shows up in my compartment. I acted as if I was asleep, so then she drops to her knees on the floor and starts crying quietly and praying, the whole rigmarole, asking God to forgive her, how she'd been carried away by fame and thought about nothing but filling her pockets and now she was getting her comeuppance, but why did it have to be her darling boy, who'd been punished enough already, why couldn't it be *her*? She was the one who deserved to be punished and no one else. Just about drove me crazy, she did, with her carrying on.

'Finally I did fall asleep and when I woke up she was gone and outside I could see snow on the trees and the fields. And you know, for the first time there was a stirring inside of me, very faint of course – I still felt a little something like anticipation: Russia . . .'

'Herr Ehrenreich was waiting on the platform when our train pulled in to St Petersburg and he was very surprised to see Mother and me clambering very slowly down from a first-class compartment. But when he saw her face – and then mine, all covered in sticking plaster – he turned pale with shock, kissed Mother's hand and didn't ask any questions. Andros was there too, and Ehrenreich exchanged a few quick words with him.

'Then he turned to me and said in an extra quiet voice: "Stilts, you must join the rest of the company in the big circus caravan I brought along, out there in front of the station. Andros will go with you – and he won't let you out of his sight."

'Andros took my hand and we walked down the platform to the second-class carriages where the three dwarfs were just scrambling out. They seemed kind of subdued, gaping around as if they were on the moon, and Max, the big one, pretended to limp – just in case. They gave me a quick glance – my face was still covered with sticking-plaster – and at once tried to attract Ehrenreich's attention. There he was, right in front of them on the platform, but he refused to notice them; he was busy.

'We were staying at a small hotel in Litanaia Street, with a view over the roofs of St Petersburg and dozens of brightly coloured onion domes. If you leaned far enough out of the window, you could see the Neva shimmering below the pink granite embankment that gave it that special colour. Branches of the Neva flowed through the whole city, and the first thing the desk clerk told us proudly was that we were now in the "Venice of the North". It was April and the famous Neva ice floes had already melted, but there was still snow on the ground and hundreds of sleighs glided through the streets without a sound except for the jingling bells on the horses' bridles.

'Herr Ehrenreich had chosen a small hotel so that there wouldn't be room for other guests and we'd have it to ourselves. The performance was to take place in five days. Five days to rest. My hands were still trembling and my left eye was all but closed with the swelling. This time I shared Mother's quarters and no one raised any objection. A dimly lit sitting-room, red velvet draperies with gold tassels, mirrors and plush furniture and silk lampshades – it could just as well have been in Nice or Baden-Baden. Everyone spoke French, and we were told that the upper crust spoke with a French accent whenever they were obliged to speak Russian. How would Herr Ehrenreich make out with his poor French during the big event? They had assured him that the Tsar understood German – his wife was a Princess of Hesse – but he was still worried. Should he perhaps send a memorandum to His Majesty respectfully listing the German names for the chess pieces? And how was he supposed to warn the Tsar against blunders? Could he whisper "Your Imperial Majesty is tottering on the brink," or was that not done? After all, in spite of the elegant French, we were among barbarians, and the Tsar held absolute power over life and death. Herr Ehrenreich spent the first night sleepless – and found the solution on his breakfast tray: a letter from the German embassy:

Count Sherbatoff, the Tsar's chamberlain, would call upon him that morning to set up the ground rules for the momentous evening. The German Ambassador was keen to ensure that the event would be a credit to the Reich.

'The Count, a weedy little old fellow with a row of medals on his uniform, sat down with Ehrenreich in the small reception room and crossed his matchstick legs. Had the company had a good journey, was the hotel adequate? Good. Excellent. He hadn't really expected anything else; after all Russia was famous for its hospitality. He hoped that even the animals had no complaints about their accommodation in the St Petersburg zoo, one always welcomed an opportunity to entertain interesting visitors from abroad, hahaha. And the machine? Herr Ehrenreich assured him he had tested it and it was functioning perfectly. Good. Excellent. He, Sherbatoff, had had the pleasure of attending our show in Berlin and it was in fact he who had brought it to the attention of the Tsar. However, Herr Ehrenreich would no doubt understand that for our performance at the Moika Palace we would need to make some slight changes in our stage routine. For instance: there would be no need for any commentary, the game should be played in silence except for the single syllable "mate" – a word with which the Tsar was quite familiar. His Majesty would sit at the table, facing the machine, as if he were playing against one of his friends.

'Herr Ehrenreich heard the angels sing and would have liked to bring the interview to a quick close, but the Count uncrossed his legs, and accepted another glass of port and in the same casual, affable tone, began to fish for information about the structure and mechanism of the machine – although it really didn't matter *how* it worked, the main thing was, of course, that it *did* work – still, he would like to be able to give His Majesty a hint or two concerning the nature of the machinery. Not that this would detract in the slightest degree from his admiration – but . . .

'But with the utmost courtesy Herr Ehrenreich kept him dangling. That was really his strong suit. He rambled on about electrical combinations, impulses and magnets, dating back to Babbage – what, the Count had never heard of Babbage? As early as 1850, in London, that man had invented a machine capable of making autonomous decisions when it was programmed for certain topics – a very limited range, of course – well, our chess machine functioned in a similar way, that is, on the same extraordinarily complicated principle. And by the way, in case the Count wished to pass along the information about Babbage to His Majesty, it might perhaps be of interest to mention that for many years he had been financed by the daughter of Lord Byron, Lady Ada Lovelace, herself a brilliant mathematician. An interesting little sidelight, wasn't it, but of course Babbage's machine was far ahead of its time . . .'

'"Stiltskin!" cried Herr Ehrenreich, bursting into our room when the Count had finally departed. "Stiltskin, no commentary! We're going to have dead silence in the little drawing-room. I don't even know whether they'll allow me to be present at all, but I'll say I have to be, on account of the machine. There'll only be about a dozen people standing around. The Tsar will sit at the table, facing you, and behind him will be one of his favourites, Prince Dimitri Pavlovich, another chess-player. And behind *him* will be the prime minister, Peter Arcadevich Stolypin, a really first-class player. He may even be allowed to play a game with you – and *then* you'll have to watch it!"

'I went to sleep again and spent the whole day in bed. You know, lying there alone and still full of pain in the dark, unfamiliar room, terrible as that was, it was less important than what was going on in my *head*: a sort of slow healing process. And I fancy, my circus life may well have helped me with that, living so close to animals, I mean, one minute scuffling and biting and the next minute mounting each other, not giving a damn whether it was a male or a female they were having fun with. I'm no psychiatrist, I'm just offering you the idea for what it's worth.

'Mother never said a word when she took my tray away with the food untouched, she just got out of the room as fast as she could. Then, on the morning of the third day, when she brought me my breakfast I sat up and drank a cup of coffee. So she plucked up her courage and took a stick of Leichner's grease paint out of her pocket. Then she carefully peeled off the sticking-plaster and covered the bruises with make-up. The swelling on my eye had gone down, I could see pretty well, and that was important on account of the peepholes in the machine being so small.

'I stayed in bed all that day too, but in the evening I got up because Sherbatoff had invited us to dinner at a famous restaurant called "The Bear" – not in the main dining-room, of course, but in a private one in the back. There we all sat at a long table: Ehrenreich, Mother and the rest of the company, all the keepers, the fellows who looked after the monkeys and the bears and the hippopotamus and the seal and the parrot, and Lord knows what else. And the two ladies, the one with the beard and the one with no underbelly; they were great friends, some said they were married.

'And, of course, the dwarfs; but they were placed in such a way that I couldn't see them without craning my neck across the table. They didn't have much of an appetite, seeing me sit right next to Herr Ehrenreich. Maybe they hoped Mother and I hadn't spilled the beans to avoid embarrassment. Big Max had tried to stop Herr Ehrenreich as he was coming downstairs in the hotel and said he needed to talk to him urgently, but Ehrenreich had brushed him off firmly: sorry, but he couldn't spare the time now; later, after our Russian tour, he would speak to him – without fail! After all we were dependent on the little bastards, that dwarf number *had* to be performed, though the mere thought of having to dance with them made me sick to my stomach. I told Andros I wouldn't be able to touch the filthy pigs, that I was afraid I'd puke right out there on stage. He could tell by looking at me that I wasn't kidding.

'The rehearsal was set for the next day. At the Moika Palace. I was still too much under the weather to take the place in. All I saw was a huge box-like stone building with pillars in front and a semi-circular inner courtyard surrounded by a colonnade where we took shelter because it suddenly began to snow again. We were conducted up a wide marble staircase to the second floor. An old man in a white smock by the name of Paul accompanied us. The other servants, all in livery, treated him with great deference, bowing and scraping like trained poodles. That fellow was Prince Yussupoff's famous butler; he alone had the honour of waiting on the Tsar whenever he visited the palace. Paul, we were told, had his own favourites among the prince's friends, and anyone he didn't like got precious little to eat and nothing at all to drink. From the word go he took a fancy to our company. In all his fifty years at the Yussupoff Palace he'd never encountered anything quite like us, never seen a hippo open its mouth on command and eat a bunch of flowers. But the parrot was the prize plum. It had to whistle "God save the King" for him over and

97

over again, and in the end the two of them croaked out the final chorus in unison.

'He ignored me – didn't care for dwarfs – had us shown into a back room where we could rehearse, and muttered when we asked for a piano.

'Andros immediately arranged the new dance routine: the three dwarfs were to do their dance alone as usual and I was to follow along behind, trying to imitate their steps as if I was "a bit daft", he said tentatively, not wanting to hurt my feelings, but I didn't give a damn so long as I didn't have to touch the bastards. And during the song I could sit by myself on the piano.

'Max actually had the nerve to ask me if I was feeling better, all solicitous, quite "concerned". I raised my fists and I'd have pushed his face in if Andros hadn't seen us and come running up.

'Later, when we assembled again under the colonnade, the others could hardly catch their breath for amazement. The things they'd seen! On the way to the private theatre where they had held their rehearsal, they'd passed an endless gallery hung with magnificent paintings, ballrooms with palms and gilding and a dais for the orchestra and columns and marble statues, and at least a quarter of a mile of glass cases full of gilded porcelain, the gift of Catherine the Great to *her* Prince Yussupoff. But no one mentioned the only thing that really interested me, the small drawing-room, and I couldn't ask because the official word was that the chess machine number had been dropped.

'All the human Wonders of Nature had been assigned to the servants' quarters on the ground floor, converted into dressing-rooms with make-up tables, while the animals were housed below us during rehearsals, in the vast cellars, and – oh my goodness, Kaspar, when you think what was to happen within those stone walls a few years later! But at that time all you heard was the snorting of our hippo and the screeching of the monkeys, not to mention the stink of the other Wonders. But just imagine, Kaspar, young Prince Yussupoff later had those very cellars converted into his personal quarters; he hung the damp walls with tapestries and covered the bare stone floors with Persian carpets piled one on top of another. Oriental oil lamps hung from the ceiling – the whole business costing thousands of roubles – and all that for a single ghastly night, for a single ghastly purpose!

'Let me catch my breath a minute, Kaspar, gimme a shot of

vodka. Do you know anything about the Moika Palace? Do you know the role it played later? Just think of it: our coach clip-clopping calmly out of the inner courtyard after the rehearsal – and then imagine that same courtyard a few years later on a December night in 1916, when a black colossus of a man came staggering over the same old paving-stones, bellowing like a slaughtered ox, with three bullets in his chest and enough cyanide in his belly to kill a couple of horses –'

'Rasputin?'

'Fantastic, no? They'd killed him down there in those very cellars. There he is, lying on the floor, dead as a doornail – or so they think – and suddenly he gets to his feet again, drags himself up the stairs leading to the inner courtyard and stumbles across to the central gateway. But by the time he gets there, the conspirators have recovered their nerve and they rush across the courtyard and fire two more bullets into his back. That does it; he collapses in the snow right by the central gateway. Later they dumped him in the Neva, just to make sure. A whole lot of books have been written about it and of course I've read them all, especially the one by Prince Yussupoff. He was the one who fired the first shot that hit Rasputin, down there in the cellar, before he crawled upstairs, "on all fours", as he says in his book. Well, that Yussupoff – Felix, his name was – I saw him with my own eyes. He was just a young fellow at the time, can't have been more than eighteen, sat in the front row during our freak show, right handsome kid he was too – well, there are plenty of stories about how he managed to lure Rasputin into the cellar of the Moika Palace, but who's to say if they're true or not?'

He sank back into his pillows and took off his spectacles, breathing hard. 'Don't be mad at me, Kaspar, I can't talk any more. . . I'm not doing it to string you along – Jesus, no, tonight would have been just fine, with you full of caviar and vodka . . . but I'm pooped and I don't want to ruin it. Come again tomorrow, okay?'

CHAPTER TWELVE

W<small>HEN THE</small> alarm went off the next morning, Kaspar went stumbling towards the kitchen, but suddenly checked himself: today was Saturday – no classes. Although he didn't like classes, he now felt completely lost. Nothing to hurry for, all the time in the world. How much longer before he could go over to Uncle Stilts's? Eleven-and-a-half hours. What a sadist the old boy was to break off at that particular point! He knew damn well that Kaspar was right there in the box with him, panting, and he had left him there last night, on tenterhooks, gnashing his teeth with frustration.

How was he to get through those eleven-and-a-half hours? Take twice the time over all activities, eat a large breakfast, read the paper from cover to cover, dawdle in the shower, cut finger and toe nails . . . what else? Some music? A book? He didn't feel like either. Friends, then? Where the hell were all his friends, anyway? His own fault. He'd said 'no, thank you' so many times that now they really were leaving him in peace, in embalmed peace. What else? Were they to ring his doorbell on spec and call out cheerfully: 'Kaspar? Why don't you join us, we're on the way to . . . We've got an extra ticket for . . .?' And what would his answer have been? 'Thanks awfully, but I'd rather not.'

Heidi then? Whenever he was at the end of his tether, Heidi came into view. Not very complimentary to her – or was it? Being the end of somebody's tether wasn't a bad role. Quick, then, before he had second thoughts: rope Heidi in for lunch at Toby's. And in the afternoon, maybe a movie – deep-freeze himself for a few hours, keeping the mild anaesthesia intact until the evening, when he could once more join Uncle Stilts in the box.

The telephone rang. Somebody wanted to talk to him! Somebody was thinking of him! His eyes were wet as he lifted the receiver.

Martinac. Even though it was the weekend, could the Professor possibly . . . Oh well, better than nothing, the morning at least was rescued. Then he called Heidi. One o'clock at Toby's. And – er –

she was off today, she added shyly. All the better; that took care of things until three o'clock, leaving only four more hours to get through.

Quite spontaneously something occurred to him, something that had always been Martha's department: today *he* would provide the caviar. And the vodka and the cognac for the old boy. The idea gave him a warm feeling – and one of alarm as well in case it might mean a thawing out of the anaesthesia. . . .

As usual the Croats arrived on the dot, Luburic with his notebook. For the first time Martinac dropped all pretence of participating in the lesson, tilting back his chair and walking it all around Kaspar's study on its two back legs, uttering little squeals of pleasure when he succeeded in negotiating the long stretch between the desk and the windowsill in a single continuous balancing act. Kaspar, who had been watching tensely, applauded, while Luburic kept his eyes obstinately on his notebook and merely raised his voice slightly as he recited: '*Das weisse Hemd, des weissen Hemdes . . .*'

Martinac executed a daring swivel and started on the return trip, got reckless and overdid the teetering, slipped, and brought down a potted cactus with red flowers in his fall. 'Easy does it!' he cried, and knelt on the floor, scooping broken pieces and scattered mounds of earth into the wastepaper-basket with his hands. Kaspar, glad of an interruption, crouched down beside him, visualizing Frau Henning's scream of dismay. After a while Luburic too knelt down to help, but there wasn't much he could do with one hand.

'Professor,' said Martinac, full of remorse, 'why don't you get mad at me?'

'My wife never got mad,' said Kaspar. 'Not even with the boys. She said it doesn't help, only makes them surly.'

Kneeling on the floor, their hands full of potting soil, the two Croats looked at him. The first personal words the Professor had ever uttered. Martinac picked the stump of the cactus out of the debris and shook the remaining bits of earth out of it.

'Your wife . . . We heard about it, Professor. We're very sorry.'

Luburic murmured something in Croatian and Kaspar nodded, satisfied: condolences for Professor Schulte in a Slavic language.

It felt quite cosy kneeling on the floor with the other two, picking grains of dirt out of the Persian rug with one's finger nails. No one

101

seemed in a hurry to get up. Then Martinac settled down finally on the carpet with his back resting against the desk. Kaspar joined him, cross-legged, and carefully took the cactus from his hand. He had given it to Martha a few months ago, all grey and prickly, and she had been delighted when it suddenly began to bloom. A pause followed, while all three stared at the prickly ball of fluff in Kaspar's hand.

'Professor,' Martinac said softly, 'there's someone waiting downstairs. Can he come up?'

'Another one?'

Martinac jumped to his feet, opened the window, whistled twice and sat down again on the floor.

'This one doesn't want lessons, Professor. We'd just like to introduce him to you.'

Kaspar looked at Luburic. 'What's this all about? What is it you want of me?'

Martinac laid his hand gently on Kaspar's arm. 'Professor, you're unhappy. We're unhappy. But you're worse off than we are. You've lost something you can never get back. We've lost something which we *are* going to get back. Easy does it. The man who's on his way up is a friend of ours. We're all friends, aren't we?'

'No,' said Kaspar. He stood up and brushed the dirt off his trousers. 'All I do is give you German lessons.'

The doorbell rang, Martinac darted out of the room. Kaspar turned to Luburic again. 'I ask you once more, Herr Luburic, what is all this about?'

'We have no choice,' said Luburic, looking fixedly at Kaspar with his sombre eyes. 'We're testing, we have to feel our way, we clutch at straws. Sometimes it works.'

'Not this time. Your problems have nothing to do with . . .'

The door opened and Martinac pushed a tall, emaciated-looking man into the room. His neck was long and wrinkled like a crane's, his shirt collar sagged half way down to his breastbone.

'Miklos,' said Martinac. 'This is our professor and our friend.'

'I am your professor, Herr Martinac, and nothing else. That is, I *was* your professor. I must ask you to make this lesson, for which of course there will be no charge, the last one . . .'

He stopped abruptly. Martinac had thrown an arm around the skinny man's shoulder, as if to protect him from Kaspar. The other hand he calmly inserted between the buttons of his jacket and pulled out a revolver from a holster attached to his braces.

'Easy does it, Professor,' he said smiling. 'Think carefully. You might be right: this may be the last lesson. This thing has a silencer and today's Saturday. The housekeeper's not here and your sons aren't in Munich.'

Kaspar was more surprised than frightened. He stared into the circular hole in the black metal tube pointed so calmly at his stomach. He could see no connection between the object and his own person, couldn't find the combination that would trigger the prescribed reaction of terror. It's only a question of time, he thought, I'll start shaking any minute now.

'Well, Professor, how about those lessons?'

Kaspar forced himself to raise his eyes to Martinac's affectionately smiling face and thought: he's about to give me a kiss.

'As I said, we have no choice,' said Luburic, who was suddenly standing next to Martinac, his good left hand in his coat pocket.

That's what's so odd about this whole scene, thought Kaspar, not the black thing with the bump on top – the silencer or whatever they call it – but the sudden stillness of the three men, as if turned into bronze statues. He was still waiting for the terror, but it was slow in coming and his anger had evaporated. He took a deep breath and exhaled loudly, then folded his arms across his chest. He would have liked to say something incisive but couldn't think of anything.

Martinac got the message though and returned the .38 to its holster, and Ante Luburic's hand too emerged from his pocket.

'Miklos,' said Martinac, 'come and say hello to the Professor. We're friends again.'

The skinny man took a step forward and shook Kaspar's hand. 'A pleasure,' he said haltingly in German. Not for me, it isn't, thought Kaspar, that's not a hand, it's a vulture's claw. He bent down and flicked a last grain of dirt from the crease of his trousers, turned away, walked calmly over to his desk and sat down on his chair.

'Well . . .?'

The three men approached and Martinac would have perched on the desk if Luburic, growling, hadn't pushed him off.

'Professor, it's really quite simple: we urgently need new friends. Some of ours have . . . er, disappeared. My friend Branco – you remember him, don't you? – often talked about you. We thought, perhaps . . . just on the off chance . . . I'm really sorry about this. If it doesn't work, I'll have to use my .38. Too bad. I really like you, so does my wife, but it's too risky. You might turn us in.'

'What's the function of a friend?'

'He lets us use his mailing address.'

Kaspar shrugged. 'Then you'll have to make friends with my housekeeper too. I don't get much mail. She'd wonder what's going on.'

'That is not good,' said Luburic quickly. 'Wondering is not good.'

'But suppose you go on giving us lessons,' insisted Martinac. 'We could meet here, and in an emergency – only in an emergency, mind – we could use your telephone, okay?'

'I'll continue to give Herr Luburic German lessons. It doesn't matter to me what you and this other gentleman talk about during those lessons. I shall be present at any telephone calls. Don't forget that I understand what you say. And that's all I'm willing to do for you, even if you do pull that thing out again.' He was pleased with his calm voice.

The three men conferred quietly. Then Martinac broke away from the group, came around the desk with his arms spread wide and sat down on the edge of it, facing him. Kaspar hastily tried to remove his hands – too late – Martinac grasped them both, stroked them and then held them fast in an iron grip.

'Professor, please sit still and listen carefully, I want to tell you about Miklos.' He beckoned the skinny man over, who, however, preferred to remain where he was.

Would Kaspar please take a good look at him. Later on, when he'd regained his normal weight, he wouldn't recognize him. Vlada was feeding him up, he'd gained three kilos since he'd been released from hospital last week. Well, not exactly released – let's say he took a walk. Not a minute too soon, either, because the West German police were waiting for him to be discharged. So just as soon as he could set one foot in front of the other, off he went, in the middle of the night. His room-mates helped him, Germans both of them, they liked him and they gave him trousers and a raincoat. Outside, it was pouring, a real cloudburst, just what old Miklos needed. Down the back stairs – smash a basement window – no one in sight. Next, he heads for my place, he remembered my address, had been told I was to be liquidated when the time came. At two o'clock in the morning our doorbell rings. Ante opens up:

Miklos is standing there, dripping wet, shaking, can't speak. Ante lets him in, takes off his clothes and sees the scars. Miklos just stands around, naked and crying. Ante gets him a hot drink and a dry shirt and trousers. Miklos can't stop his teeth from chattering, but he manages: 'I'm a UDBA man.' The first words he spoke. Not only that: an old UDBA man! Spent fifteen years hunting down Croatian activists. In Belgrade. He actually believed that we're all criminals, traitors. But *he* never liquidated anyone, that wasn't his job, he says, and I believe him. Easy does it.

Last year Miklos gets sent to West Germany. Top secret mission. They need a new face. The German criminal investigation department knows every last UDBA man, and every last Croatian too. We travel back and forth and we have no secrets from each other, hahaha. So the time comes when a few new faces are needed, and Miklos is one of them. He speaks pretty good German and he can help with the planning. It's slow, tough going, but at last everything falls into place. They finally succeed in tracking down the fellow the UDBA wants to fondle. Old Luburic here could have saved them a lot of time, he sees the guy quite often, just a young kid but in the movement from way back. He's a construction worker, illegal, of course, on the tunnel for the new subway line, not that far from here. Miklos only has to drive the car, the guy beside him is an old pal, he will take care of everything else. No problem.

So there they are in the car, parked a hundred yards from the construction site. Five o'clock in the afternoon. Pneumatic drills, buses, trucks, a terrific racket – very good, no one will hear anything. Miklos is holding a handkerchief to his face as if he'd got something in his eye, because he's parked in a no-parking zone. They wait a couple of minutes. Miklos is feeling good, tomorrow he can go home, he's been hunting Croats for fifteen years, enough is enough, they've promised him a little restaurant – the usual pay-off. In our country, the tourists in those nice little old inns are waited on by nice little old ex-UDBA men. And quite a decent pension to go with it.

Miklos sits behind the wheel dreaming of drinking his own slivovitz in his own little garden, with umbrella-shaded tables and his mother in the kitchen, cooking for the tourists – when the UDBA man beside him says: 'On your marks!' Workers are straggling out from the construction site, buttoning up their jackets. Shift change.

Miklos starts the engine, keeping his foot on the brake. The UDBA man cocks his gun, rolls his window down and takes aim.

At this very moment a face under a crash helmet appears beside Miklos. 'No parking here. What are you . . .?' The policeman sees the revolver, shouts 'Stop' and wrenches the car door open. The UDBA man shoves Miklos out, slides over to the driver's seat and takes off. But Miklos is stuck, he's caught in the door, his coat's tangled in the window handle, and he's being dragged along. He yells: 'Stop! For God's sake, man, stop!' But the fellow goes speeding through red lights, with the policeman right behind him. Miklos slips further down – his legs are banging against the wheels – the car skids and Miklos slams into other cars – he's yelling his head off, but his pal won't stop. And then finally they crash into a truck waiting at a red light.

The policeman disentangles Miklos from his coat, he's unconscious now, thank God. Later they catch the UDBA man too. Old Miklos is as good as dead, with a fractured skull, two broken legs and internal injuries.

After four months in the hospital he has his first visitor. Miklos is in a room with two Germans, they're all glad he has a visitor, a compatriot, such a nice fellow too, with flowers; unfortunately he only speaks Croatian. He sits down by Miklos's bed, takes his hand: 'Miklos, you poor man, how are you feeling?' Then, without changing his tone, he tells him that he's a bloody traitor, that it's *his* fault the UDBA man was caught, that he should have let go of the car door. No restaurant, no pension, he can look forward to a different kind of pay-off – just wait! Goodbye, friend. And he's gone again, the compatriot, with a friendly wave from the doorway.

All the time Martinac was speaking, the spindly man remained motionless, staring fixedly out of the window. Now he turned his head towards Kaspar and said slowly: 'Good man, Ivan.'

Kaspar's wrists were still held in Martinac's iron grip. Perhaps he'd release him if he said something.

'That's a dreadful story, Herr . . . Miklos. But I'm sorry, the matter is settled. I'll give lessons to Herr Luburic and you two may accompany him. No one else. My apartment is not to be used as a meeting-place for Croatian activists. In any case that would be quite impossible because I have a daily housekeeper, my sons go in and out . . . .'

'That's a lie, Professor,' said Martinac with a smile half sad, half affectionate. 'Your son Stefan never comes here and your son Werner very rarely. We've been watching your apartment for weeks. And we're not the only ones.' He hugged the violently resisting Kaspar and kissed him on both cheeks. 'Poor Professor! I must tell you something: until quite recently your son Stefan spent every evening in the Coca-Cola Bar across the street watching your windows. What he didn't know was that we were there watching *him* . . . .'

Kaspar wrenched himself away. 'Get out!' he shouted. 'The whole lot of you. At once. You've picked the wrong man. I don't give a shit for your .38 or your .83 or whatever it is. Go find someone who cares, and wave your gun under *his* nose. *I don't give a damn*, understand? Now get out.'

A few seconds of dead silence, then Luburic said quietly: 'We're going. You hear, Ivan, we're going.'

Martinac hesitated for a moment, then nodded agreement and smiled at Kaspar. 'Okay, Professor, we're going. Easy does it.'

The skinny one stepped foward and held out his vulture's claw.

'Sorry,' he murmured.

Kaspar accepted the claw. Then the three of them, in single file, left the room.

He arrived late at Toby's.

Heidi noticed immediately that something had happened. What could it be on a Saturday morning? It depressed her to think how little she knew of him, and the little was getting less all the time. Every night she lay awake for a while mulling it over, counting the days, the weeks, that Kaspar had been living alone. By now it was months. Perhaps he liked it . . .

'You've lost weight,' he said suddenly.

'Oh, I'm always going up and down.'

She shouldn't lose any more, he thought, she's pretty close to the scarecrow borderline. Oh well, there were worse things. He liked scarecrows; they had a kind of sloppy elegance and he liked to stop and look at them flapping loosely and carefree in the wind. There was no such thing as a fat scarecrow. Heidi had a slim, lanky silhouette which he really loved, especially those extra-long, graceful arms and wrists. He'd always enjoyed watching her undress and then come crawling into his arms, vulnerable and loving.

'Didn't you say you're not in any hurry?'

'Saturday. Lab's closed.'

'So . . . maybe we could go to your place?'

Later she had misgivings. She'd been too quick to say yes, made it far too obvious how happy she was to be in his arms again. Always a mistake. But she'd had misgivings of this sort before, in fact every time, during the five years of their affair. It only went to show that she'd prefer to be a different kind of person. Propping herself on her elbows, she looked at him, lying there beside her. He had hardly said a word, but the haunted look in his eyes seemed to have gone.

It was true, he did feel better. Of all the possible ways of straightening out his life and getting back to normal, Heidi was much the best bet. Uncle Stilts's story would have to end some day and what then? Heidi. As he studied her face looking down at him, he felt as if he had always known that.

He took hold of a handful of her long, thick hair and drew her head down onto his shoulder so that she couldn't see his eyes.

'Wait a little while, a few months more, for the boys' sake, and then . . . let's get married.' Before she could answer, he hastily added: 'Or would you rather not?'

The afterthought, he told himself, wasn't really his last hope, it was only being fair to *her*.

'Yes,' she said, as if she hadn't heard the afterthought.

CHAPTER THIRTEEN

UNCLE STILTS's front door was closed and he had to ring. Anya let him in without a word and without looking at him, and disappeared at once into the kitchen.

The dwarf was wearing his velvet jacket with the gold buttons. His white hair was smoothly brushed, his hands clasped on the bedspread.

'Couldn't wait for you to get here, Kaspar.'

'Same here, Uncle Stilts.'

'What's in the parcel?'

'Wait and see.'

Kaspar began to undo the string while the old man watched avidly.

'Fifty years now and I've never breathed a word of this to a goddamn soul. Never thought I could get so worked up about it. Go on, start in on your caviar. I declare, women are beyond me! Yesterday she brings a whole bottle of vodka and a great damn crock of that expensive stuff and today I have to threaten her and swear bloody murder, and then she comes back with this little spoonful and says it's all she could get. A pack of damn lies – and *you* won't tell me what it's all about, either.'

'Here you are, Uncle Stilts. Caviar, vodka and a Napoleon brandy.'

'Kaspar! The real, expensive one?'

'To celebrate the great day, Uncle Stilts – or are you going to put it off again?'

'He's on his way, the Tsar – well, nearly.'

'Tell him to get going, then.'

'It takes some time from the Winter Palace to the Moika, Inkworm, and the streets are icy.'

Kaspar removed the cognac bottle from the old man's loving embrace and carried the whole parcel into the kitchen. He searched for, and found, corkscrew, can opener, plates, glasses, ice, and a lemon. Anya's door opened a crack and for a second he looked into her wild, beautiful face.

'Anya? Good evening.'

The door closed. He shrugged, carried everything back to the bedroom and piled his treasures on the bedspread.

'We'd got as far as Rasputin yesterday, Uncle Stilts.'

'He's out, Kaspar. Sorry, but he doesn't come into my story any more. Never mind, there's going to be plenty of action today, just you wait.' Waving the glass away, he put the cognac bottle to his mouth and took a deep swig, belched contentedly and wiped his mouth on the bedspread.

'Well now: while we were rehearsing at the Moika Palace, Herr Ehrenreich had been taken on a tour of the place by Count Sherbatoff and seen the layout. Later on that day, he barged into our hotel room and fell exhausted into an armchair, "calamity" printed on his amiable horseface: Sherbatoff had shown him with great pride Prince Yussupoff's holy of holies, his personal library. As a special favour the prince was willing to place it at our disposal for the safe keeping of the machine. Admittedly one hell of a place, that library, guarded night and day by two flunkeys in powdered wigs – but miles away from our dressing-rooms.

'Sherbatoff was very much taken aback to see Ehrenreich nonplussed instead of delighted. Actually he was only racking his brain for a good excuse not to put the machine in that library – and finally he hit on one. Just a lot of cock, but what does a court chamberlain know about circus life? So Ehrenreich sighed deeply and said oh dear, oh dear, what a pity – but he always had to stay in close contact with the company at the beginning of the show. The animals were after all "special" and occasionally jumpy and it was essential for them to see him there – yet on the other hand he had to be close to the machine to keep an eye on the temperature – and so he waffled on and on, poor fellow. Sherbatoff was a bit offended, but of course, if Herr Ehrenreich was so firmly opposed to using the splendid library, *tant pis*.

'"Stiltskin," said Ehrenreich, as he got up and hugged me, "that would have been the end of us, you'd never have got past those powdered poofters."

'Finally, a special room was found for the machine on the same floor and not too far from our dressing-rooms. All the same Herr Ehrenreich was sweating blood and he said we shouldn't have come, he had a feeling it was going to turn out badly.

'I didn't share his feeling. My spirits had revived. Except for a deep scratch over my left cheekbone, you couldn't see the dark patches on my face after Mother put on my make-up in the morning. I had lost a few pounds, but so what? It would give me a bit more room in the box.

'This time we had a very strict schedule. Freak show: eight o'clock sharp. At eight-thirty on the dot His Imperial Majesty would sit down opposite the chess machine in the small drawing-room. At six we were all driven to the Moika Palace to allow the coach time to collect our animals from the St Petersburg zoo. By seven everything was in place, including the hippo, down in the cellars, in an extra large cave. Mother, in her black evening dress, was making her final rounds, the way she always did half an hour before curtain time. When she looked in on us dwarfs and saw Andros sitting beside me, she nodded, satisfied.

'Our six workmen had, of course, come with us, and now they kept us informed: the palace was sealed off. On the street, between the iron railing of the inner courtyard and the Moika Canal, hundreds of people were assembled, shouting, but whether they were cheering the illuminations or cursing no one knew. At any rate a regiment of the Imperial Guard was drawn up outside to hold them back. A red carpet had been unrolled on the marble staircase and across the inner courtyard. We all rushed over to the window to take a look – and you know, Kaspar, that carpet was exactly like a wide trail of blood on the snow, all the way to the street. Spooky, it was – or maybe it just seems that way now, looking back on it and remembering Rasputin, and the Tsar too, and how he was murdered, just a year after Rasputin . . .

'Then came more reports – the first guests were arriving. You could hear the crowd yelling. Sables and uniforms, they said, such as you've never laid eyes on. The carriage doors inlaid with coats of arms set with diamonds the size of chicken eggs. Our men were running back and forth as if they were drunk – we were all getting excited, too, although we didn't really understand why: after all, we'd seen a few palaces in Germany in our time and they weren't that dingy either. But they said no, this was something else again, something quite different.

'I leaned far out of a window and took a look. Between the white and gold uniforms I could glimpse a grey mass of people like a body of water flowing slowly back and forth, and I could hear a sort of excited buzzing like a giant swarm of bees. They didn't sound exactly happy to me.

'Then I watched the coaches driving up, one after another. It really was different, our men were quite right. Now, after all these years, everybody knows about it, but I *saw it*, Kaspar, saw it with my own eyes. It was different from anything at home because somehow it didn't hang together – the hulking Asiatic brutishness and the sophisticated French elegance. Diamonds set in wood! Upstairs in the private apartments Herr Paul had shown us a clumsy oak dressing-table. The only decoration on the drawers was a roughly carved lozenge with a huge diamond in the centre, unset, as if it had been rammed in with a hammer. From the Ural mines, Herr Paul had said offhandedly.

'The keepers were afraid that the animals would be affected by the general excitement, and indeed they were. During the performance, a little chimpanzee escaped in the middle of its number, jumped into the auditorium, plumped itself down in the lap of old Princess Dolgoruki and began grooming her grey curls for lice. The audience thought it was all part of the act and shrieked with delight. The old girl shrieked too, though not with delight. But that happened later, of course, and I wasn't there myself, just heard about it.

'By now it was five to eight and we dwarfs were led on stage. The curtain hadn't gone up yet, but the orchestra was already playing "The Blue Danube". A wonderful scent came drifting up from the auditorium, patchouli and "French Leather", and we could hear hushed conversation and laughing and the rustling of silk dresses. Herr Ehrenreich came rushing past to tell us that every seat was taken. Then the lights went out, there was a swishing sound, and the curtain went up.

'That was the first time I'd ever stood on my own two feet on stage, feeling stark naked without my box. A nightmare! I must have looked quite daft because the audience started to laugh and I came to and saw that the three dwarfs had already gone into the dance number. I hastily set off after them, trying to catch up, but I couldn't, and that made them laugh even louder. At one point I got too close to Max and he kicked out at me in the middle of a pirouette. I dropped out of character and kicked out at *him* – got him, too, right on the knee. The audience loved it.

'The last item was the song, with me sitting on top of the piano, and I piped up, squeaking for joy over the kick I'd given Max, and they evidently thought it took a lot of talent to sing that far off-key and gave me an ovation. The curtain came down – and there was Andros right beside me, beating Max to it.

'It was over. And now what? I saw Andros pushing the three dwarfs out into the corridor leading to our dressing-rooms and giving me a sign with his head: piss off. They were just announcing the second number: our ant-eater and his honey-pot.

'I sneaked along the corridor – all the dressing-room doors were closed on strict orders from Herr Ehrenreich – past the lavatories, towards the room where the chess machine was kept. Just at that moment the door of the gentlemen's WC opened and a man came out, medium height, touches of grey in his hair, a round, ruddy face. He was wearing a badly-fitting tail coat with no decorations, yet he was somehow impressive, straight as a ramrod, in spite of his *embonpoint*. He stopped for a moment and looked at me in surprise, smiled a little and stepped aside. There was nothing I could do but go into the lavatory, shaking with nervousness because I knew that Herr Ehrenreich would be counting the minutes. You see, the dwarf number had lasted twice as long as it was supposed to because of all the laughter and the ovation.

'I counted to ten, then opened the door: the man was gone, the corridor empty. I glanced at my watch: eight twenty. I dashed to "our" room right at the end of the hallway and knocked our code on the door. Ehrenreich was standing next to the machine, pale as death, with two of our men beside him.

'"Thank God!" he whispered. "I thought it was Sherbatoff coming to fetch us." I climbed into the box and closed it behind me. "Calm down. Calm down now," whispered Ehrenreich through the peepholes, but his voice was shaking so much that it came out "ca-ca-calm" and that made me laugh, thank God. After that I breathed normally, settled in as comfortably as I could, tried out my hook a couple of times, and waited.

'After a while I heard the door open. Count Sherbatoff. His voice was a bit shaky, too, because after all the whole thing had been his idea. He said the Tsar had just arrived and was being welcomed by Prince and Princess Yussupoff. The machine was to be brought into the drawing-room immediately.

'I was picked up and carried up a staircase covered with soft carpeting. All I could see through my peepholes was the flickering of hundreds of gaslights and candles. Then another door opened, the one leading to the private drawing-room, because I could hear men's voices oohing and ahing at the sight of the machine. I was set down on a table and heard Sherbatoff introducing Herr Ehrenreich. The air was lousy with Princes or Dukes, I counted fourteen. Only one commoner, Peter Arcadevich Stolypin, the prime minister. He stepped forward and I saw a stout gentleman wearing no orders – the man from outside the WC! He was talking to Herr Ehrenreich in fluent German.

'Once more the sound of a door opening – and at once silence. Footsteps. The figure of a man, then another. I couldn't see everything through my peepholes, but I knew that the first one must be the Tsar and the one behind him most likely his favourite Dimitri.

'Again Herr Ehrenreich was introduced. The Tsar said something in halting German in a soft, pleasant voice, then spoke a few friendly, slightly self-conscious words in French to the others. At last he stepped over to the table and examined "me". Now I could see his uniform and his orders, not many of them but very precious ones. I thought I recognized one of them, and would have loved to call out: "I've got that one too, Your Imperial Majesty."

'Then he sat down and I finally got a look at his face. He was a rather pretty gentleman, with his brown hair and moustache and his little goatee. His nose was narrow and quite straight and his eyes had a friendly, shy expression. He looked like a well-brought-up younger son of a good family, who was glad his elder brother would inherit the money and the position. I must admit I'd rather have seen a more imposing figure of a man, some sort of Cossack or Tartar, full of blood and thunder. This one here seemed to me miscast as the absolute ruler of a hundred million souls, with power over life and death.

'He looked at the machine with interest and a certain self-consciousness that obviously was part of his nature, and reached out rather diffidently to touch it – and, would you believe it! Herr Ehrenreich sprang forward and boldly exclaimed in German: "Careful, Your Majesty. The machine is recharging."

'"Oh, *pardon*," said the Tsar, snatching his hand back. Everybody watched respectfully except for the stout gentleman. He looked thoughtful, with a frown on his face, but he said nothing.

'"Let me know when we can begin," said the Tsar in French over his shoulder to Sherbatoff, who repeated this to Ehrenreich in German.

'"Immediately. *Tout de suite.* We're ready," warbled Ehrenreich. "The machine offers His Imperial Majesty white."

'Oh. A little contretemps: His Majesty didn't want to accept the chivalrous gesture. The Little Father wasn't accustomed to being patronized: he was in the habit of offering his opponents white. Herr Ehrenreich held a quick palaver with Sherbatoff: unfortunately the machine was set up for black because . . . well – a thousand apologies – but the odds were on its side in any case . . . because – another thousand apologies – it always won!

'Mutters and murmurs. Subdued exclamations of *"Parbleu!"* *"Quel chien!"* *"Vraiment, c'est un peu trop!"* But the Tsar smiled, this time quite spontaneously, and nodded. *"Très bien. Merci. Allons-y."*

'I glanced quickly at Stolypin. The frown was gone, but his expression was just as speculative and certainly not amused.'

Kaspar raised his hand, as if to say something, namely, that this was one game the old man was welcome to describe, move for move, in every detail, but the dwarf misunderstood the gesture and shouted: 'Shut up, Inkworm, I'm not about to cast my pearls before a moron, I'll just give you the bare facts: he began very decisively, he'd probably thought it over carefully beforehand: P–K4. My hook darted out – and he jumped! Must have instinctively thought it was an attempt on his life, poor fellow, and I could also hear a few exclamations behind him, but they were quickly hushed. Anyway he immediately regained his composure and just smiled and exclaimed: *"Mon dieu!"* while his Dimitri behind him tried to demonstrate his *sang-froid* by leaning forward and calling out: *"Mais c'est épatant!"* Similar murmurs came from the supporting cast in the background. I couldn't watch Stolypin's reaction because I had to concentrate and couldn't allow my mind to be distracted. It's not that easy, you know, Inkworm.

'I responded to his opening move and he followed up with his second pawn and I was forced to take the first one. This didn't bother him: he moved his queen to Q4 – and *then* I knew what he was leading up to: the so-called Centre Game, the one the German chess-master Mieses uses sometimes in tournaments, and which begins with the pawn-sacrifice. Not bad. The man knew what he was doing. I liked that and I gave him his head instead of choking him off.

'During the first half of the game Herr Ehrenreich confined himself to a few respectfully murmured *"Merveilleux!"* In the second half, as things slowly began to go downhill for the Tsar, he gurgled a couple of *"Ah, quel dommage!"* into the room, but he cut out his usual ecstatic praise for the machine. Once or twice the Tsar quietly consulted his Dimitri, but it didn't help him much. When I knew I had the game in my pocket and was just stringing it out for a few more minutes for courtesy's sake, I looked around for Stolypin. Unlike the others, he hadn't moved in closer but was still standing slightly off to one side, his hands behind his back. He wasn't frowning any more: he looked interested – and somehow satisfied.

'After a quarter of an hour I was getting bored and my hook knocked three times on the board. "Mate?" said the Tsar in German, leaving the question dangling. They all stepped forward, studied the board and stepped back without a word. "Checkmate," the Tsar confirmed, smiling in the nicest possible way. I withdrew my hook and the game was over.

'"Wonderful!" he said, still in German, clapped his hands approvingly and raised himself slightly as if to bow to the machine. Sherbatoff stepped up and said something in French. The Tsar nodded and turned to Ehrenreich, smiling.

'"Congratulations, Sir," he said in German. "Your machine is a master. And a masterpiece." Then he turned around in his chair and called: "Stolypin, won't you have a try? Would you like to?"

'I'd like to, I thought, and I was delighted when the stout man took the Tsar's place. The Tsar remained at the table – they hastily brought another chair – because he was set on watching the game.

'Don't worry, Inkworm, that was a game I couldn't begin to describe, far too complicated – give me some more cognac, will you? – a variation on the Spanish Game. Give me another one – I'll need it in a minute. Well, this time I did take an occasional risk. I could hear Herr Ehrenreich groaning, but I was in no danger, not even for an instant, I knew exactly what every move was leading up to, and that, Kaspar, is the key to the game. Think ahead! Always think ahead. You can't afford to rest on your laurels for a single second, or you're in *Zug-Zwang* – know what that means?

Zug means move, and *Zwang* means obligation. It's a tragic predicament. Try to imagine it: you've made a couple of brilliant moves and there you are, invulnerable from every direction, but it's your *Zug*, your move; you're under the *Zwang*, the obligation to do something, anything – and worsen your position; you have no choice, see? Too bad you don't play chess; it would do you a lot of good, you know.

'Anyway, we fought it out for a good half-hour, but then I had to cut it short because my legs were asleep. When the hook gave the three knocks, the whole room broke into shouts of "Bravo!" and the Tsar clapped enthusiastically. Must have been glad he wasn't the only one to take a licking from the machine. Stolypin clapped, too, like a good loser.

'At once Herr Ehrenreich launched himself into a very respectful but firm address about how the machine must be removed instantly – in-stant-ly – because it was getting overheated, and I admit it was a great relief to me when I saw our two workmen come through the door and into my field of vision, bent double with awe. The door opened, one last round of clapping and bravos, then it closed again and along the hall we went and down the back stairs to the ground floor. I could hear Herr Ehrenreich's footsteps trotting along beside me. "Quick, quick," he whispered to our men until they were actually running. And finally the last door opened and closed – and I opened up the rear panel.

'"You'll have to lift me out, Herr Ehrenreich. Oh, my legs!"

'"I thought so! I thought so!"

'He stood me carefully on the floor, but I immediately fell down, as if I had no legs at all. He towered above me, laughing, and I lay on the floor, laughing – both of us quite hysterical with relief.

'And then, suddenly, behind me, the door opened. All I could see was Herr Ehrenreich's face, the colour draining from his happy, flushed cheeks and his eyes closing so as to shut everything out for a second. In his excitement he had forgotten to lock the door behind our men. Who could it be? Mother? But she always used our secret code-knock. Who would just walk in like that?

'And then I knew: I didn't even need to turn around.

'The man closed the door behind him and locked it. "You are careless, Monsieur," he said to Herr Ehrenreich, who hadn't moved and was looking so ill that I got alarmed. My legs were awake again and I was able to get up and walk over to him.

117

'"Herr Ehrenreich," I said, taking his hand, "come and sit down, Sir."

'He did; there was really nothing else he could do. Having seen him safely to a chair, I turned around and said: "Won't you be seated too, Excellency?"

'He took a chair not far from the box. There it stood, with the rear panel swinging open, looking like the cheap trick it was.

'"I expect you prefer to stand, you've been sitting down long enough," said Stolypin. I was rocking back and forth on my heels, you see, trying to stop the pins and needles. He called me "du" as if he was speaking to a child. Then he turned to Herr Ehrenreich. "You don't look well, Monsieur. I hope it's not on my account. You have no need to be apprehensive – not on my account."

'Herr Ehrenreich immediately looked better, and found the strength to wipe his face with his handkerchief. He'd already seen himself – and me – being led from the Moika Palace in heavy chains, headed for Siberia.

'I can't exactly tell you, Kaspar, why that man didn't inspire any fear in me. I had played against him, eyeball to eyeball as you might say, mind to mind, guile to guile, and believe me, you get to know someone pretty well when you play chess with him. It's not called the game of kings for nothing. The Tsar, for instance, had played like the decent little piker he was, but this man had reserves to draw on, hidden stock-piles, if you know what I mean. High-powered he was, and sound as a bell – you could feel it, and above all he had a sense of humour. I tell you, what happened later in Kiev was a tragedy for the whole world!

'He inspected the machine, held the back panel open and peered into the empty case. "Aha! So that's it! Quite simple. Pretty much as I thought. Still, if I hadn't encountered you outside the lavatory, it would never have occurred to me that someone might be sitting inside it. And another thing: if you hadn't had that scratch on your cheek, I might not have paid much attention to you, but it made me think: however did the boy get beaten up like that? Or maybe he is a dwarf? So you were still floating around in my mind when your machine was carried in. All that nonsense about magnetism and electricity that Sherbatoff was blathering about didn't take me in for a moment, although of course I'm familiar with Babbage's experiment in 1850. So that's where you put your legs? You poor little devil! You're a monumental chess-player and I don't care a hoot whether you play sitting in a box or not. But tell me, why *do* you do it?"

'"Your Excellency," whispered Herr Ehrenreich, his voice still hoarse with excitement and shame, "that's a long story."

'"Well, I don't need to hear it," said the man slowly. All this time he had never taken his eyes off me. "I think I have a pretty good idea." He drew me towards him and stood me between his knees. "Poor child – what a life! What's your name?"

'"Stilts."

'"Well, Stilts, I knew immediately that it was you sitting in the box. The Tsar doesn't know and I don't think we should tell him. But you're not to trick him again. I can't allow that; it would be as though I were tricking him myself. I'm his first minister and he trusts me." Then he turned to Ehrenreich, who had pulled himself together, standing at attention, listening. "I hear that you are to receive another invitation tomorrow. The Tsar wants a return game and he also wishes to show the machine to his wife. Though not here in the Moika Palace: the Tsarina and Princess Yussoupoff are not on good terms. You are going to be invited to their private quarters at Tsarskoye Selo, an honour which you are not to accept, you understand?" Herr Ehrenreich nodded violently and flashed his yellow teeth in a devoted though unhappy smile. "I'm sure I don't need to tell you that I would have to do everything in my power to prevent your accepting it. Find a good excuse to decline and leave our country as soon as possible – tomorrow rather than the day after."

'Someone knocked our code at the door. Mother. Probably it was intermission time at the freak show. I went quickly to the door and opened it. Before she had even crossed the threshold, she called out: "Well, laddie, how did you do? How did it go?"

'Then she froze, and took it all in at one glance: the machine – wide open – me, and the stranger.

'"My mother," I said to Stolypin. "Mother, this is His Excellency, Prime Minister Stolypin."

'"Pleased, I'm sure," she said tonelessly.

'"Congratulations, Madame," said Stolypin with a bow. "You have an amazing son."

'She glanced wordlessly at Ehrenreich, who made a large vague gesture that covered everything, including: I'll explain it all later.

'Stolypin turned back to me and said: "I'd have liked a return game with you myself. Perhaps there'll be an opportunity some other time."

'There wasn't one. He had already survived two assassination attempts by the skin of his teeth. Three years later they got him in Kiev during a gala performance at the theatre. A single shot. The Tsar was right beside him.'

The old man took off his glasses and ceremoniously polished them on his velvet jacket. 'The Tsar was right beside him,' he repeated, shaking his head. 'Yussupoff says in his book that he wasn't very deeply affected, the silly clot.

'So we were supposed to leave Russia the next day, and we really wanted to do just that. Believe me, Kaspar, all we wanted was to go home – but it just wasn't possible.

'And this time we all lost our nerve, without exception, even my mother. I need another drink. Thanks. We had telegraphed the Tsar, expressing our most humble thanks, but "Regrettably the machine has reacted adversely to the climate and has to be taken back to Germany immediately to be repaired." We had finished packing and were sitting in Ehrenreich's hotel room. Just as he was putting on his coat, the bomb exploded.'

The old man beat his tiny fist against his chest and whispered: 'That was something none of us would ever have dreamed of – the Tsar! Such a nice little fellow – but still, the Tsar. Orders from the Winter Palace: Russian technicians would repair the machine – better than the Germans, the best in the world – strictly confidential – hand over the machine immediately.

'Hand *me* over! I crept into the closet. Siberia!

'Ehrenreich watched from the window as a coach rolled up to the hotel door and two men with long, grey beards got out. Shortly after there was a knock at the door: "Open up! Orders of the Tsar."

'We barricaded the door, pleaded, shouted, begged through the keyhole: "We can't! Don't you understand? The secret of the machine must not be disclosed!"

'*Nitchevo!*' The Tsar was an honourable man. Strictest discretion. . . .

'My mother sat in the farthermost corner and prayed, I stuffed my fists in my mouth to keep me from screaming, Ehrenreich kept arguing through the door. It took hours, on account of the interpreter.

'They didn't want to use force, not yet anyway, those were obviously their orders – but finally they lost patience. One hour to think it over, while they went to lunch, then they'd break in the door.

'All was lost. I climbed out of the wardrobe and said in as firm a voice as I could manage: "All right, I'll go to Siberia. I'll survive, you'll see." And Mother said: "I'll go with you. It's no more than I deserve. It's God's will."

'Ehrenreich walked over to the machine and stared at it for a long time. Then he said: "I'm going to burn the bloody dud. And then I'll shoot myself."

'Mother and I nodded. It was the right thing to do. We embraced and held each other tight. Then we looked for matches and couldn't find any, but Herr Ehrenreich did find his pistol in his suitcase. We watched him load it, turn it around and look down the muzzle.

'Then he said, quite quietly: "When they come back, throw the machine out of the window, Stilts. Wait until no one's passing underneath and drop it into the street. Then open the door. Put the blame on me, maybe it'll help. It's true anyway: it was my idea."

'We embraced him again.

'Nothing to do now but wait. I opened the window and heaved the box up on the sill. It was warm outside; the snow was melting on the roofs. Down on the street people were strolling past. I waited. Silence in the room. I waited a bit more – there were still a couple of people about – and now a coach came up at full speed and stopped directly below me. Another delay. The concierge came rushing out, two hotel footmen opened the door of the coach and stood to attention. Aha, I thought, here comes someone to fetch the machine – well, I'll save him the trouble. I picked it up – it wasn't heavy – while down below three pairs of hands respectfully reached out to support the man who was rather awkwardly getting out.

'I waited; I didn't want to drop it right on his head. The man stood erect for an instant and I could see quite plainly – a bird's eye view but still, quite plainly – that it was a stoutish man with a bit of an *embonpoint*.

' "Stolypin!" I yelled.

'Ehrenreich rushed over to the window and watched him disappear into the hotel.

'Mother asked quietly: "What does this mean?"

'"The end," said Ehrenreich, taking the revolver out of his pocket.

'True. Stolypin knew, and he would tell the greybeards that it wasn't the machine they needed to take away but me.

'Ehrenreich released the safety catch with a click – and I threw myself upon him. To this day I can't rightly say why, Kaspar, but I suddenly knew that it *wasn't* the end.

'"Wait," I yelled. "Wait! At least until they start breaking the door down."

'You should have seen the look he gave me! His eyes were already far away – but I hung on to his right arm and we all looked towards the door.

'Minute after minute passed; neither of us dared to move, we just kept staring at the door. And then, suddenly, the sound of running feet, frantic beating, knocking, screaming in German – Andros! He shouted something through the door–I can't remember what – but Ehrenreich rushed over to the window. Down below, they were opening the door of the coach once more and the man with the *embonpoint* got in again – followed by the two greybeards! The footmen closed the door, stood to attention, and the coach rolled away.

'We remained at the window, crying, clutching each other, unable to speak, Ehrenreich, Mother, Andros and I. We watched that coach ramble down the road until it was no bigger than a black beetle.

'Later, on the way to the railway station, we got the full story from Andros: he had immediately rushed over to the German embassy, where they had managed to get through to Stolypin on the telephone and allowed Andros to speak to him. Stolypin had just listened and said: "I'll come right over." And then he had added one more sentence, intended for me – a message from him to me: "Tell the boy to come out of his box and take a stand." That's the word he sent to me, Stolypin, he asked me to come out of my box. . . .

'In the train going home I had plenty of time to think about it. But I couldn't do it, Kaspar, I needed my box. After all, I'm a dwarf . . .'

'So am I,' murmured Kaspar.

The old man made no reply. He half turned over on his side,

fumbled unsuccessfully with the buttons on his velvet jacket, gave up and immediately fell asleep.

Kaspar gradually slid down the bedpost until he felt the soft pillow under his head. The bed was big enough, they wouldn't be in each other's way.

CHAPTER FOURTEEN

LYING crosswise at the foot of the fourposter in the early dawn, Kaspar felt full to overflowing. He'd simply have to take a break, catch his breath. As he was about to steal away, unwashed and unshaven, the old man croaked after him:

'Lots more happened after that, Inkworm, you've no idea what's still to come.'

All the better. But first he needed to digest what he had heard. Half the night had been spent vodka-impregnated in that box with the little dwarf, and now *his* legs were asleep.

There were very few people in the streets; it was barely light. He zigzagged home, negotiated the stairs, and left a note on the kitchen table that considerably baffled Frau Henning: 'Don't wake me. Still in the box.'

He slept for four hours, and when he woke up he felt fine. Hungry, too. He prepared a huge breakfast, taking care not to look at the clock; under no circumstances did he want to know the time – this was going to be a day off from timetables and lessons – though when it came to boiling his eggs, he was up against a problem. How about covering one eye with his hand and forcing the other to focus on the second hand of the big kitchen clock? It worked. Four-minute eggs were done and he still didn't know what time it was.

Today was to be devoted exclusively to the dwarf; today he didn't need anyone – he just wanted to 'live in the story', to immerse himself in the details, experience it all once again and only for himself, passionately – though at second hand. 'You're a good listener, Kaspar.'

It felt, uncannily, just like the days immediately before the war, when his father's nightly stories became his sanctuary – in the teeth of his mother's fierce opposition: she wanted the boy kept on a steady diet of Wotan and the Niebelungs; to her all non-Germanic fairy-tales and legends were sabotage. She wasn't entirely wrong there; those stories acted like a smokescreen between him and the Hitler Youth.

Ordinarily he avoided introspection – he couldn't afford unorthodox discoveries – but just now he had made an interesting observation: even as a child he had had the ability to anaesthetize himself. Not exactly a glorious endowment, but a useful one. Outwardly he had done everything required of him, sang, cursed, shouted, in a language which remained so many disconnected syllables. But in the evening, when his father sat down by his bed and began to tell him a story – did that man know what he was doing? – he would come to life and *live* the story.

The father. All of a sudden he had acquired a new profile, superimposed, like a Picasso portrait, on the familiar full-face one. And this new profile, 'that Leopold', was a stranger, and it disturbed him. It was natural and useful to discover new profiles in your children, but not in your dead parents. With parents it was a shattering experience, and one remained attached to the fragments. His father, that silent man who hardly ever spoke except in the evenings, when he was sitting by his son's bed – had he really once been that enterprising do-it-yourself handyman who spent his days and his nights in the circus and the freak show in the company of trapeze-girls? When had 'that Leopold' turned into the taciturn Herr Schulte, and why? 'Lots more happened after that, Inkworm', and 'lots more' had to include the metamorphosis of Leopold.

He'd have to wait for that until the little dwarf came out with the next instalment, but so far as the other characters were concerned, the big shots, he had plenty of books in his library: Tsar Nicholas II, Stolypin, Rasputin, Yussupoff – the pre-history of the Russian revolution.

He spent the whole day lying on the sofa, with several fat volumes on the floor beside him. He read as if he were re-living his own memories, as if *he* had trudged through the snow in St Petersburg, as if *he* had beaten the Tsar at chess and shaken hands with Stolypin. By the time he laid down the volume he had reserved for last, the murder of the Tsar and his family in Ekaterinburg, it was already dark.

Dead. All dead. Uncle Stilts was probably the only survivor of that gala evening at the Moika Palace – he and perhaps the parrot. Parrots lived for ever. Could it still whistle the national anthem? He folded his arms behind his head and lay still for a long time. 'A dreadful story', the dwarf had called it. So dreadful that it had blown away the last remaining wisps of Kaspar's protective anaesthesia. And yet – how very strange – this was his first good day since Martha's death, the first day he hadn't felt forced to breathe extra deep to get rid of the feeling that his lungs were short of air.

The telephone had rung several times, but he didn't feel like answering. Today was to be entirely devoted to the little man who had made his way, forging stubbornly ahead like a tank. Where did he get that stubborn streak? From his mother, of course – though it might just as well have turned out contrariwise, with the boy rebelling against the powerful mother.

As it had in his own case. His own stick-in-the-mud character was certainly a reaction against his get-up-and-go mother. What could any son of hers do except dodge her punches? For one thing, she was so tall! She and his father stood neck and neck – because he seemed to grow shorter next to her. Why had he ever married her? Did a lot of people ask that question: why did my father ever . . . how could my mother ever . . .? Impossible to imagine the two of them in bed. By the time he was old enough to think about such things, he was convinced that nothing of that sort went on between his parents. Not any more, at any rate. His mother had been obsessed by Adolf Hitler and used to pant when he spoke on the radio. When he ranted and roared, she would ecstatically close her eyes. He remembered the broadcast of a Hitler speech at the Party rally in Nuremberg. As the Führer was about to explode in frenzy, his father had leaned forward, shaken his mother's arm and whispered: 'Wake up, Trudi!' How old would he have been then, just before the war? They had recently returned from Belgrade, to 'be a part of it', as his mother had put it, with tears of pride in her eyes, so he must have been eight. A year later, his father was in the navy, his mother a troop leader in the Nazi girls' association, he himself in the Hitler Youth. He'd had a tough time those first few months, continually getting demerits at school and slaps in the face at home for using Serbian words by mistake. That's when he'd started living his snail-like existence, not so different really from a box.

A good thing his father had been discharged soon after the war ended, because he himself had been too young – barely fourteen –

to cope with his mother after Hitler had killed himself. She had refused to see anyone for weeks and ate practically nothing. But she drank beer. Where she got it he didn't know; she probably stole it. On his return, his father left the boy with neighbours and went off with his mother 'into the mountains', both of them with rucksacks. When they came back a month later, his mother had gained ten pounds and one could talk to her again.

Before long they were better off than many other people because his father had found a good position in the newly established Perutz plant in Munich – in spite of his wife's reputation. She was still getting anonymous letters from time to time calling her a Nazi. She read every one of them several times, then put them safely away in the box in which she once kept her gold Party badge, laid to rest, when the war ended, on a piece of pale blue cotton wadding. Four years after the end of the war she was still a bit dazed, as if she had suffered slight brain damage.

She contributed to the household expenses by writing recipes and weekly horoscope columns for small magazines, under a pen-name, of course. Kaspar attended the academic high school. Things went really well for them in Munich – until the winter of 1949, when his father came down with pneumonia. His mother proved to be such a reliable, not to say self-sacrificing, nurse that his father would sometimes stare at her in disbelief.

He survived the crisis that was inevitable in every case of pneumonia in those days – penicillin was not yet available – but died two days later during the night, while Kaspar was watching by his bed. Trudi Schulte punched her son in the face. Why hadn't he called her? He didn't dare to admit that he'd probably fallen asleep.

And then, from one day to the next, the water was up to their necks. Was there really no one they could turn to for help? Uncle Bernie was long dead. Kaspar had never laid eyes on him, and his father had hardly ever mentioned him. That had something to do with the Uncle Stilts legend – Uncle Stilts, who was a dwarf, no higher than this, as his father had once told him while his mother was in the kitchen. That was all Kaspar knew about him. Maybe he was long dead, too? His mother shrugged her shoulders and refused to make inquiries: she'd rather starve than ask *him* for help. Though why?

His father's death certificate gave Landshut as his place of birth.

One Sunday Kaspar set out with a rucksack on his back and hitchhiked to Landshut, a hundred kilometres away from Munich. There he searched for and found the Schulte house, or rather the former Schulte house. Herr Franz Schulte had sold it several years ago. So the dwarf's name was Franz. No one could tell him where he'd moved to.

His mother had already given notice on the flat and Kaspar was about to drop out of high school when the anxiously awaited news arrived: Frau Schulte had been awarded a war widow's pension after all! Their family doctor had certified that in 1945 Naval Lieutenant Leopold Schulte had returned from six years of war service with severely impaired lung function. The doctor had a soft spot for Kaspar.

So he got his high school diploma after all. For a long time he had been reading all the Serbian and Croatian books he could lay his hands on and his mother raised no objections, even though she still had nothing but contempt for anything to do with 'the Balkans'. He wanted to become an instructor in Slavic languages at the University of Munich and get out of Poor Street fast. In spite of his dislike of her, his mother impressed him: the way she made the rounds of the editorial offices every day and wrote her recipes and columns at night . . . It kept him from taking any steps to trace Uncle Stilts.

Only after she died, in the autumn of 1962, did he commission a private detective to find the whereabouts of a Herr Franz Schulte – if he was still alive.

Within a few days he was informed that the gentleman – assuming that this was the right person, that is, a very old gentleman, and – could he perhaps be a dwarf? Yes? Well then, the gentleman in question was to be found on the second floor of No 31 Kaiserplatz, right here in Munich.

CHAPTER FIFTEEN

HEIDI was again lunching regularly with Kaspar at Toby's and once or twice a week he would come up to her place, but he always went home later and had still not spent a whole night with her, as she so fervently wished he would.

She said nothing when he rolled off the far side of the bed and disappeared into the bathroom as if it were the most natural thing in the world, and she watched without a word as he sat on the edge of the bed, getting dressed again, preoccupied, concentrated, quite unself-conscious. Underpants, socks, trousers, shoes, shirt, and tie, always in the same order, intently concerned with himself, not with her. Once or twice she'd seen him to the front door, naked or wearing only her nightgown, her feet bare on the cold floor of the hallway, handed him his hat and kissed him once again, but it had made no difference, so now she stayed in bed and let him wave goodbye to her.

When they made love, he gave it his full attention and was gentle and tender, the way she liked it, again with hardly a word, and that suited her fine. It was his stony silence afterwards that left her feeling dried out. When she heard his car drive off, she would sometimes get out of bed and drink a whole glass of milk from the refrigerator, to replenish herself.

In the course of the week she noticed that she was being followed again. She stopped once more suddenly in the middle of Leopold-strasse and Harold Wegmann almost bumped into her.

'Again? What do you want? You promised . . .'

'I know I did, but it's something urgent. Really urgent, please believe me. Could we . . .?'

They wound up at Lottie's again. He ordered coffee for her and mint tea for himself, or rather he ordered hot water, he'd bought the mint leaves with him in a little bag. From his herb garden. 'Better for you than coffee.'

'Well,' she asked, 'what is it this time?'

'I simply have to try and stop you making a fearful mistake. At least I have to warn you, as – as passionately as I can . . .'

'Well?'

'I'm sure you know that Stefan's living with me. He's going to be a landscape gardener too. I managed to get him in as a regular trainee so I'll be able to keep an eye on him. We've become real friends. He says it's made a new man of him.' Heidi made no comment and took a sip of coffee. 'Yesterday he went to see his brother and Werner told him . . . Is it true?'

'That his father and I are going to get married? Yes.'

'Heidi!' The people at the next table turned around. He didn't notice, but grabbed her hand, resting on the tablecloth beside her cup.

'Let go of my hand,' she said quietly.

'First you must listen to me, I've got to be sure you won't run away, that's why I'm holding your hand.'

'I won't run away.'

Reluctantly he let her go, imploring her with his eyes. 'Heidi, you don't need to answer, just listen to me: if you marry Kaspar Schulte, you'll be a very unhappy woman. This isn't just my opinion and – please believe me, it isn't prejudice on my part, it's a fact. I *know* it.'

'Why, Herr Wegmann?'

'Because he himself is an unhappy man and he makes everyone around him unhappy – everybody, without exception – and because you can't save him. It's not within your power.'

For a while she stared into his agitated face and the beseeching, deadly serious eyes. 'You may be right, Herr Wegmann. I may not be the right girl for him. But I'd like to give it a try.'

'Heidi! You're ruining your beautiful life.'

'You think so? But even if you're right, I'd like to give it a try.'

CHAPTER SIXTEEN

T HE DWARF sent a message that he'd lost his voice. Would Kaspar please be patient for a few days? Anya would telephone.

When he hadn't heard from her after five days, Kaspar telephoned himself. She went off, dragging her feet, and was soon back. Yes, the day after tomorrow at eight.

Kaspar was looking forward to it. Now they were moving into the PR – Post-Russia – period. There were still a lot of loose ends to be tied up and, according to Stilts, all kinds of things still to come. The day after tomorrow . . .

When he returned home from the Institute that afternoon, he found a letter waiting for him, with a note from his housekeeper:

'Frau Henning found this letter slipped under the door although she's been here all day, slaving away. Mystified, yours sincerely, Frau Henning.'

On the envelope no return address; inside, a torn scrap of paper with a typewritten message in Croatian: 'Professor, please telephone. Something bad has happened. Call 78424. Urgent. L.' L for Luburic. And all the 's's were missing.

Luburic's deep voice answered, so husky that Kaspar hardly recognized it. 'Professor? Thank God. Come to Pasing – at once.'

'Now? What's wrong?'

'I can't tell you. Better not . . . you understand? At once, please.' And when Kaspar didn't reply: 'You're human, aren't you, Professor?'

'What's happened, Luburic? I'm not coming if you don't tell me.'

A long pause. Kaspar hoped the man had hung up, but then he heard, almost inaudible: 'Ivan's dead.' Then a click.

On the way to Pasing he asked himself why Luburic wanted him there, of all people. Damn. They hadn't given up on him, they were still trying to involve him in their problems, to get him to be their 'friend', to make him one of them. Certainly it was tragic that Martinac was dead – whatever could have happened to him? An accident? Murder? But what could *he* do about it? Give them money. All right, he'd send off a cheque at once. Much better than showing up at the flat, and less painful, too.

He stopped, relieved, and was waiting for a chance to turn around and head for home when he suddenly heard Luburic's voice again: 'You're human, aren't you, Professor?' He sighed and drove on towards Pasing.

Outside the block of flats was a group of people and a policeman. He had to identify himself. Okay, pass. The sign on the elevator still said in two languages: *Out of Order. Shit.*

A white-haired woman in a dark tailored suit tugged the heavy door open and looked at him questioningly.

'My name is Schulte, Professor Schulte. Herr Martinac was a student of mine.'

'Yes?' She still wasn't going to let him in.

'Herr Luburic called me.'

'Who?'

She stood there unyielding, barring his way, and he was about to give up in relief when a dark figure emerged from the kitchen: Vlada, carrying a glass of milk.

'Oh,' she whispered. 'Howyouttoo.'

The white-haired woman stepped aside. Vlada pointed silently to the living-room door and led the way. He suddenly noticed how quiet it was. 'Where's the dog?'

'Dead,' said the white-haired woman behind him.

The three elder children were standing by the living-room window engrossed, watching the police car and the people down below. When their mother came in they hastily turned around and tried to look unconcerned, bowed to Kaspar and hurriedly left the room.

Vlada remained standing in the middle of the room, holding her glass of milk like a fat white candle. She allowed the other woman to lead her over to the sofa, an arm around her shoulders, but when she held the glass of milk to her lips, Vlada turned her head away.

'My name's Popper. Frau Popper. I'm from Caritas, the Catholic Aid Society. Won't you sit down? I'm trying to help out a bit here. Unfortunately I don't speak Croatian, but we're expecting someone from the consulate. We've been waiting since nine o'clock this morning. In the meantime I'm helping take care of the children. You know how it is with children! They're thrilled, I'm afraid – and delighted to be out of school. Of course they don't even begin to understand.'

'Do you know where Luburic is? Or Miklos?'

She shook her head. 'Who are they? You must remember that I don't know the family. I was just sent over, the way such things are handled, you know. Who are those people?'

'Friends of Martinac. One of them called me.'

For the first time Frau Popper gave him a searching look. 'Really? How strange.'

'Yes, isn't it?' said Kaspar.

His eyes fell on Vlada. She was sitting with her head dropped, her hair falling forward, merging with the ink-black of her dress. She was as good as invisible, nothing but a patch of darkness. He couldn't possibly go off and leave her like this.

'What happened? Was Herr Martinac – assassinated?'

'I think so,' said Frau Popper, holding Vlada closer. 'They didn't tell me anything either. The neighbours telephoned our office – that's what we're there for, isn't it? – they said: "Croatians! Be careful," and that's really all I know about it.'

Aha. At any rate it was advisable to speak German.

'Could we get one of the children in here, the oldest perhaps?'

'Oh – do you think we should? He's only a child . . . .'

'Yes. I want to ask him something.'

Frau Popper gently disengaged her arm and propped Vlada against the back of the sofa. She let it happen, even picked up the glass of milk again. Her face was devoid of colour, transparent-looking, her eyes half closed, her lips even paler than her skin.

Frau Popper returned, holding the oldest boy by the hand. He glanced uncertainly from one to the other; his mother did not even look up.

'What's your name?' asked Kaspar, drawing him over to his chair, while Frau Popper again tried to get Vlada to drink the milk.

'Ivan.'

'Ivan, do you know where Ante Luburic is?'

The boy shook his head.

'Or Miklos?'

No again.

'Ask your mother.'

He turned his head and murmured a few words. Vlada opened her eyes and gave Kaspar a long look. Then she replied to her son, never taking her eyes off Kaspar's face. She spoke for quite a time without stopping, in a hoarse, monotonous voice, so that Kaspar had trouble understanding what she said.

While she was speaking, the boy stared at the floor. When she stopped, he raised his eyes and recited, very fast and with no trace of a foreign accent: 'My mother says I'm to tell you Uncle Ante had to go away. She says he won't be coming back. Papa won't be coming back either because he's dead. She says Uncle Ante and Miklos aren't dead, but they won't be back.'

Apparently Vlada realized that he was using the boy as an interpreter, trying to make Frau Popper think he wasn't connected with them.

'Do you know what happened?'

Again Ivan shook his head.

'Ask your mother.'

Frau Popper protested. 'No, really! He's only a child . . .'

But Kaspar persisted. 'Go on. Ask her.'

Vlada seemed to be waiting for the question. A spark of life showed in her dark eyes and she firmly pushed Frau Popper's protective arm away. Thus, Kaspar heard the story twice, first from Vlada, then from the child, who translated carefully, and as factually as if he were talking about strangers.

The three of them, Martinac, Luburic and Miklos, had driven into the car park behind the flats at two o'clock in the morning. Luburic was at the wheel because – well, Uncle Ante never had a drink and Miklos didn't have a German driver's licence.

Kaspar interrupted. 'Was the dog in the car with them?'

No, it was waiting for their father in the car park, the way it always did. The shots . . .

'With a silencer?'

Consultation with his mother. Yes, probably, otherwise a lot of people would have heard them. The shots had been fired into the back seat of the car, obviously intended for Luburic, because his father usually drove. Uncle Ante had no driver's licence, on account of his hand. But that particular night . . . well, better only one hand on the wheel than too much slivovitz. His father had been sitting in the back, or not so much sitting as leaning against Miklos, asleep. That's what had saved Miklos's life. Luburic and Miklos had rushed upstairs into the apartment and woken his mother up. But they told her not to call the police or go running down to the car park. Uncle Ante had given her strict orders not to.

Kaspar nodded. 'What could she have done?'

Ivan junior looked at him in bewilderment. Was the question addressed to him?

'Go on.'

But the boy had lost the thread of his story.

'Uncle Ante didn't want your mother to see your father in the car – like that.'

'Really, Professor!' exclaimed Frau Popper.

Ivan had caught up again, without paying any further attention to the thought of his father's body in the back seat of the car. Uncle Ante and Miklos had hastily packed a few things and were gone before the police sealed off the house. It had taken them a good half-hour to get there, anyway. The shots had sounded like sharp cracks, and only an elderly couple who lived on the ground floor had been awakened. And by the time the husband had put on his dressing-gown, found his flashlight and stumbled out into the car park in the pitch darkness, shining his light into every car until he found the right one. . . .

'And the dog?' asked Kaspar.

'He was lying in the bushes. He won't be coming back either.'

Kaspar cleared his throat, and was about to say something in Croatian, but checked himself just in time. Too late now. What would the woman from Caritas think?

He said to the boy, in German: 'Ivan, tell your mother that Uncle Ante asked me to come here. But he didn't say what I should . . . how I could . . . Ask your mother what I can do to help her.'

Suddenly Vlada was sitting up straight; the numb apathy had vanished and her eyes darted from Kaspar to her son. Her answer came promptly: many thanks, there was nothing Kaspar could do at the moment, but Luburic would be in touch again and then, she hoped, he himself would take care of things.

Frau Popper wanted to know whether they could manage without the child now. Yes. Kaspar had no more questions and the boy bowed and ran out of the room. Communications with Vlada were therefore cut off. Why had she played along?

He got to his feet and was about to leave, when Frau Popper

motioned him to sit down again and, without beating about the bush, asked him for a contribution. Caritas and the Croatian organization would pay for the funeral, but what then? Vlada might get a widow's pension and supplements for the children, but all that took time and in the meantime . . .

Kaspar took his cheque-book out of his pocket and wrote a cheque for a thousand marks, very generous by his standards. Vlada's black eyes staring past him, empty, utterly mortified, together with the unnatural silence in the children's room next door, made any smaller amount unthinkable. A thousand marks made a decent showing on a cheque, less humiliating than, say, seven hundred and fifty. He handed it to Frau Popper. She inspected it carefully and thanked him. This would take care of the family for a month. He would have to excuse Vlada, she was in no state to express her gratitude.

Kaspar shook his head, took Vlada's hand and pressed it, said goodbye to Frau Popper and left. But while he was still struggling with the front door, Vlada suddenly came running towards him down the hall, Frau Popper protesting in vain behind her. Pushing Kaspar aside, she threw herself on the door and wrenched it open with all her strength, as if the effort might relieve both the pressure on her mind and her burden of gratitude. Then she grabbed his hand and held it tight, engulfing him in a flood of sobbing, incomprehensible sounds, her eyes fixedly staring into his face.

Behind her a door opened. Ivan junior stood in the doorway, the round heads of his brothers and sisters clustered around him like grapes, the two smallest children holding on to his knees.

'Mother says she wants you to promise . . .'

'I know,' said Kaspar loudly in Croatian, with a quick glance at Frau Popper's bewildered face. 'I won't run away. You can count on that.'

CHAPTER SEVENTEEN

'I SUPPOSE you think it's all over bar the shouting, don't you?'
'Well, I certainly don't see any more caviar or vodka.'
'What do you expect, for goodness sake? We're on the way home now and pretty soon we'll be back in Landshut and there you'll get a decent glass of beer, but that's about it. Go and fetch yourself one out of the fridge.'

Kaspar knocked cautiously at the kitchen door. With any luck Anya would already be asleep. Darkness and dead silence. He returned to the bedroom carrying three bottles of beer. The old man hadn't even noticed his absence and was still talking.

'. . . for the first time in years,' he was saying emphatically and thought hard for a moment. 'But, you know, holidays weren't a common thing in those days, not regular ones every year, I mean. Also, we weren't that keen on holidays, we spent our days travelling anyway and besides, we always had a break between engagements, and our caravans were just like home. My brothers usually had something going with one of the little trapeze-girls and I had my Lisa, and Mother would say "holiday" as if it was a dirty word.

'But after the Russian caper we all felt like going into hiding somewhere. Even Herr Ehrenreich was thinking about going to visit his family on the Riviera, but then he decided to go to Paris with Lisa instead. Now that I'm telling it all in the proper order, I have to say I wish he'd been more of a family man – but who could have guessed then what was coming?' The old man sighed and shook his head. 'Chance, blind chance. You happen to look in a certain direction, something happens to catch your eye – and your whole life is changed. And not only yours, because it's all linked up and hooked into other people's lives. If Herr Ehrenreich hadn't happened to stumble over a suitcase on the railway platform in Paris, Lisa wouldn't have looked around for someone to help him up, because he'd put on a bit of weight, you see, in the last few years. And of all the people passing by at that moment, her eye has to fall on *him*.

'You know, sometimes I dream that I can re-run my life like a film, back to the moment when Herr Ehrenreich tripped over that suitcase – and then I'd just take Lisa's little head and turn it in the opposite direction . . .'

'Uncle Stilts, if it hadn't been him, it would have been . . .'

'I know, Inkworm, I know. But you don't know a goddamn thing. It didn't have to be someone like the fellow who happened to be walking towards her down that railway platform. Hold your horses, will you?' He sat for a while in silence, gnawing his upper lip.

'Never mind, we'll get to it in the end. One thing at a time. Anyway, we arrived in Berlin by train from Moscow. Lisa was waiting for us at the Eden Hotel, but I didn't get to see her because it turned out that Mother was hell-bent on going straight through to Munich. She was sick of travelling, she wanted to get the whole trip over with in one go. All of a sudden she just went to pieces, and insisted she had to sleep in her own bed in Landshut, she'd been away too long.

'I was sick as a pig with disappointment. I'd planned to get out of that train and take a cab to the Eden Hotel – I'd been counting the hours till I'd see Lisa again – but I couldn't say anything. Maybe they all knew and were trying to break us up. What do you think?'

'Could be.'

'Would you have gone along with them? Would you have tried to break it up between me and Lisa?'

'No, I wouldn't have interfered.'

The old man's head swayed gently back and forth. 'You always stay out of things, don't you, Kaspar? You think that's the safest thing to do. But it's also the loneliest, and I have a feeling it's beginning to get to you a bit, isn't it?' Kaspar nodded. 'Oh well, you're still young. You've still got time to catch up.'

'Young? At forty-seven?'

'The way I look at it, you are. But don't make the mistake of trying to catch a young whippersnapper. That'll only make you feel older. You're not going to marry that Heidi of yours?'

'Probably.'

The old man gave him a long, grim look. 'I don't know the girl, but you're a damn fool if you do it, a born loner like you. I'm glad I won't live to see it. Give me a shot of brandy – hardly any left. Did you bring me another bottle? Anya won't buy me any more – says it'll be the death of me, the silly bitch.'

'From now on I'll keep you supplied, Uncle Stilts.'

'But not the really expensive one, mind. That was a special for the Moika Palace. I think I'll skip the long journey to Landshut because I spent the whole time shut up in my compartment, sobbing. Never once did Mother knock on the door to get me to eat something, the way mothers do. She let me alone. She knew we weren't done with the tears and the bad things, and she knew that roast beef and omelettes wouldn't help me cope with what was in store for me, inevitably.

'My brothers were waiting on the platform in Landshut, waving like mad, dying to know how I'd made out with the Tsar, while we were still getting off the train.

' "Did Stilts win?"

'Mother nodded, but sort of reticent, and I said not a word. They realized something was wrong and didn't ask any more questions. Later, when I was asleep upstairs, back once again in Grandfather's bed, Mother told them the whole story.

'The idea was to have a month's rest. She needed it, and it would have done me good, too, if I hadn't always been lying in wait for the postman. Lisa was writing about once a week from Paris, very nice letters, and that's what kept me alive because I really didn't know what to do with myself all day long. To be on the safe side, I let it get around that I'd retired from chess, to the great disappointment of the pastor and the doctor. I don't have to tell you that we'd never ever given a guest performance in Landshut. Too many people might have remembered the dwarf who used to be such a whiz at chess. . . .

'Yes. Well – I suppose I can't put it off much longer, might as well get on with it. Where's my brandy?' He took a big gulp. 'I know what you're thinking, Kaspar, you're thinking: best part of seventy damn years ago – and the old fool's still eating his heart out. I'm not, you know; it takes it out of me, that's all.' He took another swallow. 'So then – one morning Mother gets a letter from Paris, from Ehrenreich. She stopped reading in the middle of a page and gave me a quick look.

' "What's wrong?" I asked.

'"Nothing," she said, and read on.

'"What does he say? Does he want something?"

'"Nothing," she said, carefully folding the letter. "We're starting again June 1. In Lübeck. Two days. And then a private performance for the Duke of Schleswig-Holstein at the palace."

'"Will Lisa be going with us?"

'"Maybe," said Mother, and I began to seethe because she hadn't said: "Of course."

'My brothers were jumping around the room for joy because things would get going again, and I grew even angrier and suddenly I burst out: "To hell with the Duke of Schleswig-Holstein! Who the devil's he? Get me the Emperor or I'm not playing."

'Jesus, Kaspar! You should have seen that Leopold's face, I mean your father's face, I mean – goddammit, I keep forgetting –'

'Don't worry, Uncle Stilts, I remember all right. "That Leopold" is my father.'

For a moment the old man looked confused and began to chew his upper lip. 'I can't help it, to me he's that Leopold, don't get me all mixed up now . . . Well, Bernie and that Leopold stopped jumping around and looked at me as if they wanted to kill me. Then they started shouting, asking if I'd lost what bit of sense I used to have, who did I think I was, God Almighty? Only Mother kept calm and acted as if the Emperor was nothing out of the ordinary. "Why not?" she said. "He'll get pipped at the post in no time." And then she calmly put away her sewing and went out. From the window I could see her going after the weeds in the garden, though not in her usual way, carefully examining every stalk, but pulling up everything within reach, flowers and even carrots and peas.

'The two women Herr Ehrenreich had engaged to keep house for us – remember, I told you about them right at the beginning – well, she'd thrown them out in no time flat, said the whole place was filthy and the dishes all chipped. Then somewhere or other she came up with this funny little old girl, Ida – you'll be hearing a lot more about her. Ida had feet like omelettes and she waddled about the house like a duck, with her long neck poked forwards and her mouth sticking out like a real beak. She'd have been a natural for the freak show, but Mother took to her right from the start, and that was most unusual, because Mother never had any friends.

Now she took to spending a lot of time in the kitchen gossiping with her, and we could hear Ida quacking gaily away, and Mother was laughing.

'The afternoon Herr Ehrenreich's letter arrived, she went to church with Ida. Usually she only went on Sundays, but when she suddenly appeared at my bedside after supper, I understood why she'd absolutely had to go to church that day. You see, Herr Ehrenreich had also told her something else in his letter: Lisa had got herself engaged to a Monsieur Grandet, Alphonse Grandet, a very fine young man from a very good family, very well educated, with very good manners, and very much in love with Lisa and Lisa was very happy. I threw myself flat on my back and pulled the big feather quilt over my head. I couldn't stand another "very" any more.

' "Get out of here," I shouted.

' "Go on," she said very quietly, "go ahead and hit me if it makes you feel any better, but the way I see it, it's good news for you."

'And I did hit out at her, I really hit her, and she edged closer on the bed to make it easier for me.

' "Go on, hit me," she said, as if she was really enjoying it. "It does you good – and me too." But I soon gave up and hid under the quilt again. When I had to come up for air, she'd gone, leaving the letter on the bedside table.'

He sank back on his pillows and lay quiet for a while. When he began to speak again, his voice was calm. 'I'm thinking how I can shrink the next few years together so I won't bore you, because they were all pretty much alike, travel and guest performances and more decorations to nail on the box. I never lost a game, and nobody except Stolypin ever suspected anything.'

'What about the Emperor?'

The old man smiled. 'I was so busy crying about Lisa that I'd forgotten all about him. Anyway, he didn't play chess.' He sat up and rubbed his forehead roughly with both hands. 'Now I have to tell you about Herr Ehrenreich. When we arrived in Lübeck, he was different, somehow. He didn't really look at me, didn't ask me any questions, didn't even give me a hug. . . .

'But hold on a moment, Kaspar, I was trying to make a long story short, wasn't I? Maybe I'd better tell it to you as if I'd had some kind of bird's eye view of everything, like the good Lord, including things I didn't see for myself, things I only learned about later.

141

Now let me think where I should begin. I know: in Paris, when Lisa got engaged. Yes, that's it. Well, soon after the announcement, she comes rushing to Herr Ehrenreich at the Ritz Hotel, weeping and wringing her hands: her fiancé had taken her to visit his parents at their place in the country. They had driven right past a wonderful chateau that had once belonged to his family, but now they all lived in the carriage-house. They received Lisa with open arms – such a beautiful young lady and so well brought up!

'Then they'd discussed the wedding date, and Lisa said quite innocently, she hoped it would be before the circus season began so her uncle could give her away. Circus season? What on earth . . . And then it turned out they hadn't realized that Herr Ehrenreich actually *managed* the circus, they naturally thought – since he stayed at the Ritz Hotel – he was a gentleman! And suddenly they all looked suspicious: had she, Lisa, ever taken part in "that sort of life"? She'd started to stammer and said: yes, sort of, and then quickly: no, of course not – but there was an awful silence and her fiancé told her to come for a walk with him. Hardly out of the door he asked if she was still "innocent".

'"Good Lord," said Herr Ehrenreich. "What insolence! Well, I hope you told him – "

'Then and there she broke down and "confessed". Get this now, Kaspar, she confessed the same story to Ehrenreich she had told her fiancé: a wicked dwarf in the circus company had invited her to drink a glass of wine with him, and she'd felt sorry for him and didn't want to hurt him by turning him down – and suddenly she'd come over all queer and lost track of what was happening and – oh God! – something *had* happened.

'Naturally Herr Ehrenreich asked why she hadn't come straight to him and why on earth she'd continued to see the wicked dwarf in her caravan, but she came up with several good explanations: first, she was ashamed. Second, she had to learn chess, hadn't she? And third, she threw herself into Herr Ehrenreich's arms, crying her heart out.

'So what now? Had that cooked her goose with the Frenchman? Was the engagement off?

'Lisa pointed to the door. Monsieur Grandet had been waiting outside all the time. In he walked, twirling his black moustache, and Herr Ehrenreich had to swallow a lot of insults about circus life, depravity, loose living – and, above all, letting his own kin, his niece, an innocent angel, visit him and fall right into the sink of iniquity! Criminal! Someone should bring charges against him – in fact, that's just what he was going to do: bring charges.

'Quietly Herr Ehrenreich said: "You do that. Bring a charge. Are you going, Lisa, or are you staying?"

'But Lisa didn't move and there was a long pause. You could almost hear the tide turning, but that was all you could hear. Finally Monsieur Grandet gave his moustache a last agitated twirl and pronounced himself ready to put mercy before justice for the sake of his love for Lisa and overlook this – er – blemish on her person. The dwarf, however, must be punished and dismissed from the company. And now, if Lisa would please leave the room, there were some formalities to be discussed.

'The formalities cost Ehrenreich a hundred thousand marks, twice the dowry that had been agreed on, and a promise that the wicked dwarf would never be featured in the programme again – which was no problem because my name never *had* appeared in the programme.

'The wedding took place soon afterwards, but Herr Ehrenreich didn't attend it. He hadn't been feeling well for some time, ever since the Russian trip, in fact. He, not the machine, had been affected by the climate.

'Now, don't forget, Kaspar, when I knocked on the door of his caravan in Lübeck, I didn't know anything about that business of Lisa and the wicked dwarf. So there we stood, facing each other – but why was he giving me that funny look? He didn't say a word, not even "Hello, Stiltskin." He wasn't looking at all well either; overweight, and his lips bluish-pale.

'Finally he said: "Stilts, do you know anything about opium or any other narcotic?"

' "No," I said. "Do you need some?"

'He shook his head and gave me a faint smile. "A stupid question. Forgive me." Then at last he stepped forward and hugged me very tight. "Stilts, did you have an affair with Lisa?"

' "Yes."

' "Did you seduce her?"

'I broke away and said: "I don't know what you mean, Herr Ehrenreich."

' "Did you – force her?"

' "*Force* her? *Me?* "

'"Was she still innocent?"

'I didn't answer, just thought to myself: if it comes to that, I too have very fine manners.

'"Ah well," he said and nodded, and then he quickly went over to his armchair. When he was comfortably settled, he said again: "Ah, well." That was all, but I remember it because the whole thing seemed so strange. I sensed that something was wrong, but he never told me what had happened in Paris. I didn't learn the full story until much later.

'And so we began all over again, Kaspar, first in Lübeck, then at the Duke's – same old routine. Only Herr Ehrenreich's commentaries weren't as dramatic any more. It was getting to be too much for him, but he wouldn't hear of giving it up. We limped along for a couple of years or more and every evening we said to ourselves: he'll never make it tonight, he's going to collapse, he's already blue in the face . . .

'And then one night it happened, right after the performance, in Mainz. He was about to set foot on the steps of his caravan and had one hand on the banister. Andros found him hanging there.

'We spent the whole day outside his room at the hospital, the entire company, including the freak show, although the hospital staff made a fuss and threatened to drag any "strange-looking persons" off to the operating-room and amputate everything they earned their living with.

'About four o'clock in the afternoon the end came and we were allowed to go in and see him. The evening performance was called off and the remainder of our Mainz performances were cancelled.

'Herr Ehrenreich's lawyer telegraphed that he was coming to Mainz, would we meet him at the Hotel Krone the next day, "the Schulte family", and Andros as representative of the circus company. "Other parties" would also be present for the reading of the will. My brothers sat around whispering, gesticulating, speculating.

'Mother and I spent the intervening time in our caravan. I couldn't stop crying, couldn't get it through my head that he was gone. What about the future? Well, there were my brothers, they would have to take over the commentary. But that wasn't it. I missed Ehrenreich, missed him the way I ought to have missed my father when he died – if I hadn't been so callous at the time. And suddenly I noticed that I'd become much thinner-skinned, much more vulnerable, than I used to be. I don't believe that unhappiness and suffering improve one's character, Kaspar; only happiness does that. Happiness is the only thing that can thaw out a frozen nature like mine was. And the box was where it began. When the audience first broke into that wild shouting and applause, something drilled itself through to me, a kind of delight I'd never experienced before, something – well, I suppose you might call it a feeling of happiness. And another thing, Kaspar – and of this I was really proud – I'd come to terms with myself. I was no longer torn apart by that giant-dwarf tug-of-war. I knew there were a lot of things I'd never have, but in exchange, secret and watertight, I had something else: my self-esteem. You can call it arrogance if you like.

'I'd cried buckets when I lost Lisa, and the pain was still there, but now I'd lost Ehrenreich too, and I learned the difference between getting worked up because you're in love with a pretty girl, and losing an irreplaceable father who's given you life itself. Because that's what Ehrenreich had done for me, much more than my real father ever did: he'd given me my life.

'Mother didn't cry, but she sat at the window a lot, looking out at the other caravans, all orphaned and silent. It seemed to me that even the animals had noticed something and weren't bellowing and screeching as much as usual.

'Who were "the other parties" at the Hotel Krone? Ehrenreich's wife? No, she was dead. His daughters? Lisa perhaps?

'Our appointment was for 10 a.m. precisely. We all assembled for breakfast in Mother's caravan; nobody spoke. None of us had slept much, Mother because she dreaded anything to do with lawyers, my brothers because they were worried about their future, and me because of Lisa.

'Andros came to collect us, all dressed up in a stiff collar and bow tie. He too never opened his mouth. Herr Ehrenreich had been not only a father to him, but also his child. His face was so drained of colour that the old scars left by lion and tiger claws around his mangled nose stood out like fresh wounds.

'We walked across the lifeless circus grounds in silence. The curtains were drawn back in all the caravans, everyone watched us pass. To be or not to be for the Sarasate Circus, for all the circus folk and all the animals.

'At the Hotel Krone we asked at the desk for Doctor Pollart, the lawyer. Second floor left, room thirteen. "Unlucky number!"

muttered that Leopold at the same moment that Bernie exclaimed: "Thirteen for luck!"

'Outside the room all five of us stopped and took a deep breath. Then Mother knocked.

'"Come in."

'At first you could hardly see anything because the heavy draperies were half drawn. An imposing drawing-room, very dignified. Behind the desk a thin gentleman with glasses. "Pollart of Pollart & Sperrholz – a pleasure." He bowed. Then, indicating a sofa against the wall: "Frau Schulte and sons and Herr Andros – Monsieur and Madame Grandet."

'We didn't even have time to close the door before the gentleman on the sofa jumped up as if stung by a wasp.

'"*Comment?*" he cried, his moustache jiggling up and down. "Is that him?" he shouted at the lady in pink at his side. She nodded. We stared at him blankly. So did Doctor Pollart.

'"*Petit chien puant!*" Monsieur Grandet screamed, his face turning purple.

'Bernie hurriedly closed the door. Doctor Pollart got up from his desk and was just starting to say: "Now, now, what's all this?" when the fellow with the moustache swooped down on me and grabbed me by the throat. I didn't even have time to let out a yell, but the Monsieur too wasn't allowed enough time to get a really good stranglehold on me because he suddenly found himself sitting on the floor, with Andros twisting his arm behind his back until he yelled "Aaiee!"

'Doctor Pollart, who had hastily retreated behind his desk, called out: "Please, gentlemen, please!" but Andros wasn't about to let go; his face had regained a very nice colour and he looked almost happy as he snarled: "Well, Stilts, have you anything to say to this gentleman?" Nothing momentous sprang to mind and anyhow the gentleman was yelling "Aaiee!" again.

'Lisa jumped up and screamed: "Andros, let go of my husband this instant. How dare you!"

'But Andros didn't let go; he was enjoying himself. He just said casually over his shoulder: "Madame Lisa, tell your husband not to touch our Stilts again or I'll break every bone in his body. Kindly tell him that, please."

'She said something in rapid French, probably remembering how Andros had crushed two ribs of a young African lion, while the lawyer called out: "Ladies and gentlemen, please be seated."

'"You heard what the man said, Madame Lisa," said Andros.

'Lisa sat down again, murmuring: "Let go of him. He won't do it again."

'Sorry, Kaspar, that's not quite true: she didn't murmur it, she hissed it from underneath her pretty pink veil, just in time to harmonize with the third "Aaiee!"

'Well, finally we were all seated, at appropriate distances, at a round table. My brothers were still completely stupefied and kept staring from the Monsieur to Lisa and then back at me. Mother was looking down at her folded hands and Andros was sitting beside me, his face stony again. Lisa raised her veil, but I couldn't look at her properly because I was unobtrusively trying to rub my neck. The Monsieur was massaging his elbows as obtrusively as possible and not looking at anyone, not even his wife.

'Doctor Pollart got up from his desk. The will – if that's what it was – was lying in front of him, already opened. In that small envelope?

'"First I should like to explain to those present why certain others are not present," he began, still a bit shaky. "You may not be aware that the deceased had concluded a written agreement with his daughters, both of whom reside in America and have re-nounced their share of the estate." He took a sheet of paper out of the envelope and held it up. "Available for inspection later, if you so wish. The testator subsequently made a new will."

'We all sat in a curious sort of dead silence, and I'm willing to bet that that silence was Doctor Pollart's idea of heavenly music for the solemn ring-a-roses he had set up around the big table. Finally he woke up from his trance and took another piece of paper out of the envelope, a small, thin sheet, and read it out, enunciating so precisely that he sounded like a sheep bleating:

'"The sole heir to my entire estate and beneficiary of all my unencumbered assets shall be the Sarasate Circus under the sole direction of Herr Gyula Andros and the Schulte family. All profits from the operation of the circus proper shall go to Herr Andros and those from the freak show to the Schulte family. To Madame Lisa Grandet I bequeath the sum of ten thousand marks. I bequeath my own circus caravan, complete with all furnishings, to Herr Franz Schulte in the hope that he will live in it and not forget me. Frankfurt, 23 September 1909, Joseph Gottlieb Ehrenreich. Signa-

147

ture witnessed by Pollart and Sperrholz, attorneys at law. That's all, ladies and gentlemen. Any questions?"

'We had no questions; we just sat there stiffly without a word.

'But the couple on the far side of the table had jumped up and were remonstrating with Doctor Pollart at his desk, Monsieur in French, with Lisa translating and adding a few choice phrases of her own. But the man just looked at them calmly over the rim of his glasses; this sort of thing he could handle with ease. When they paused for breath, he reminded them that there was a probate court of appeals to which they should kindly address themselves. And now, if they'd be good enough to sign. . . .

'At this, Monsieur knocked the paper out of his hand and Lisa cried she refused to accept "charity".

'"Then if the Schulte family and Herr Andros will be good enough to sign. . . ."

'We marched over to the desk in closed ranks and for the first time in years I found myself standing beside Lisa. She was still using the same perfume and it disturbed me quite a bit.'

CHAPTER EIGHTEEN

IT WAS one o'clock in the morning when Kaspar pulled into Gellerstrasse. For a few moments he remained seated behind the wheel; he was tired and he had three bottles of beer inside him. Finally he pulled out the ignition key and opened the door. Instantly a tall, thin shadow materialized beside it, preventing him from stepping out.

'Miklos?'

'May I get in, Professor? Just for a minute or two.'

Without waiting for an answer, the shadow glided around the car and slid into the passenger seat. 'Luburic must talk to you, Professor. Very important.'

'Important for whom?'

'Professor, you want Luburic be dead too?'

'How am I supposed to prevent it?'

'He want to meet you. Not at your place. Other people place, friend's place. You have friends?'

In the faint light from a street lamp, the face beside Kaspar seemed to consist entirely of bones and deep, dark hollows. Other people's place? What right did he have to involve his friends in the Croats' troubles?

What kind of reception would he get if he went up to a single one of them saying, 'Is it all right if I use your place to meet some Croatian activists on the run?' The trouble was he simply didn't have the right kind of friends, the 'tolerant' sort, mildly dropped out, the counter-culture types.

'I'm sorry, Miklos, I can't think of anybody.'

'We know good, safe place, Professor.' The death's head beside him was automatically turning from side to side, keeping watch. 'Thirty-one Kaiserplatz. Your uncle.'

'What? How did you come to think of *him*? What do you know about . . .?'

'Martinac said, remember? He knew about uncle. Thirty-one Kaiserplatz. We can . . .'

'Out of the question. My uncle's very old, and besides he's bedridden.'

'Bedridden is good! He don't need to know. Cook is foreigner, too, perhaps . . .' The vulture's claw, ice-cold now, was laid tentatively on his knee. 'Only one more time. Luburic say not again.'

Kaspar was too sleepy to be brutal. In any case he wasn't going to get away scot-free. 'Call me tomorrow evening about six. If there's any way . . .'

The vulture's claw pressed his knee hard. 'Say only when. Nothing else. Thanks.'

Miklos slipped soundlessly out of the car, taking no notice of Kaspar's warning: 'Mind, I'm not promising anything.'

Early next morning, before leaving for the Institute, he made a telephone call.

'Anya?'

'Master is sleeping, dammit. I don't wake him.'

'I know. That's why I'm calling now.'

'What?'

'Anya, I'd like to borrow your kitchen to meet two people.'

'People?'

'They're in danger, they have nowhere to go. Only this once, Anya. My uncle doesn't need to know about it. Just for half an hour.'

Silence at the other end of the line.

'Anya? May I bring them tonight abut nine? Yes or no?'

'But don't ring.'

People in danger count the seconds, even when they're not crucial. On the dot of nine the two men were standing outside Uncle Stilts's door, impatient and jumpy, waiting for Kaspar, who came sauntering up the stairs a good ten minutes late. He nodded to Luburic and knocked softly.

Anya opened the door, barring the way. No one spoke. Without deigning to glance at Kaspar, she gave the other two men, the thin one and the stocky one with the deep-set eyes, a long, searching look, taking no notice of the unavoidable surprise in their faces. Then she let them in, pointed silently at the dwarf's bedroom door with a finger to her lips and led the way on tiptoe to the kitchen.

There was only one chair. Kaspar brought another from Anya's room, glancing quickly at the covered, silent birdcage. He leaned against the window, Anya perched on the table, and the two Croats sat down on the chairs, darting sidelong, slightly bewildered looks at the young woman, who was watching them with a frown, her long, blue-jeaned legs dangling.

'They must eat,' she declared abruptly, and jumped down to fetch a loaf of bread from the breadbox, butter and salami from the refrigerator, plates and knives from a drawer. No one spoke.

The two Croats watched her every movement, counted the slices as she cut the bread, each slice more than an inch thick, and held their breath as she smeared on a generous layer of butter with a single movement of the knife. She hacked the salami into thick pieces and laid them beside the bread.

'There.'

Luburic had lost a good deal of weight, too, but he took his time, unlike Miklos, who just opened his mouth, crammed in everything on his plate and gulped it down.

Anya gave Kaspar a hostile look. 'Why you not bring these two before?'

Miklos set his empty plate down on the table, stared at the girl with the long, thick Palomino mane of hair and sank slowly to his knees. 'Holy Mother of God,' he whispered in Croatian.

'What he say?'

Kaspar translated. She studied the kneeling man attentively and shook her head. 'He die soon if he not eat more. You tell him.'

She buttered two more slices of bread, then two more for Luburic, who ate them in silence without raising his eyes from his plate.

'Okay,' she said as she cleared away the plates. 'You like to talk now. I am next door. Knock when you finished.'

Miklos stared at her as though he had been visited by the Holy Ghost and then abandoned again. 'What's her name?'

'Anya. Herr Luburic, you wanted to talk to me?'

The Croat nodded, leaned back in the hard kitchen chair and closed his eyes for a moment. He probably hasn't slept, thought Kaspar. Where the devil can he be living? But he didn't ask.

'I'm leaving, Professor. I'm going home, to take a rest. Later I'll be back – to work.' He broke off, exhausted.

'Where is "home"? Is there anything I can do for you?'

'Thank you, I already have my ticket. I live in Bled, not far from the frontier. Do you know it?'

Kaspar shook his head.

'Very beautiful. Many honeymooners,' said Miklos.

'Do you have a place to stay?'

'I have friends. My father taught swimming at a hotel there before the war. Some of the boys he taught are still friends – you understand what I mean?' His eyes closed again.

'You can't travel in the shape you're in. Get a good night's sleep first.'

'Sleep? Ivan's dead. I wanted to ask you two favours. Go and see Vlada occasionally. She doesn't know anybody except other "friends" and all she hears is: revenge, revenge for Ivan. Talk to her about the children and the future. Perhaps you can help – no, I don't mean money. And then Miklos. The UDBA's looking for him, the German police are looking for him, he wants to shoot himself, but perhaps you could . . . I can't take him along: he has no papers. I can't sleep because of Ivan and Miklos.'

'Shooting is fast. Starving takes long,' observed the skinny man, his eyes still fixed on Anya's door.

Kaspar suddenly had an idea. He got up and knocked on the door. Anya appeared in her long woollen nightgown, her half-braided hair hanging down over her breasts, a hairbrush in her hand.

'Finished?'

'Anya, this man's name is Miklos. He wants to die because he's hungry and because he has no place to stay.'

She looked at Kaspar crossly and muttered something unintelligible. Then she went over to Miklos, who was slumped limply on his chair, bent down and tapped him lightly on the shoulder with her hairbrush.

'Why you not stay here? Utility room over there, for ironing-board, sewing-machine, junk. We throw it all out and you sleep tonight on floor with pillow. Tomorrow we see about bed.'

Slowly he raised his head and looked at her. Kaspar wasn't sure whether he had understood a single word and quickly translated into Croatian, but Miklos still seemed unable to take in anything except the girl.

Straightening up, Anya glanced at Kaspar. 'I ask the Master. Okay?'

He nodded. The little dwarf would wonder what he was doing in the kitchen, but she was right, they must get his permission before allowing in a strange bird like this.

Several minutes passed without anyone saying a word. The two Croats sat stiffly on their kitchen chairs with their eyes closed and their arms hanging limply at their sides. Luburic's black leather glove swung gently back and forth.

'Can't your – your organization do anything for you?'

Luburic shook his head without opening his eyes. 'I'm on the black list. They say it's all my fault for going out with Ivan that night. But you knew Ivan, Professor; Ivan did what he wanted. I couldn't stay behind in the apartment; I had to stay with my bodyguard. Damn funny joke, isn't it?' He opened his eyes and looked at Kaspar, frowning. 'If only he hadn't had so much to drink that night . . .' After a pause he added: 'What a punishment for a few glasses of slivovitz.'

'But then you wouldn't be here now.'

'Ivan had five children. I'm not married.'

'And Miklos? Why can't they do anything for him?'

'Miklos was a UDBA man. They don't trust him.'

Anya appeared in the doorway. 'The Master wants to see you. All of you.'

Kaspar translated, adding that his uncle was not only very old, but he was also a dwarf. They nodded. A dwarf. Why not? Anya pushed the two Croats into the old man's bedroom, stood aside for Kaspar, then followed him in.

'Good evening, Uncle Stilts,' said Kaspar, quickly crossing the room and propping himself against his familiar bedpost. The old man glanced at him briefly, then turned his attention to the two men, standing hesitantly in the dim red glow, half way between the door and the big fourposter.

Anya tried to push Miklos forward. 'This one here, Sir, the thin one.' Grasping his vulture's claw, she drew Miklos closer to the bed and straightened him up like a puppet. 'His name Miklos. Eaten three sandwiches already.'

The dwarf looked up at the silent, rawboned scarecrow, then at Luburic, still standing in the back, barely visible in the semidarkness. 'And that one?'

'This is Ante Luburic, Uncle Stilts. He's going back to Yugoslavia first thing tomorrow morning. They've been after him for a long time. He's a Croatian activist.'

'Why doesn't he come closer?'

Kaspar turned his head and said a few words in Croatian, but

Luburic didn't move. 'It's better people don't see me. I'm only waiting for Miklos.'

Kaspar translated.

'But he interests me,' cried the dwarf indignantly. 'He's the one that counts, I can see that. Tell him to come over here, to the bed.'

Kaspar spoke again, somewhat impatiently, and Luburic advanced and stood next to Miklos. The faint gleam of the night-light fell on his huge head; his dark eyes rested without curiosity on the dwarf.

'He looks like a Roman emperor,' the old man exclaimed delightedly, leaning forward to get a better look. 'Kaspar, tell him he can stay here, too. We'll find room for him, it'll be fun.'

'Uncle Stilts, the UDBA has just assassinated his bodyguard, he's got to get away immediately.'

'Damn.' He gnawed disappointedly at his upper lip.

'May the other one stay here for the time being? He hasn't exactly had a ball either.'

The dwarf glanced quickly at the thin man and nodded. 'If it's not too much for Anya.'

She grabbed Miklos's arm from behind and was about to drag him out of the room, when Luburic caught hold of him, asking in Croatian: 'He can stay? Good. I have to go now, but I must have a few words with him first. Outside.'

Stepping forward, he held out his left hand to the dwarf, but the old man pointed fascinated at the right one in the black leather glove.

'Kaspar, ask him if I can look at it. Tell him I once used an iron hook myself.'

Luburic frowned and Kaspar had to explain a few things before he hesitantly held out his right arm. The dwarf grasped the glove without the least embarrassment, fingering it and feeling around inside Luburic's sleeve to find the place where the artificial hand was attached.

'Lousy job,' he muttered. 'Tell him they could do much better than that. I'll pay for it.'

Kaspar wearily translated.

Luburic withdrew his hand and shook his head. 'I must go.'

He inclined his head to the dwarf, murmured 'thank you' in German, shook hands with Kaspar and gestured with his head to Miklos to follow him.

Pausing briefly in the doorway, he added: 'Thank you, Frau.'

Kaspar swung himself up on the bed and leaned against a bedpost, while the dwarf polished his glasses reflectively.

'Second thoughts, Uncle Stilts? You still have time, they're still out there in the hall.'

'Tell me about that skeleton, Inkworm.'

Kaspar told him as much as he could remember of what Martinac had told him. The old man listened attentively, nodding from time to time.

'Yes,' he said slowly. 'Yes, I've heard quite a few stories like that. I lived for a while with people who'd been through that sort of thing themselves, for one reason or another. I always wondered how a fellow like that can survive and eat and drink, and sleep at night, and think about girls again.' He paused for a moment. 'Not me. It took me a long time to get over it. Years.'

Kaspar waited, not asking any questions. He heard the apartment door open and close again. Luburic had left. Where had he gone? It looked as if he had no safe place to stay. Perhaps he'd keep himself awake by walking about the streets, or maybe he'd crawl behind a bush in the park and sleep until daylight, when he could make for the station. Once he got there, he'd be safe. The UDBA couldn't touch him on the train.

He heard Anya's voice talking to Miklos. Apparently he could not understand her for she tried again, twice as loud. Then the kitchen door closed and everything was quiet. The dwarf was staring at the bedspread, rubbing his hands together as if he felt cold.

Kaspar decided to risk a cue: 'Did you spread the good news around the circus right away?'

But the old man was far away. 'What good news?'

'About Herr Ehrenreich's will. Did you go on with your engagement in Mainz?'

'Mainz? Mainz?' the dwarf repeated vaguely, still rubbing his hands. Suddenly he let them fall on the covers and looked at Kaspar. 'Do you know what Lisa said to me? "Stilts," she said, "I leave it to you. You see to it that I get my fair share. You know why." She actually said that to me, in German, while I was standing next to her at the lawyer's desk waiting my turn to sign the papers. Her husband at once pulled her away; he was a nasty piece of work if ever I saw one. "We'll sue you," he yelled in French and kicked at me with his foot. "One doesn't talk to vermin of your sort." And at that they took off, fast.

'It certainly spoiled my day. Later, when we returned home to the circus with the great news, the jubilation and the dancing about cheered me, too. It was like finding everybody safe in the lifeboat after the ship's gone down. Andros even told the news to the animals, going from cage to cage with a bottle of brandy, singing and rattling the bars.

'My brothers didn't come back with us, they stayed on to talk business with Doctor Pollart. Later Mother went to church; she tried to take me along, but I couldn't bring myself to go. I just wanted to sit alone in our caravan and think about Herr Ehrenreich – though I couldn't stop Lisa from popping into view now and then. She was as beautiful as ever, you know, though she suddenly seemed awfully big, as if she'd grown since the old days. I tried to imagine her in bed with her Monsieur and his moustache.

'Then I walked over to Herr Ehrenreich's caravan – Pollart had solemnly handed over the keys. There, at last, I was rid of Lisa and alone with Herr Ehrenreich. I sat down in my little chair opposite his big one, where we'd sat and laughed together. "Stiltskin, Stiltskin," he used to say in that low, teasing voice – nobody would ever say it again that way.

'Later, Mother came in to make me go back for supper. It was the last evening we'd all spend together in her caravan because the next morning I was going to move into Herr Ehrenreich's for good. The brothers had separate ones, anyway. Mother would be lonely, but she knew it was inevitable. Andros was missing. Somebody finally found him snoring in the elephant tent and he was brought over to Mother's too.

'We crowded around the little table, each of us with a glass of champagne, and drank a toast to the memory of Herr Ehrenreich. Then Mother served the roast beef, but my brothers were too excited to eat; first they had to tell us the great news. It turned out that Herr Ehrenreich had been worth a hell of a lot of money, I've forgotten the exact amount, but it was several hundred thousand marks. We all looked at each other, sitting there in front of our plates heaped with food, Leopold, Bernie, Andros, Mother and Stilts, five rich people around a table. Andros started to cry, and his tears were neatly channelled into and then down the furrows of his scars. He missed his Ehrenreich. My brothers each took an arm and hauled him back to his own caravan.

'Talk about rich! That wasn't the word for it, Kaspar. We began a new life the very next morning. Mother opened a bank account for me and it grew and grew. We continued with the tour for the rest of the year, just the way Ehrenreich had planned it, and my brothers took turns doing the commentary for the chess machine. It wasn't great, but it got by, and in time I got used to it. A few months later Doctor Pollart wrote that Lisa and her husband were trying to have the will declared invalid but he thought they wouldn't have much luck.'

The old man chewed violently at his upper lip, suddenly discovered that his pyjama jacket was buttoned up the wrong way, fiddled with it impatiently and pulled a button off.

'I feel so hot, Kaspar – though we're still in 1911 and nothing awful had happened as yet. On the contrary. Mother and I were leading the grand life, taking two months' vacation every year. We went to Italy and once to Egypt, always first class. Mother was now the rich Frau Schulte, though she refused to believe it. She had a brand new caravan to live in, expensive clothes, a fur coat – all presents from us, of course – but she didn't really enjoy them, said it was "sinful" and talked a lot about the camel and the eye of a needle. She still made her regular evening rounds before the performance and . . . oh yes, that reminds me of something: "our" workmen, the ones who'd been sworn to secrecy, well, when their three years were up Andros had paid them their premiums, with interest, and renewed the agreement for another five years. We never had any problems, imagine! Nobody ever blabbed; it worked because we were all in the same boat.

'Until the beginning of 1914. Now I feel cold again. Hand me that old cardigan over there. You button it, I'm too fidgety. January 1914. I guess everybody remembers that year, but for me personally there was a special little something, on top of everything else. It had been a particularly cold winter and we were playing in Berlin, a draughty place. We couldn't heat the caravans properly so Mother and I moved into the Eden Hotel. She took to her bed with a touch of bronchitis.

'Well, one night after the performance they sent up a bellboy with a message. We were having our supper, Mother sitting up in bed with her tray on her lap and I beside her with mine. The boy

said there was a lady downstairs asking to speak to Herr Schulte. I
knew at once who it was, and I also knew what she wanted. In
those three years since I'd last seen her, in Mainz, it had occurred
to me once or twice that this might happen. And, you know,
maybe it had occurred to Mother too. She wasn't a bit surprised,
that's for sure. You should have seen the way we looked at each
other when the bellboy brought the message, and the way she
slowly nodded her head.

'"Ask the lady to come up."

'We went on with our supper, and Lisa walked into the room.
"Good evening," she said, standing in front of Mother's bed.

'"Won't you take off your things?" said Mother. "You'll have to
excuse me, I've got a bit of a cold."

'"Oh," said Lisa, looking at me. I slowly got to my feet and
helped her out of her fur coat, thinking: Mother has a better one.

'"Do sit down," said Mother.

'Lisa pulled the hatpins out of her cartwheel hat covered with
ostrich feathers and settled into an armchair, crossing her legs
elegantly, a very handsome shape. I returned to my tray.

'"Will you excuse me if I go on eating?" I said. "I don't want it to
get cold."

'"Please do," she said.

'Mother went on with her soup and Lisa looked from one to the
other. For a time no one spoke, then Mother laid down her spoon.

'"To what do we owe the pleasure, Madame Lisa?"

'"I expect you can guess all right. As you know, the probate
court has ruled against us so we have no choice but to obtain justice
by other means." She paused, but we didn't inquire what "other
means" she had in mind. "You may remember, I participated in the
chess machine number for a time."

'Mother waggled her head from side to side. "I surely do
remember," she said, as though it were a painful subject. "Not
much good either, I'm afraid, not exactly cut out for the stage, if
you don't mind me saying so."

'Lisa's cheeks turned red. "We're not talking about my acting
talent but about my legitimate claims. I am Herr Ehrenreich's
niece and I demand at least an equal share of the revenue.
Retroactive for three years, of course, to the date of my uncle's
death. Otherwise . . ."

'"Otherwise?" repeated Mother.

'Lisa hesitated and looked at me. I met her eyes, keeping my expression as neutral as I could and taking in her hair style, puffed up high, with a tight roll around the head and a lot of frizz across her forehead, and underneath, her eyes, so lovely, blue-grey and blazing with anger, and her little nose, and her pale mouth which was trembling violently.

'"Could I have a few words with Stilts – alone?"

'"What for?" I asked, reaching for my dessert. "I have no secrets from my mother."

'"Stilts, you and I could come to terms, I'm sure. After all, we were fond of each other once, weren't we?"

'"A long time ago," I said, in between spoonfuls of apple sauce.

'She made one last try. "I'd like to settle this in a friendly way, that's what I've come for. I'd hate to have to . . . er, bring up the big guns."

'She certainly had an elegant manner of speaking. Mother was very impressed. "And what kind of guns might those be?" she asked, like someone with a genuine thirst for knowledge.

'"I shall inform the appropriate authorities that your so-called chess machine is a complete fake, an outrageous deception of the public and therefore the solicitation of money under false pretences. They will not only put you out of business, they'll also bring criminal proceedings against you."

'Mother nodded. "Quite right," she said. "There's just one little snag, Madame Lisa – though I must say you've cooked up a pretty good case there with all them fancy words. But that little snag kind of spoils it a bit. What I mean is: didn't you do your share of defrauding the public? If I remember rightly, you said just now how you were one of the team for a time. So I guess they'll have to bring their criminal proceedings against the whole lot of us, won't they? It's quite all right with me. How about you, Stilts?"

'"I can hardly wait," I said.

'Lisa didn't answer, but her bosom heaved and I allowed myself some memories . . . Then she picked up her hatpins and ostrich feathers and stood up.

'"We'll see," she said so softly that Mother had to ask: "Beg pardon?" "You'll regret it, I assure you."

'I got up to help her into her coat, but she wouldn't let me.

159

'"My husband is quite right," she said – no, I'm telling it wrong again, Kaspar – she didn't *say* it, she spat it out the way our large cats in the cages would spit when they got angry: "Filthy vermin!"

'Very effective, that exit of hers. Though Mother and I had given a fine performance, too – you'd think we'd rehearsed it – but when she was gone, my feathers drooped a bit.

'"This is going to be a real knockdown fight," said Mother. "You can count on that. It might be better to give her her share or pay her a lump sum. It could turn real nasty, if a little viper like that gets nothing at all."

'"A lump sum won't work, Mother. She'll just blackmail us for more. Same with giving her her share. Once she tastes blood, she'll never give up."

'Mother nodded and sighed. "So what are we going to do?"

'"Go to jail," I said, "if we have to. But not one single cent."

'My brothers took the same view and so did Andros. Not a goddamn penny. They couldn't turn us in, it was just bluff. Goddamn nerve! But Mother kept shaking her head and saying: "Better safe than sorry. If a dog's real mean, give it two bones." But she couldn't move us; we were like a stone wall.

'Only four more days in Berlin. Mother was better, but we stayed on at the Eden for safety's sake. On our last day, a Saturday, I went strolling down Unter den Linden, watching the pretty women and the elegant carriages and automobiles. It was a glorious day, blue sky, though still a bit chilly. By this time I'd been a dwarf so long – twenty-four years – that I didn't even notice how people behaved when they saw me in the street. It was always the same: goggle-eyes, and then the reaction depending on their upbringing, ranging from pretending not to notice to actually stopping for a good hard stare. As for me, I saw nothing and heard nothing. Wherever I might happen to be, I was sitting in my box.

'Well, on that particular Saturday morning, I was standing on the corner of Wilhelmstrasse when somebody came a bit too close to me and said something. I caught a glimpse of a skirt and turned away.

'And then, above the noise of the traffic I heard: "Please, Stilts!" She *must* speak to me, she said, just for a minute. She had tears in her eyes and she repeated very quietly: "Please, Stilts." There was such a bedlam of honking and rattling around us that I almost had to read her lips.

'So we sat down in the Café Bauer on the corner of Friedrich-strasse. I found a corner table right in the back because she was crying so hard. I ordered hot chocolate and finally she blew her nose and felt able to talk. You can imagine how it tore me up. All those nights crammed full of grief and rage! And now *she* was sitting there, crying. It gave me not even a crumb of satisfaction, I had to keep telling myself: don't touch her, don't stroke her hand, just sit quiet and wait.

'And then it all came out, Kaspar. In between tears and hot chocolate, she confessed the story of the "wicked dwarf". And at that point I'd have choked if I'd kept my mouth shut any longer, so I asked her how she could possibly have thought that anybody would have fallen for such a load of bullshit. Hadn't she realized that both men had only pretended to swallow that story. Ehren-reich, because he was a gentleman, and her Monsieur, because he was a cad? I said cad, Kaspar, I wasn't in the mood to pull punches.

'Well, maybe I always misjudged her, maybe there always had been a hidden source of acting talent in her, for she insisted with eyes blazing that her husband implicitly believed every word about the wicked dwarf, and that he hated me like poison.

'I sat back and shut up, and she quickly came to the point: why she'd waylaid me on that street corner. They were hard up; the lawyer had taken everything they had; she didn't know what they were going to live on. In her husband's family no one *worked*, for God's sake, he wasn't trained to do anything and she wasn't either. What was going to become of them?

'We sat in that damn café for at least two hours, I can't tell you all the back and forth arguments. In the end, after she'd downed three hot chocolates, I promised to talk to my brothers and see what we could do for her.

'"What about your mother?"

'"She's in favour of it anyhow."

'"She is?" said Lisa, giving me a funny look. "I'm surprised. She never liked me."

'I couldn't contradict her there, so I kept mum. Then came a long pause and after that, with a completely different expression in those pretty eyes: "How much?"

'"I don't know, Lisa, but if my brothers won't agree to it, I'll see that you get part of my share."

'"How much?" she asked again.

'I sat there like a fool, confused by the change of role from the ewe-lamb to tough business woman, and then she said quite slowly and plainly: "My husband knows that it's *you* sitting in the box, Stilts. I've told him." I must have looked like a stunned ox in a slaughter-house because she repeated it again, carefully and slowly. "Don't forget that, Stilts," she said. "And tell your mother and your brothers too. He knows." Then she got up and left without even saying goodbye.

'I sat on in the café for a while. It was empty now and I moved to a window table and looked out at the street. It too was almost empty. Lunch time. I sat there for at least an hour and watched the sun shining through the bare linden branches, making patterns on the pavement. I came to a decision. I wanted to be completely sure, see, and in the end I was.

'At night after the show, our last performance in Berlin, my brothers and Andros came up to Mother's room with me because I had something important to discuss with them. I told them about meeting Lisa and that I was willing to give her something out of my share, but my brothers interrupted and began shouting: "Stilts, you're crazy! Why ever would you want to do that?"

'"Because she has the upper hand," I said. "And because she's going to push my teeth in with that upper hand."

'"What the hell can she do? She can't denounce us."

'"She'll find some way, you can count on that. And that's why I want to get out of that box."

'Then they all began shouting at once – except Mother, of course – and Andros was cursing and swearing, which he normally didn't do in front of Mother, about Lisa and her Monsieur, but I hadn't finished: "Let me be quite honest: it's not just on account of Lisa. I'm sick of that damn box. I've been sitting in it for nine years now and I'm sick of it."

'There was a dead silence. Then Mother nodded and a moment later Andros followed suit.

'Then that Leopold said: "Well, for God's sake, what are you going to do with the rest of your life?"

'"I want to get out. I want to travel, drop out of sight for a few years, maybe go to America. Give them time to forget all about the chess machine. And then I can come back and play chess in public. Enter tournaments. Become world champion."

'"But what about the freak show?" asked your uncle Bernie, all confused. "You can't just leave us in the lurch."

'"The freak show can survive even without the chess machine," said Mother.

'"No!" shouted that Leopold. "We've signed contracts and the machine's the big attraction, you know that."

'"How much longer?"

'"Three weeks," said Andros. "Next week Magdeburg, then Brunswick, and then back to Potsdam. The programmes are already printed and sent out."

'"All right," I said. "I'll stay with it for three more weeks. That's all." But you know what, Kaspar? It was those three weeks that did it.'

He sank back into his pillows, took off his glasses and closed his eyes. 'I'm all in too, Kaspar. I'm pooped.'

'Uncle Stilts – you can't do that to me.'

The old man opened his eyes and looked at him in surprise. 'What is it, Inkworm, don't you understand? I'm tired.'

'You want to send me home *now*? Do you think I sit here listening to you and then just wipe it out of my mind as I walk downstairs?'

The dwarf smiled, stretched out a tiny hand and patted the bedspread reassuringly, as if it were Kaspar's hand.

'Good. Good. I'm glad it takes it out of you. It takes it out of me, too, you know. After you've gone, I lie awake for hours, thinking and thinking. . . .'

He put his spectacles back on and struggled up until he could settle comfortably against his pillows. 'All right, then, I'll give it a try. Let's see how far I can get tonight, it isn't really all that much, only – it . . . it . . . well, you'll see in a moment why it's hard for me to . . . by the way, did I mention the letter waiting for me at the hotel when I got back after the performance? Now that's important, mustn't forget that. It was just a note saying: "How much and when? Reply immediately to our address." No greeting and no signature. Lisa's handwriting. I wrote underneath: "Not a penny and never." Didn't sign it and sent it off.

'I had long talks with Mother whether she should carry on the freak show without me. She'd had enough, too, and my brothers didn't press her; their share would be all the bigger. But poor old Andros, he took to getting soused every night and crying because he'd be left all alone. Mother wanted to go back to Landshut, she missed her garden and Ida. She was only forty-eight, but she looked a whole lot older, with her hair all white – maybe from having to be an adult so early on. She spent the three weeks saying goodbye to all her Wonders of Nature, man and beast alike, and there were tears aplenty every night while we played.

'And then came Potsdam. The last week . . . I'll do my best to tell you about that quite calmly, and I'll make it short, or I won't last to the end. Five days we were supposed to play there. So – we're getting to it now, Kaspar, and I can see already I haven't a dog's chance of remaining "calm"! I've got a good strong heart, you know, but now I can feel it thumping, dammit. Oh well, too late now, I'll just have to press on.

'On the third day, during my first game, I heard a bit of a commotion down in the audience, on the left, and people shouting "Quiet!" That Leopold was doing the commentary that night and he called out very loud: "Ladies and gentlemen – my goodness me! Herr Griebler can't castle now. He has to be very, very careful, we must have absolute quiet, please! Aha, I see Herr Griebler wants to exchange queens. Very good move, Herr Griebler! Bravo!" I castled neatly, moving my king to safety. He was a good player, Herr Griebler, but whatever was going on down there, on the left, wouldn't calm down, so I polished him off fast and gave the three knocks for checkmate. "Bravo, Machine!" shouted that Leopold. "Well played!"

'The audience began to clap. Herr Griebler bowed and was stepping down from the stage when someone in the audience yelled: "Fraud! Swindle! They're a bunch of crooks." And a second voice, with a Berlin accent, shouted: "That's not a machine. There's someone sitting inside it. Somebody go up there and take a look."

'That Leopold rang down the curtain, but the audience began to shout: "Curtain up! Curtain up!" Our two workmen were trying to get the machine off stage as fast as possible, but they were blocked by a handful of people who had jumped up on to the stage and surrounded the table.

'From down in the audience the second voice, with the Berlin accent, yelled: "Go on, boys. Open up the back panel!" Most of the audience were on their feet and everybody watched tensely to see if they'd manage it and to find out what was really inside the machine.

'But it couldn't be opened from outside and I could hear them scratching at the panels trying to find an opening, cursing that their fingers were already bloody. More and more people crowded on stage. I could see their faces through my peepholes and I was scared, I tell you. The man with the Berlin accent yelled: "Get a knife and break the goddamn thing open."

'That Leopold tried to force them back, while our men pushed their way to the table. He kept shouting things like: "Careful, for God's sake – the machine is priceless! Get back! Watch out for electric shocks," and "I'll sue anyone who lays a hand on it," but then all of a sudden somebody pulled out a pocket-knife and stabbed the blade through the back panel. It caught me at the left shoulder and it went in deep. I bit my lips hard, trying not to cry out from the pain and the fear of being stabbed again –don't forget, I couldn't move, couldn't dodge – but now our men ploughed into the people crowding around the table, hitting out right and left, and threw themselves on the fellow with the knife and wrenched it away from him.

'Then somebody shouted: "There's blood on that knife!" and there was a sudden silence. Someone else yelled hysterically: "Look! There's blood! Down at the bottom of the box – that's where it's coming from!"

'No one on stage moved; even that Leopold and our men stood as still as statues – but only for a second, and then I heard someone running and one of our men yelling: "A crowbar. Quick!" The man down in the audience shouted again: "It's a fake. There's someone sitting inside it. A dwarf!" – but at that moment a voice said quietly: "Someone's hurt in there. Open it up immediately. I'm a doctor."

'That was the last thing I heard. They say that Leopold kept shouting: "Open up, Stilts. Open up quick," but I know nothing about that, they told me about it later. Finally someone rushed up with a crowbar, sobbing; he thought, of course, I was dead, since I wasn't answering. I was told that Leopold went completely to pieces and just kept whimpering: "Quick, quick!"

'Everybody on stage stepped back to make room for the doctor, who was taking off his coat. More and more people were trying to climb up because they all wanted to see what was in the box, but the doctor had a very commanding voice and he insisted that no one was to come too close while our men were prying the boards apart with the crowbar.

'When they finally got the back panel open, there I sat, a limp form held in place by the rigid structure. The doctor lifted me out carefully and my head lolled to one side and blood trickled over his hands. They were all convinced I was dead and they just stood there, struck dumb with horror. Someone shouted: "Where's the man with the knife?" But he had disappeared.

'And then the first voice in the audience started up again: "What did I tell you? It's all a fake. They're a bunch of swindlers!"

'But nobody wanted to get into that, they all stayed where they were, on stage or down in the audience, whispering together, too fascinated by all the excitement to leave, though some were worried that they might be held responsible later for incitement to murder.

'The doctor carried me backstage, laid me down on the floor and took off my shirt. Somebody had gone for an ambulance, and while he waited, the doctor bandaged me up, cutting my shirt and his own into strips.

Mother was in her caravan, about to go to bed, when she heard the ambulance bell. I only came to in the hospital, and she was sitting at my bedside. . . .

'Okay? That'll do for you, Kaspar? I can't manage any more tonight. Want to sleep here again? Go ahead, stretch out. It's warm enough and we're not going to disturb each other.'

Though they did, when the dwarf pressed the bell the next morning and Anya appeared to draw back the curtains, wearing a kitchen apron over her woollen nightgown, her hair still in braids.

'What's going on?' mumbled Kaspar irritably. He was curled up tight at the foot of the fourposter. Some time during the night he had pulled off his jacket and shoes, loosened his tie and undone his collar button. Anya was looming high above him, hands on hips.

'You want me get *his* breakfast too?'

'Goddammit to hell, woman, do you have to have it in writing? Ask the Professor what he'd like and get going.'

The Professor wanted coffee, plenty of coffee, nothing else. He sat up drowsily, but made no move to tidy himself. The dwarf watched him, grinning.

'I've been awake for ages. The bathroom's free. You'll find a new toothbrush in the cabinet. In a plastic container.'

Anya was bringing in the breakfast tray when Kaspar emerged from the bathroom. 'What time is it? I forgot to wind up my watch last night.'

'Seven o'clock.'

'Do you always have breakfast so early?'

'I don't like sleeping for a long time at a stretch. Later, when you're gone, I'll sleep some more.'

As Kaspar drank the hot coffee, the events of the previous evening began to come back to him: Luburic, Miklos . . .

'Uncle Stilts, did that Croat spend the night here?'

'Why? Do you want to speak to him?'

'I must tell you that I hardly know him. I can't vouch for him.'

The old man rang the bell and the girl reappeared, her hair brushed now and hanging, a shining yellow-white, over her shoulders.

'Getting dressed,' she said crossly. 'Please don't disturb now.'

'Is that man still here?'

'Miklos? Eating now. Please don't disturb.'

'Anya, my nephew tells me he doesn't know him, so watch your step.'

'Is a good man, don't worry. Now I wash.' She slammed the door behind her.

The dwarf shrugged. 'It makes no difference to me. Anyway, what could he do? Anya'll clout him if he tries to start anything.' Kaspar said nothing, but the old man guessed something: 'And if she lets him, because she needs a fellow – that's all right with me, too.'

'Aren't you going to eat anything, Uncle Stilts?'

The dwarf looked thoughtfully at the slices of toast in the silver toastrack and the butter and honey beside them. 'I'm not hungry this morning, don't know why. Usually I eat it all, every crumb.'

'Because you're still in the hospital in Potsdam, with a knife in your shoulder, that's why.'

The old man nodded, leaned back on his pillows and stared at the ceiling.

'Did they catch the men who started it? There were two of them, you say? The first one and then one with a Berlin accent. Was the first one Lisa's husband?'

'Inkworm! He couldn't speak a word of German. But he'd hired them, all right, that Frenchy, paid them to raise a stink.'

'And the man with the knife?'

'He was the third one. You see, that was no ordinary pocket-knife. It had a long steel blade, not the usual kind you carry around with you.'

'And they never caught any of them?'

The dwarf shook his head.

'But – but Father was there. He saw him do it! Didn't he report it to the police?'

The old man remained silent as if he hadn't heard and continued to stare at the ceiling.

'What did he tell you when he came to the hospital?'

'He never came to the hospital.'

'What?' Kaspar set down his cup and leaned forward so that he could peer into the old man's face. 'What do you mean, he never came to the hospital?'

'He never did, and Bernie didn't either. I never saw them again – no, wait a minute, I did see that Leopold once more, much later, from a distance; but I never spoke another word to him.'

Silence. Then Kaspar forced himself to ask: 'And Andros?'

'He came to the hospital, of course. He wasn't there when it happened; he was in the big top supervising the elephant number when our men called him. First he went looking for the man with the knife and then for the other two, and the people in the audience helped him. They were all still standing around – nobody wanted to go home – and they gave Andros a complete description of all three of them, but they'd disappeared off the face of the earth. So then he ran over to Mother's, but of course, she'd already gone off in the ambulance. Next he tried my brothers' caravans and they were empty too – but they had *not* gone off in the ambulance. That Leopold had been seen running into Bernie's caravan in a hell of a hurry and then back into his own, next door. And right after that they took off as fast as they could, both carrying suitcases.'

'Uncle Stilts, have you got a cigarette?'

The old man groped for the bell, but before he found it, Kaspar jumped up. 'Never mind. I'll go and ask in the kitchen.'

In the dark of the hall, outside the kitchen door, he stopped and closed his eyes. That Leopold. . . .

The girl and the man were sitting at the kitchen table deep in conversation; broken German, Danish, Croatian, and sign language. Miklos, barely recognizable, fresh from the shower, his hair wet and carefully parted, wearing an old dressing-gown of Anya's, was working on a bowl of oatmeal. Anya sat opposite him, in blue

jeans and a blouse. She looked up crossly, but brought out a packet
of cigarettes and even gave Kaspar a light. He leaned against the
window, smoking in silence. In the next room the blackbird was
singing away.

'What's the matter, Professor? You not look good,' said Miklos.

Kaspar shook his head. 'May I keep the packet?'

He returned to the bedroom, swung himself up on to the bed
and leaned back against his bedpost. The dwarf was lying exactly
as he had left him, still staring at the ceiling. He turned his head
and watched Kaspar silently smoking.

'Sorry, it's your father, Kaspar. He and Bernie knew right away
what was coming: next morning, as soon as the doctor had been to
look at my shoulder, the nurse told me that a gentleman from the
police was asking for me. Mother and Andros were with me when
he came in and interrogated me. He took both of them back to the
police station, but they let Andros go right away, thank God,
because he had nothing to do with the freak show. He rushed
straight back to the hospital, and it was a good thing he did because
they had had to tie me down, I was in such a frenzy. He swore to
me that Mother would just be questioned and asked to sign a
statement and then they'd let her out on bail. That same day. He'd
already informed Doctor Pollart, and he was due to arrive next day.

'I'll have to skip a lot now, Kaspar. Anyhow you have to go to
class, don't you?'

'Not till ten, Uncle Stilts.'

'It's not all that interesting, anyway. I was discharged from the
hospital ten days later and they let me go to Landshut, to Mother's.
On bail, too, of course, ten thousand marks if I remember right.
Andros had already begun to wind up the freak show. Everything
was beginning to fall apart, like an old sweater unravelling when
you pull the right thread. It's a good thing Mother and I weren't
around when the Wonders of Nature were finally sold up. They all
cried buckets, the poor souls, although Andros went to a lot of
trouble to find good openings for them. But they'd never again
have it so good as with Mother, and they knew it.

'The charge against us was fraudulent practice and obtaining
money under false pretences, just as Lisa had said. Maybe they
wouldn't have been so hard on us if so many prominent people
hadn't been taken in. They didn't give names, of course, during
the trial, but they hinted a lot and the Russian Ambassador

kicked up a terrible fuss – behind the scenes, of course – and the judge made references to my "travels abroad" and the damage I'd done to Germany's reputation. The newspapers were full of it: the case of the chess machine and the dwarf. But the damn fools forgot to mention one thing: how well I played chess. Nobody ever said a word about *that*. In the end they slapped a fine of a hundred thousand marks on Mother and me, because they couldn't round up my brothers. They'd left Germany the next morning, leaving everything behind. Everything except their money; they'd made a stop at the bank on the way out.

'A hundred thousand marks or a year in jail. I chose jail. I wanted to be locked up, really wanted to, absolutely – can you understand that, Kaspar? Let me tell you one thing: if ever you want to do something that may cost you your neck, if you ever feel in your bones that you've *got* to do it, then go in head first. Mark my words, Kaspar. Never mind how cold the water is, think of me and dive in – head first. That's what I did, and it was the only thing to do.

'Mother wanted to go to jail, too, but when she found out that she'd be in a different prison, a long way from me, she decided to pay the fine so she'd be free to send me food parcels and visit me. She and Andros came twice a month, and sometimes they brought Ida with them.

'It was the end of May, Kaspar, when they put me inside, and to me it seemed a world-shaking event, but three months later, in August 1914, something happened that really did shake the world, and after that nobody gave a tinker's curse for me any more.'

PART TWO
Kaspar

CHAPTER ONE

SUNDAY was such a hot blue day that Kaspar and Heidi decided to drive out to their favourite lake, the Wiessee. But instead of taking the *autobahn*, Kaspar made a detour via Grünwald. Heidi didn't ask why; she felt utterly contented, leaned way back in her seat and never looked at the road. Not until the car slowed down and Kaspar began checking the gardens on either side of the road did she sit up and ask what he was looking for. For a nursery. Now she was wide awake. Wegmann's nursery? Yes. Werner had told him that that fellow had set up in business for himself, in some kind of partnership with Stefan.

'I just wanted to see what it looked like, this place of theirs.'

Taking one side-street after another, they criss-crossed Grünwald and eventually wound up far beyond the residential development, where the woods began. WEGMANN & SCHULTE, NURSERYMEN. A sprawling, single-storey bungalow, half a dozen greenhouses, and, behind them, row after row of trees and shrubs, from stiffly severe silver firs to floppy laburnum.

Kaspar drove slowly by and stopped a hundred yards past the building. No one around. A dog barked; otherwise unbroken Sunday stillness.

'Don't know what to make of it,' he murmured, rolling down his window, and leaning out. 'Do you think this fellow Wegmann is gay?'

'No. You never know, of course, but I don't think so.'

'What's he up to with Stefan? Werner says all he wants is to hold on to something connected with Martha. He says Stefan's become a fanatical gardener, takes courses in fruit-tree pruning and the cultivation of special varieties and Lord knows what else.'

He continued to look around, hoping to detect some sign of life, but now even the dog was quiet. 'Where do you suppose they are, the two of them, on a beautiful Sunday morning like this? Out in the wood, botanizing?'

'Come, let's go, before the traffic gets worse on the *autobahn*,' said Heidi.

They found the right spot to picnic in the forest and afterwards stretched out side by side under an enormous beech, Heidi's favourite tree. Even through its dense canopy, they could feel wafts of noonday heat. It smells so good, thought Heidi, I'll doze off, here, right next to him.

Kaspar lay on his back, his arms folded beneath his head, staring into the flickering, impenetrable tracery of leaves high above him.

'I'm a lousy father,' he said suddenly, 'or rather, I'm not a father at all.'

'Not true. And in any case, better too little than too much. It took me years to break free of my father. He's convinced to this day that I stole something from him.'

'What?'

'Me. I was his property, wasn't I?'

'Was he a good father otherwise?'

'He thought I ought to love him and trust him absolutely. I lied and faked it as best I could, but, of course, he knew. Maybe a different daughter would have seen his stranglehold as love and concern, and probably that's the way he intended it, but I wasn't that kind of daughter.'

'And your mother? You never talk about her.'

'There's nothing to say. She had a boy-friend, as far back as I can remember, and she lived for him alone. She was always extra polite to my father, perhaps because she . . .' An early dead leaf drifted gently down and Heidi·followed it with her eyes until it reached the ground, still covered in spring moss and seedlings so that it lay there as if in a strange land. Then she went on gingerly: 'She's a bit vulgar if she doesn't watch herself. Not quite in Father's class, and she's aware of it; she's far from stupid.'

'You talk about her like a casual acquaintance.'

'That's right, an acquaintance, but a casual one. She never paid any attention to me except when I was ill. I can still see her sitting by my bedside when I had the mumps, with Father on the other side, facing her, both of them reading, never exchanging a word. I kept looking from one to the other, and only when I couldn't stand it any longer, I'd ask for something, because they'd both jump up simultaneously and fight over the glass of water or the cold compress or the potty, all in deadly silence. The doctor wondered why my fever didn't break. And then, as soon as my temperature did go down, my mother would disappear again. But he would sit on. I'd have liked to be rid of him, too, so that I could lie in my bed with nobody watching me, biting my nails, scratching myself or tossing and turning without having to explain why.'

'Do you still see your mother?'

'Now and again. She lives alone, her boy-friend died some time ago.'

'Does she know about me?'

'Yes.'

'And your father? Is he still living?'

'And how. He has a girl-friend, not much older than me. Every evening she has to give an account of herself and he gives her a grade for conduct. She enjoys it just as much as he does. Suits me, too. Because now at last I'm free without having to feel guilty about it.'

'I feel guilty about the boys. All the time.'

She turned on her side to face him. 'Are you sure they'd rather have a different kind of father?'

'One who'd be faithful to their mother, for example. Didn't you resent your mother having a boy-friend?'

'No. It was clear to me – most of the time, though not always – that I didn't fit into her life, and that that was *my* tough luck rather than ill will on her part.'

'The boys think I didn't love their mother the way she deserved to be loved.'

'It's not a matter of deserving. My father deserved a better daughter.'

He looked at her thoughtfully. She's beautiful and she's wise, he thought. She reminds me of Martha.

'Do you still want to marry me? After six years you think you know me. But let me tell you something: *you* deserve someone better, too.'

She rolled over on her back again and they both stared up into the canopy of leaves.

'I don't believe in this business of "deserving" – any more than I believe in rewards,' she said softly.

After a while he started up again. 'You realize, don't you, that the boys hate you. At least Stefan does. Werner's less primitive.'

'I can understand it. I'll try my best . . .'

'Don't! For goodness sake – don't! Think of your father sitting up with you at night. Love's Labour Resented.' Heidi said no more. 'It's really only a matter of moving. Pack up your belongings and move in with me at Gellerstrasse and we'll go and sign the marriage licence. Do you want to keep on working in the lab?'

'I think I should.'

'Well then – everything can stay the way it is. Frau Henning will show you where things are kept and carry on as usual. Okay?'

'Okay.'

'Not a very romantic proposal, was it?'

'Better than none.'

'I'm a lucky man,' he said after a while. 'I'm lucky that I don't have to make an effort with you. That's a great compliment."

'I know.'

He sat up and stroked her face and hair. 'I really don't know if I should do this, it might be a big mistake . . .' She looked up at him questioningly. 'But I'd like to take you to visit Uncle Stilts.'

'He means more to you than the boys, doesn't he?'

'It would mean a lot to me if you understood why.' He took a cigarette from the packet in his coat pocket and slowly exhaled the smoke. 'I haven't seen him for a week. Anya says he sleeps with his eyes open and doesn't move except when she brings his meals. It worries me.'

So he *can* worry, thought Heidi, pleased.

Kaspar gnawed his upper lip, but hastily stopped when he realized what he was doing. 'Suppose we got married next week . . .' A pause, then in a rush: 'We could go over and see him right afterwards.' He stopped – but now it was too late.

He loves him and he's afraid of him, thought Heidi. She couldn't wait to meet the dwarf.

And Anya, of course, who opened the door and stared at her. Heidi stared back; she had never seen a girl like this one.

'The Master expecting *Professor*,' said the archangel, pointedly.

Kaspar nodded amicably and helped Heidi off with her coat. 'How is he, Anya?'

'Not too good,' she growled, keeping an icy stare fixed on Heidi. 'He see only family. No strangers.'

'Of course,' said Kaspar.

Anya pointed to a chair beside the mirror. 'She wait here.' Slowly and threateningly her glance swung back towards him. 'Better still, downstairs, in the car.'

He gave her a quick, searching look before answering. Poor Viking, so heavily armoured and so vulnerable. 'This is Heidi, my wife. Family.'

Anya opened her mouth, seeking a word to hold on to. Kaspar could think of no way to build a bridge for her, and Heidi, who understood it all, didn't dare to follow her impulse and step forward and embrace the girl, who was standing there in the hall like a damaged statue.

A man's face, someone whom Kaspar didn't immediately recognize, peered out from the kitchen doorway. Miklos! At least ten pounds heavier, and beaming. 'Professor!'

'This is my wife, Heidi. Heidi, this is Miklos.'

'Wife? Good, good! Lep!' Loud exclamations of joy. Kaspar was kissed, and Heidi too, until Miklos caught sight of Anya's face and subsided.

The dwarf was lying flat on his pillows, without his glasses, and slowly turned his head. Kaspar stepped up to the bed, holding Heidi's hand.

'Uncle Stilts, it's twelve days since I've seen you – twelve long, empty days. Here are your glasses – and here's Heidi. Take a look at her. We were married today.'

The old man struggled to sit up, fighting off Kaspar's helping hands. He put on his glasses and looked at the girl without speaking. Heidi had been prepared for appraisal as well as hostility, but this was worse.

'Good afternoon,' she said tentatively. 'You've no idea how much I've . . .'

'Yes, I have,' muttered the old man. 'I've a damn good idea.' But his muttering sounded different, more muted than usual, thought Kaspar, and his stomach suddenly felt cold. This was it! The dwarf was preparing to make his exit. Had he himself sensed this and was that why he'd married Heidi in such a hurry? What an exchange!

'Everything all right, Uncle Stilts?' he asked in a flat voice.

'As far as I'm concerned – yes,' growled the old man. Then, close-mouthed and addressing himself to Kaspar, as though the girl were not even present: 'So you've gone and done it!'

Heidi felt the tears spring to her eyes and quickly looked at the floor so that Kaspar shouldn't notice. After all, he had warned her.

'Inkworm,' murmured the old man, 'you still haven't caught on, have you?'

Heidi raised her head, tears running down both cheeks into her hair. 'I'll wait outside,' she said, and turned to leave the room. But then she remembered that girl lurking out there in the hall. She stopped, gulping with fear and rage, and Kaspar caught up with her and drew her back to the bed.

The dwarf looked her over once again from head to toe and said slowly: 'I've got nothing against you. You have nice red cheeks. But that fellow . . .' – he pointed his tiny index finger at Kaspar – 'don't you see that he mustn't be made to join anything?' The owlish eyes behind the glasses peered at her, not without sympathy. 'Can't you tell he's – single?'

'I know he is. But maybe I can teach him . . .' she whispered so softly that the dwarf couldn't understand her. She had to repeat the sentence more loudly, and then it sounded so inane that Kaspar turned away and stared out of the window.

'Teach him what?' croaked the little man. 'What the devil do you think you can teach him, if you don't mind me asking? What you need him for can't be taught, and you know that, don't you?'

'I'd like to give it a try,' whispered Heidi, remembering that she had said the very same thing to Harold Wegmann – and how fine it had sounded then.

Nobody spoke. Finally Kaspar said: 'Uncle Stilts, may I come over tomorrow night? Just for half an hour?'

The dwarf sank slowly back onto his pillows and shook his head. 'I'm locked up in my cell now, in Berlin. Remember? Just arrived there. They run a tight prison, those Prussians. No privileges for your first month, no visitors, no mail. I'll let you know when they give me my privileges, then you can come. Why don't you go on a honeymoon?'

'Has the doctor been to see you?'

The old man nodded. 'I like the old boy. Plenty of common sense. Never lays a hand on me. We play a game of gin rummy and then he clears out. If he wins, he sends me a bill, but I never pay.'

'I behaved like a fool,' said Heidi as they were going downstairs. 'Though – what does he have against me?'

'He's not against *you*, he's . . .' He broke off. 'Wait here a minute, will you?' He ran back upstairs and rang the bell. Anya opened the door, barring his way.

'Miklos,' he called loudly, over her shoulder.

'Professor?' Miklos appeared in the kitchen doorway.

'Miklos,' switching quickly to Croatian: 'What's the name of that place in Yugoslavia you were talking about? The romantic one, for honeymooners, remember? Where Luburic was born.'

'Oh, Bled! Very beautiful, Professor. Good food . . .'

'Do you know a hotel there?'

'Hotel?'

'Yes. Maybe the hotel where Luburic's father was the lifeguard.'

'Oh yes. Hotel Godice. Right on the lake. Very good food.'

'What you say?' Anya, not understanding a word, came between them like the angel with the sword. 'What you want of Miklos? What you say?'

Kaspar took out his pocket diary. 'Don't worry, Miklos isn't going anywhere. Hotel Godice, you say . . . .'

The next day he went over to Kaiserplatz directly from the Institute. He hadn't telephoned first, yet, to his surprise, Anya greeted him as if she had been waiting for him.

'Doctor with Master now,' she informed him anxiously.

'That's good.' Leaning against the living-room door, he lit a cigarette. Miklos appeared from the kitchen, but Anya shooed him away.

'I worry for Master. Doctor don't say me anything. *You* ask. Perhaps he say you.'

From inside the room came the sound of the old man's laughter.

'That's good,' said Anya. 'Won't die when he laughs, right?'

'It's a good sign, but he's very old, you know.'

'I sleep on mattress beside him. Often he not sleep. Sighs but says he have no pain. Once he said: "It's broken loose, I can feel it."'

'What has broken loose?'

'Something on his lung. A little bag, he says, full of blood. He has it many years. No harm. But if it break loose – not good. I worry. What about Miklos if bag break loose . . .?'

'What about *you*, Anya?'

'Oh, me! Many things I can do. Miklos – no papers, no friend.' He had never known her so eloquent.

'Oh well, we haven't come to that yet. I'll talk to the doctor.'

Anya nodded vigorously, biting her lips like a child trying not to cry. They stood there in silence, until at last the bedroom door opened. Anya slipped past the doctor into the room.

'Ah, Professor Schulte, how are you?' A fat man with a bald head and a black bag, which he handed to Kaspar to hold, while he hurriedly put on his coat.

'Doctor, could you spare me five minutes?'

'My dear Professor, I've already spent so long playing gin rummy . . .'

'I came over here specially to . . .'

'Did the Danish Musketeer send for you?'

'Yes,' Kaspar lied.

'Oh, well then.' The fat man dropped heavily into the chair beside the mirror and said what he had to say as fast as he could. They were dealing with an aneurysm, a sac in the wall of an artery, in this case the aorta. It was impossible to say without an x-ray whether the aneurysm had separated or not. In any case Herr Schulte was not suffering any pain; he felt a little weak, but strong enough for gin rummy. Even with an x-ray, there wasn't much they could do. After all, at eighty-nine, what can you expect?

'How much time do you give him?'

'He might go on for months, but it could equally well happen quite suddenly.'

'Without any pain?'

Snatching his black satchel from Kaspar, the doctor escaped, calling back as he ran downstairs: 'Possibly. Possibly. Let's hope for the best.'

Anya was standing by the bed, her arms around a bedpost, gazing worriedly at the dwarf, who was propped up against several extra pillows.

'Come on in. I've just beaten the old quack two games running. You're alone? Don't want any females around tonight. Got that, Anya?'

She left, reluctantly, and Kaspar swung himself up into his regular place.

'Nothing doing, Inkworm. I'm not telling you any more stories.'

'How can I leave town before I've visited you in prison, Uncle Stilts? Don't they ever make an exception? What was the rule in

those days? Were you kept behind bars? And how long would I
have been allowed to talk to you?'

The old man smiled and shook his head. 'Nothing doing. You're
not going to trick me into it again.'

'Uncle Stilts, you can't let me dangle like this, I've still got so
many questions to ask, so many loose ends . . .'

'Don't upset yourself, you'll know all about it in good time.
Today I'm too tired. Don't feel like it. I'm mad at you, anyway, for
going and doing it. Nothing against the girl, matter of fact, I'm
sorry for her, nice little thing. It's the same old story: you've put
another great big stumbling-block in your path and some day
you'll want it out of your way – and then you'll think of me. You're
that Leopold's son all right; he never had any guts either. Well, he
got what was coming to him. It's a miracle you've turned out the
way you have. I knew nothing about your existence, you know,
when you showed up out of the blue that day, and all the time,
while you were sitting there, I watched you and thought: he's
Mother's grandson! And all of a sudden it dawned on me that you
were kin to me! That I had a relative! And you know, it didn't take
me long to figure out that you too were sitting in a box and I began
to wonder whether you ever would get out. At last your boys
cleared out and Martha kicked the bucket . . .' he beat his forehead
with his tiny fist, 'and you have to go and get hitched up again, you
fool. I suppose one can blame your father and mother for that,
though, Lord knows, *their* marriage was nothing to brag about. So
now you've got to be married too, everybody's got to be married!
Jesus! Well, you're the one that'll have to deal with it, not me.'

Suddenly his face looked grey and ancient, and he sank back,
closed his eyes and lay still for a while. Then he murmured so softly
that Kaspar had to bend down to hear him: 'I wish you'd forget the
whole lot of them, just wipe 'em out, every last one, and remember
nobody but me, as if I were your father and your mother, both. Will
you do that for me? Promise?'

He struggled to open his eyes and stretched out his hand.
Kaspar took it and held it in both of his own. It was as weightless as
a feather and it felt the way the hands of very old people feel,
lukewarm.

'I promise.' Should he tell him, could he afford to say it aloud,
the very day after his wedding? 'No one in the world means
anything to me, Uncle Stilts – except you.'

'I know, Inkworm, but I like to hear you say it.' His eyes closed again, although he was trying hard to keep them open. Finally he gave in, the tiny face became peaceful again, and he whispered: 'When you do break loose, remember one thing: the easiest way is head first.'

Kaspar laid the tiny hand carefully back on the bedspread and sat for a long while looking at the old man.

On the same afternoon Harold Wegmann was standing in the lobby of the paediatric clinic, waiting for Heidi. He had asked for 'Fräulein Wennerstett, or rather Frau Schulte', and had been told that she would be down in a few minutes. Shortly afterwards she stepped out of the crowded elevator, called 'Ciao!' over her shoulder, and caught sight of him. Her face, just now open and laughing, became guarded. Today she would put an end to this whole business.

And yet, a short time later, there they were at Lottie's just as before, and she was asking herself why she always gave in to him.

He was obviously very agitated, kept reaching for her hand, but checked himself at the last moment, repeating again and again: 'Heidi, Heidi, why in the world did you do it?'

'I told you I wanted to give it a try, Herr Wegmann, don't you remember?' Her tone was harsher than she had intended, because the old man's wrinkled face on the white pillows and the mocking, owlish eyes interposed themselves between her and the young man.

As if from far away, she heard him reproaching her: 'You're experimenting with your own good life!'

She forced herself to smile. 'You're a gardener, aren't you? You must know something about experimenting. You graft one plant on to another and hope that it turns out well. Don't forget that Kaspar and I have had an affair for six years. That's not virgin soil in our flowerpot.'

'You're treating it as a joke.' He covered his face with his hands, unmistakably a gardener's hands, square, red with scrubbing, fingers covered with scratches, nails trimmed too short. Heidi was more moved by those hands than by his beseeching voice or his despairing eyes.

'I'd like to tell you something, Herr Wegmann – although I really don't know why – something even my husband doesn't know.

About two years ago I got pregnant and, without telling him, I had an abortion.'

Wegmann dropped his hands from his face and stared at her, then said almost inaudibly: 'You don't look like that.'

'What do you mean?'

'Like somebody who would abort a child.'

'Would I look better if I had told Kaspar? Then he'd have had to choose who was to get the short end of the stick, his wife or me. I made the decision for him. One thing's certain: being pregnant is a bad reason for getting married, bad for both parties – or don't you agree?' He shook his head helplessly. 'How old are you, by the way?'

'Twenty-four.'

'Never been caught in a trap like that, have you? It happens all the time, though, to thousands of people.'

He bent his head. After a while he said quietly, without looking up:

> '"A young man loves a maiden
> Who's in love with another man . . ."

'Know what that is?'

'Heine.'

'So far it fits. Now come a couple of complications that don't fit; it doesn't matter, though.' In a rapid, monotonous voice he recited:

> '"The other man loves another girl
> And marries her while he can.
> The maiden marries in anger
> A likely looking lad
> Who happens to strike her fancy . . ."

'That doesn't fit, but it will again in a minute:

> ". . . Who happens to strike her fancy.
> The young man's heart is sad."'

His eyes filled with tears as he looked at her and repeated softly: '"The young man's heart is sad." Do you know what comes next? It fits too:

> "This is an old, old story,
> And yet for ever new.
> And the one to whom it happens
> Feels his heart will break in two."'

Putting her hand on his arm, Heidi forced him to look at her. 'My heart was broken in two when that happened and I promised myself I'd make up for it.'

'You want a child?'

She nodded and looked at him steadily. He bent his head until his forehead was resting on the back of her hand, rubbing against it in utter despair, and she couldn't quite bring herself to pull it away.

CHAPTER TWO

THE PORTER at the Hotel Godice in Bled, a fussy old man, gave them the wrong key and, tired as they were, they had to take the lift back down to the lobby. The wrong key? Confusion, denial, futile rummaging, until finally the manager, Herr Alexis, appeared and found the right one. The old man, upset, tried to make excuses; Kaspar spoke up for him in Serbo-Croat, much to the surprise of the manager, who accompanied them upstairs. Kaspar told him about his childhood in Belgrade. Ah, so that was it! Herr Alexis opened the door and proudly showed off first the modern bathroom, then the rather small room with furniture finished with dark, high-gloss lacquer. He opened the door to the balcony and motioned to Kaspar and Heidi to step outside. He himself remained inside the room, smiling modestly as though he had personally selected and composed the landscape and wished to let his work speak for itself. It was indeed a masterful achievement, he had left nothing out: a small, greenish-blue lake surrounded by mountains, some wooded, some romantically craggy, and, towering behind them, the Triglav, snow-capped winter and summer alike. The finishing touch was provided by a tiny island in the middle of the lake, so densely covered in shrubs that all one could see was a church spire. Woods and meadows lined the shores of the lake, but hardly any houses. The first few sailboats of the season dotted the water like butterflies.

'Well?' said Herr Alexis, joining them on the balcony. 'What do you say?'

Heidi shook her head slowly. 'It's overwhelming.'

'That's the swimming beach over there, isn't it?' Kaspar asked.

'Have you been here before?'

'No, but I happen to know someone who learned to swim there, a long time ago.'

Herr Alexis withdrew. Kaspar and Heidi stayed out on the balcony until the last rays of the sun died away, plunging the lake abruptly into inky darkness. Neither of them had the strength to unpack; they just stretched out on the beds. They had left at eight o'clock that morning and hadn't even stopped for a picnic lunch. Heidi had cut sandwiches up into small bites and fed them to Kaspar as he drove. They were held up for some time at the Yugoslav frontier, although their BMW was the only car in sight. A heavily-armed customs official stepped forward and motioned them with his submachine-gun to step in the customs office, where their passports were grimly scrutinized. Heidi reacted in the prescribed manner, standing wide-eyed with alarm until the two passports were pushed back as though they might contaminate the inspector's clean desk. But they were still not allowed to return to the car: first they must change their money.

In the currency exchange office, little more than a shack, the atmosphere was more relaxed. The two officials had unbuttoned their jackets and loosened their trousers and were playing cards, a bottle of slivovitz within easy reach. One was laughing, the other singing. 'Please be seated.' The singer continued to sing, the other one swore; neither of them looked up. Kaspar began to feel at home; he remembered the swear words from his childhood. The cards came slapping down on the table: the level of slivovitz in the bottle fell; but the singing lost its mellow tone, for the singer lost the game. Flinging his last card down on the dirty floor, he poured the remains of the bottle down his throat and left, roaring. Kaspar exchanged two clean, crisp hundred-mark bills for a bundle of greyish, crumpled scraps of paper, at which both parties burst out laughing. Then they were finally allowed to get back in the car. By the time they arrived at the hotel, it was early evening but still light enough for them to catch that last glimpse of the lake and the island.

'I never imagined it could be so beautiful, did you?'

Kaspar forced himself to open his eyes. 'Yes,' he said. 'Let's go and have dinner.'

They left the key at the desk and descended the wide staircase leading to the restaurant. The dining-room was half empty; the season hadn't yet begun. The decor was modern and functional to the point of austerity. The only touch of glamour was provided by the lighting fixtures: large golden hedgehogs, a light bulb in every prickle.

Heidi was amazed. This was a hotel in a Communist country? She had expected something far more modest. The guests were all dressed up, the men in their good blue suits, the women in long skirts, their hair permanently and tightly waved. No jeans or open-necked shirts. Subdued conversation; not a single loud laugh.

The food – enormous quantities of it – was good though over-cooked. Kaspar had dark rings of tiredness around his eyes, so they didn't stay for coffee, left the dining-room and picked up their key. Upstairs, they discovered that the porter had given them the wrong one again.

'Never mind,' said Heidi. 'I'll go down.'

He gratefully leaned back against the wall and closed his eyes. Honeymoon . . . .

She returned, accompanied by Herr Alexis, who looked as if he held in his hand the key not only to their room but to the prestige of his entire country. Kaspar disappeared into the bathroom, while Heidi tried to console the distressed manager.

'What am I to do?' he said, on the verge of tears. 'I'm going to fire the fellow right now.'

'He's an old man,' said Heidi.

'I'll have to find someone younger – or shut down the hotel altogether.' He slunk out of the room.

Heidi opened the door to the balcony. The moon had a halo – bad weather tomorrow . . . He won't want to sleep with me tonight, he's too tired . . . How few lights there are, and it's only ten o'clock. I suppose everyone goes to bed early to save electricity. They look like sturdy people, the Yugoslavs . . . That bright light over there must be from the island, from the little church . . . Should I make it clear that I'm not expecting anything tonight? Should I say: Kaspar, darling, there's no need for you to . . . I mean, you mustn't . . . Or will he take it the wrong way, as if I think he's too old to perform after the strain of a long trip? I'd better just say: goodnight, darling, I'm *so* tired, I'm practically asleep already. Would he see through it? I'll add: I'm very happy – you too? That's a must for the first evening of a honeymoon – or would it be even better *without* the 'you too'?

Bled, 20 May

Dear Werner,

It's raining so you needn't wonder why I'm writing to you. In any case I wanted to thank you for being a witness at our wedding. Stefan will never forgive you. Funny that he should be so vindictive. How does he manage to be always so sure he's right?

We take long walks even in the rain. It doesn't bother Heidi. She goes around with her hair soaking wet, water dripping down her face – and I walk beside her in my hat. Today it occurred to me to ask myself whether you have a girl-friend. Do you? Too bad I'm not the type other people confide in. I wonder why. Do I keep them at arm's length? Do I ooze lack of interest? Give me an honest answer when I'm back in Munich. By the way, I'm better at that sort of thing than you might expect, ask Uncle Stilts; he says I'm a good listener.

Bled, 22 May

Glorious weather today but I'm writing to you just the same. We're sitting on our balcony. Heidi's reading and I'm bored. No reflection on Heidi. She's never bored, she can always find hundreds of things to do that interest her 'intensely'. My own fault, of course, I'm always expecting something to come round the corner . . . And, except for Uncle Stilts, nothing ever has.

How is he? You were going to call Anya, in fact you promised you would. I'm apprehensive every time I walk past the desk here in case there's a telegram for me.

We're doing everything one is supposed to do, and Bled is really quite beautiful. I even tried to swim across the lake – with Heidi close by in a rowing boat, of course, but I didn't quite make it.

Occasionally, just now, for instance, when I look up, I think it's your mother sitting beside me. Have you ever noticed that Heidi looks rather like her? (I know I can ask you that without your immediately assuming this is an insult to your mother.) I noticed it before, and I'm becoming more and more aware of it all the time. Don't tell Stefan; he'd be so furious he'd gobble up a flowerpot.

Back next Tuesday. We look like two doughnuts, tanned and plump.

All the best,

Father

P.S. Heidi is pregnant.

CHAPTER THREE

THEY arrived back in Munich about nine o'clock at night. For the last couple of hours Kaspar had been driving too fast, which wasn't like him at all. Heidi sensed the reason and, when he muttered something unintelligible and disappeared, immediately after dropping off the suitcases at the flat, she asked no questions. But he was too late. Much too late; the dwarf had been buried the day before. Anya let him in as though she had been expecting him, late as it was. She could hardly speak, except for a few scraps of Danish, accompanied by wild, despairing gestures.

Kaspar sat down beside Miklos at the kitchen table and got the whole story in Croatian, though barely audible because the girl suddenly began to run the vacuum cleaner out in the hall, as though Kaspar had trailed in great piles of dirt. 'She runs it all day long,' said Miklos apologetically. 'The noise does her good.'

The dwarf had been unconscious for the last few days and had been failing ever since Kaspar's departure. Anya and Miklos had taken turns sitting up with him. Last Thursday he had suddenly come to himself and looked at Anya with perfectly clear eyes and said a few words to her in a perfectly clear voice. Unfortunately Miklos didn't know what he'd said. Then he'd lapsed into silence again, his eyes wide open.

Kaspar got up, went out into the hall and switched off the vacuum cleaner. 'What did my uncle say at the end? What were those last few words?'

She ran into her room. On the bedside table was a note. 'I wrote down right away because I not understand the words. Lawyer not understand either.'

Kaspar read the note. 'First head, ink.'

'You understand?' she asked anxiously.

'Could he have said: "Head first, Inkworm"?'

Yes, he could. Did the Professor know what he meant? Kaspar said that it wasn't easy to explain and would she stop vacuuming. Then the three of them sat around the kitchen table drinking coffee. Miklos tried to speak German so that Anya could follow: 'Professor, you think I have to get out?'

'It depends on whether the flat has to be given up or not. He'll certainly have made some provision for Anya.'

Miklos bent over his coffee cup to hide the tears running down his face. The sadness of the moment didn't prevent Kaspar from noticing that he now had a double chin.

Roughly Anya brushed the thin hair back from his forehead and wiped his face with the back of her hand. 'I have saved money, Miklos. No worry.'

Under the terms of the will Anya inherited everything except a small suitcase, which was left to Kaspar. The dwarf had bought the flat outright years ago and had lived on a monthly income from a Swiss life insurance policy, which, however, would cease with his death.

'Sell the flat, Anya,' said Kaspar. 'It's worth a lot of money.'

'I stay. With Miklos.'

Kaspar took his hat, hesitated, turned back and re-entered the bedroom, the suitcase in his hand. He had opened it and quickly checked the contents: several dozen hand-written pages in two manila folders. In the upper right-hand corner of the first one were the words 'Moabit State Prison, Berlin, Kingdom of Prussia, 6 July 1914'.

The bed was newly made but without the bedspread, the numerous pillows neatly stacked. He swung himself up into his old place, leaned against the bedpost and closed his eyes for a moment. That was exactly what he had intended *not* to do, pledging himself never to set foot in this bedroom again.

'You come when you feel like,' said Anya from the doorway. 'Read here when you want.'

'How do you know. . .?'

'Master said: keep carefully, letters for my nephew. You leave suitcase here. Nobody will read.'

Kaspar shook his head. Dead means dead, he thought, how can I sit here and read his diary, as if he were talking to me?

He slid down from the bed, put on his hat and picked up the suitcase. 'Where's Miklos?'

'In my room. He cries.'

'Goodbye, Anya.' He put his arms around her for a moment.

'Good luck.' Her eyes, red-rimmed under the long, wet lashes, dropped from his face to glance again at the empty bed.

'Put the bedspread on now,' said Kaspar.

It would have been a macabre touch to study the dwarf's 'letters' on his own fourposter bed, but it was a practical one too. Where else could he read them? His own flat was impossible, he needed isolation. Any noise, however hushed, any sound of voices, door bells or footsteps, would drown out Moabit Prison.

Although Frau Henning was there only occasionally, Heidi, unfortunately, was home all the time now. She had given up her job at the lab because of her pregnancy. She had serenely accepted the congratulations of her colleagues, and when her boss, Dr Lamprecht, said: 'You can come back any time, Heidi, later, when the baby can spare you,' she had embraced the woman and thanked her, thinking: Never. Why ever should I? Kaspar earns enough for both of us, enough for the three of us – and anyhow I want another child right after this one and that'll make four of us – exactly as it had been with him and Martha.

The same thought occurred to Kaspar as he walked across the Prince-Regent Bridge, and, although he was walking in blazing sunshine, he felt suddenly very cold. He had transferred the contents of the little suitcase to his briefcase and wanted to use his lunch hour to read at least the first few pages. Occasional passers-by and the noise of the distant traffic he could easily tune out. He found an empty bench under the tall trees in the little park next to the monument of the angel of peace and took out the folder of papers, but once again he got no further than 'Moabit, 6 July 1914.'

He leaned back and closed his eyes. It was the postscript to Werner that was paralysing him. No sense in shoving it aside any longer in the hope that it would somehow go away. The news of Heidi's pregnancy, which she had broken to him in Bled, seemingly nonchalant but obviously elated – *her* postscript – had shaken him like an earthquake. At first it was like one of those earthquakes one watches on television, the kind that happen in far-away places, so far away that you felt the shock only while you were watching the picture. That's how it had been in Bled. She had said: 'By the way, I'm pregnant. Three months already.' 'No!' he had exclaimed. That could have meant surprise or joyous disbelief – or exactly what he meant: *No!* The last possibility didn't occur to Heidi, of course, as she turned her blushing yet triumphant face towards him. What were women so proud of on such occasions? Martha had looked exactly the same; he remembered it perfectly. What had they done that was so remarkable?

He had silently pressed Heidi's arm, which seemed to satisfy her. And then he had switched it off, like the TV earthquake. Not now! First he had to go home, see Uncle Stilts.

But Uncle Stilts had left him in the lurch, and now the earthquake, seven on the Richter scale, was shaking him. Why hadn't he been expecting it? Heidi was still quite young, after all. But she'd never mentioned children, must have been on the pill all these years. And suddenly she'd stopped taking it? They should have talked it over, he should have warned her. . . .

It meant starting all over again, a repeat performance twenty years later, twenty years more intolerable. Furnishing a nursery, admiring tiny clothing that set his teeth on edge, accepting the congratulations and the knowing winks of his friends, some of whom already had grandchildren.

She would have to get rid of it. But even while he thought it, he knew Heidi would never do it and that he could never suggest it. He needed advice. Who from? Alfred Bannheimer or Else? Or even Werner? And what could they offer except dismay at his dismay?

Uncle Stilts, now – *he* would have had plenty to say. Get the hell out. Drop everything and clear out. This is your chance. Be a son of a bitch. Don't just dream about it, be one! Walk out on her? Don't be a ninny, use good plain language: fuck off. A dirty trick? Sure thing. Go the whole hog. She'll despise you and hate you. Let her, it's good. It'll help her and it'll help you.

All right. Suppose I do walk out, walk out on the whole lot of them, Heidi, Werner, Stefan, my students, everybody – and then what? Where should I go? I can't just shoot off into the blue, I have to have a target, a refuge, some kind of motivation . . . Inkworm, we're not talking about a change of scene. What you've got to do is start a new life . . . I know, Uncle Stilts, I know. But where? You don't expect me to stay on in Munich, do you? How? Who with? . . . How about that fellow you brought to see me one night, the Roman emperor? . . . You mean Luburic? . . . Yes, that's the one. You helped him when he was on the run, he owes you a favour. I bet he wouldn't even be surprised if you showed up. He's used to trouble of a different calibre, I could smell that.

Luburic. His student. *Ich bin, du bist, er ist, wir sind....* Something inside, his professorial self, baulked at the idea. Good morning, Herr Luburic, I'm in a bit of a fix. I wonder if you could....

Is that really the only possibility?

What if I get a grip on myself and somehow survive the months of pregnancy, the birth, the little bundle of joy, back home to the Gellerstrasse, the three of us, Heidi beaming on her pillows – and me, going to the Institute every day like a good boy and listening to the baby crying at night . . . even if I manage all that, won't I be counting all the time, counting the days until I *do* feel able to get out?

Stop stewing over it, Inkworm. Go!

How right you were, Uncle Stilts. Why in God's name did I marry again? Because it was the logical thing to do and I'm a logical man. And a decent one, too. Decent. Absolutely. Unfaithful to Martha? Nothing to do with decency; a different category altogether. I've always behaved decently so that I'd feel comfortable with myself. That was the one thing I could always rely on, fall back on when in doubt. Very important to me. Not acquired, just the way I'm made – I think. Please try to understand that, Uncle Stilts.

He looked at his watch. The lunch hour was long over, but he didn't feel able to move. Very similar to the way he'd felt after Martha's death: at the end of his tether. Even more so now. Did other people ever have that feeling? Did Alfred Bannheimer know what it was like to sit and wait for someone to come along and say: Kaspar do this, Kaspar do that?

What am I doing here? At the Institute twenty students are sitting waiting for me. The way they handle me with kid gloves – it's scandalous! When I'm late, when I don't show up at my classes – no one complains, they offer me sick leave. They know I've not been myself since Martha's death. Although, lately, ever since we got married, they've been tactfully trying to get me back on the right track again.

A passer-by looked at him suspiciously. Fair enough, I *am* a suspicious character, sir. I don't think I can get up. Why not? That's a long story and I wouldn't know where to begin. With 'your father, that Leopold'? With Martha? With the box? I don't know the beginning of the story, only the end, the earthquake.

I can't get it into my head that this is happening to me, that I'm sitting here in the sun as if I were chained down, and that I literally can't move. There's a word for this: catatonic. Now, let's see: do I still know who I am? Of course I do: Schulte, 36 Gellerstrasse, salary DM 80,000 a year, pension plan with benefits, etc., etc. See? I'm all there.

But it has happened to me, that thing one is always hearing or reading about: losing touch with yourself. I always used to make fun of it, I'd say: 'Show the poor kid his driver's licence, then he'll know who he is.' Fat lot of use my driver's licence would be to me now. So this is how it feels! Not at night, drunk or flipped out in the gutter or in a lavatory at the railway station, not at all. To a decent man like me it happens in broad daylight, cold sober, during the lunch hour. Isn't that something, Uncle Stilts? You're not surprised? Well, I am. I feel terrible. I'm going to be sick.

As he turned around to look for a suitable bush, the folder slipped from his lap. He bent down and picked up the scattered papers. Thank God, he thought with relief, I've moved, I can stand up! I feel terrible, I'm going to be sick – *ergo sum*. I'll go home and lie down. Then I'll plan how I'm going to get out.

CHAPTER FOUR

He examined and rejected a dozen best ways to go about it and finally realized that there was no best way. What about the worst way then? That would have the advantage of making Heidi despise and hate him. But would she?

First he dropped all his private students on the grounds that he was suffering from a circulatory disturbance, a slight cerebral anaemia, difficult to confirm and not too worrying, even to Heidi. Appalling how understanding everyone was. His friends went out of their way to make it clear that they 'understood'. First Martha's death and now, so soon afterwards, a young wife and a new baby . . . It's not easy, Kaspar, old man. These things take some getting over.

Just you wait, he thought, before long you won't 'understand' at all. Soon you'll be saying: What? Kaspar? The son of a bitch! You'd never have thought him capable of such a thing.

None the less he proceeded in his usual methodical fashion. First he took Heidi to the bank to register her signature so that she could draw on his account. What ever for? She was astonished and touched by his thoughtfulness; never before had he shown any interest in money matters. The balance, DM 68,400, didn't represent a fortune, but still . . . Then, without telling her, he named her beneficiary of his life insurance policy for a hundred thousand marks. He didn't have to worry about the boys: Martha had left what money she had to them, and that would take care of them for the next five years.

So far, so decent. Now it was time to think about himself. He made the rounds of travel agencies and looked at brochures. Everywhere the sky was blue, the beach sparkling clean, the people radiant against a background of stately pines or palms. The city photographs emitted up-beat dynamism – all very seductive, but not for him. Then one day, as he was looking at a brochure of the Ivory Coast, his breathing suddenly became laboured and he felt dried out and shrivelled; in the distance, still far off yet unmistakable, he could detect the now familiar deathly, numbing lull in the air. Dropping the brochure, he fled from the African travel agency. On his way home he talked aloud with Uncle Stilts and agreed that it would have to be Luburic.

But where was he? A short visit to Anya and Miklos didn't help; they hadn't heard from him. Would Vlada know? His conscience bothered him when he thought of her. He bought a dozen carnations and went to see her, without calling first. A child's voice asked who it was, then Vlada opened the door, this time without any difficulty, for the metal facing had been removed. She was obviously glad to see him, spontaneously spoke Croatian, sent the child away, and brought Kaspar a cup of tea with lemon. She and the children were getting on nicely, no complaints. She was receiving a monthly widow's pension, with supplements for the children, enough to live on if she was careful. He put down his cup and looked at her. She was still entirely in black, but her face wasn't as pale and watchful as it had been while her husband was alive, and her eyes had a dark shine to them. Sexy, thought Kaspar; I wonder if she has a lover.

'Vlada, do you know where Luburic is?'

She looked at him in surprise and answered slowly and hesitantly, as if she would have liked time to think it over. 'He may be in Bled. I got a postcard from him not long ago – from Bled. But he may have left again by now.'

'Where could I get in touch with him if he's still there?'

She shrugged, then brusquely turned her head and looked out of the window.

'It's important, Vlada.'

'For the Ustasha?'

Kaspar recognized the name. 'Ustasha' was the name of the original Croatian underground movement, the one fighting for an independent Croatia. He decided not to tell her a direct lie and simply repeated: 'It's important.'

Slowly she turned towards him again, and her face wore the old, rigid mask. Reluctantly and in a low voice she said that there might be a possibility – then she faltered and looked out of the window again. There was a woman in Bled. . . .

'Yes?' said Kaspar insistently.

This woman acted as a sort of message centre for the movement. Her husband had been liquidated by the UDBA several years ago.

'And this woman knows where Luburic is?'

'Could be.'

'What's her name?'

'Bogdan. Mariana Bogdan.' Her tone became suddenly harsh. 'I don't know her address.'

'You know her?'

'No.'

'But you don't like her?' No reply. 'Is she a friend of Luburic?'

'She's everybody's friend.' Hardly audible, but full of bitterness. Not surprising, thought Kaspar. Tied down to five children, a widow, eyes glowing with love of life. He looked at the hands in her lap, clenched fists, white around the knuckles.

'A friend of Ivan's too?'

She sat so long without moving that Kaspar needed no further answer and decided to prepare his exit. And then the words came bursting out from her tight lips, eyes full of tears that suddenly rushed down her cheeks. 'Of Ivan, of Ante, of my brothers . . . Whore! And she has two children. And she's married . . .'

'I thought you said her husband. . . .'

'That was her first husband. She married again.' Vlada rubbed her wet cheeks viciously and in vain, the tears kept coming.

'And her second husband's name is Bogdan?' The only thing that really interested him.

'Mirko Bogdan, poor devil.'

He couldn't get up and leave, not yet, couldn't just walk out on her like this, with those tears and those clenched fists.

'Vlada, all that doesn't mean anything, your husband loved *you*. He told me so himself.' A lie, but perhaps assuaging. To his surprise she brushed it off contemptuously: 'I know that. Ivan never loved anyone but me. Mariana was – trash.'

Suddenly she jumped up, her fists pressed to her mouth. 'But Ante! Ante!' Convulsively and incoherent, for now the tears were choking her. She ran to the window and pushed her forehead against the pane, sobbing loudly, without constraint.

Kaspar looked at her back and marvelled at his blindness. After a while she returned and sat down again, twisting her wet handkerchief. The dark pupils had widened to fill her eyes, as though they were melting altogether. 'Did you know?'

'No.'

She said nothing. Perhaps his answer disappointed her; perhaps she thought – even hoped, as a way of getting even with Ivan – that Luburic's feelings for her were too plain to be overlooked.

'I didn't know, Vlada. But it's – understandable.'

She took no notice of the insinuation.

'I married very young. I had two younger brothers, my father was dead. I knew nothing about men. I was pregnant all the time, every year. That's the way Ivan wanted it. I began to hate him.' She met Kaspar's eyes and added calmly: 'You're thinking back and you wonder why I went to pieces when he was killed. It wasn't because he was gone. *Ante* was gone.'

'I see. Yes. And will he be back?'

Gradually the tears had stopped and her voice was steady again. 'Soon. Maybe in a month.'

'And in the meantime he'll be in Bled?'

'I don't know. I hope not.'

At the door he kissed her lightly on the cheek. 'If I find him, Vlada, have you any message for him?'

'Tell him there's no need for postcards. I'll wait.'

Off to Bled. At once.

But how? He still had no definite plan – when did you ever *plan* anything, Inkworm? – and every day he examined his feelings carefully to see whether there had been any change, whether his decision was still firm, whether he felt any temptation to stay. But however much he probed, the voice inside him demanded with the same intensity: out!

Heidi . . . If he hadn't been so firmly convinced that in the long run it would be the best thing for her, too, he might never have gone through with it. (How far off was 'the long run'? A year? Two years? Longer? Would the baby help or would it rub salt into the wound?)

Heidi . . . He shut his eyes and shook himself. How could she suddenly be so blind and so deaf? Was it something to do with being pregnant? She used to have an antenna, an awareness of anything that got on his nerves. Now she seemed to run wild, jumping about, spreading jollity, cock-a-hoop all day long. And another thing: she was so taken with Frau Henning's notes that she had adopted their style for everyday conversation and now addressed him exclusively in the third person. 'Would the beloved man care for some vegetable soup?'

He waited for the day of her monthly doctor's appointment. She always made a point of coming straight home after it, but was never back before twelve-thirty. Instead of going to the Institute that morning, he took his umbrella, strolled through the pouring rain to his bench near the Friedensengel, and used his newspaper to sit on. Today, then! Now all he had to do was get rid of Frau Henning.

No one in sight. He liked the sound of the raindrops beating on the umbrella, it helped him to think. All kinds of ideas presented themselves . . . By the time the damp had penetrated to his skin, he had a plan.

Frau Henning was rolling out pastry dough on the kitchen table. Her radio was going full blast and she didn't hear his key in the lock. When he spoke to her, she jumped and exclaimed: 'Holy Mother of God!'

'Frau Henning, I'm having bad pains here.' He pointed to his breastbone. 'I've just been to the doctor – no, no, nothing to be alarmed about, but I'm supposed to lie down. Would you be kind enough to get this medicine for me? Unfortunately the only pharmacy that carries it is Gerd-Möller's, 25 Gerd-Möller-Strasse in Pasing. Would you mind . . .'

Frau Henning looked at the scrap of paper. 'No prescription?'

'It's a homoeopathic medicine, you don't need a prescription. No hurry, you can take the bus.'

'If there's no hurry, could I finish my pastry?'

Instead of answering, Kaspar half closed his eyes and leaned against the door. Even if she took a taxi, she wouldn't be back before one o'clock, because the Gerd-Möller pharmacy didn't exist.

She rushed off – but came back a few minutes later for her umbrella, just in time to meet Kaspar in the hall with a suitcase in his hand.

'Whatever are you doing with that suitcase, Professor?'

'The suitcase? Oh yes, well – as a matter of fact I thought I might have left a few of those pills in it – I mean, when we returned from our honeymoon.'

Together they opened the suitcase and confronted its gaping emptiness.

'Never mind,' she said reassuringly. 'I'll get you some. You leave that thing here and go and lie down.'

Clutching her umbrella, she dashed out of the door, and Kaspar hastily began to pack. The scare had shaken him so severely that he thought he really did have a pain in his chest. He felt humiliated and angry. Out! Quickly! Let me out of here!

He packed very little: jeans, a few cotton shirts, sandals, a sweater, his raincoat, pyjamas and underwear, socks, hand-kerchiefs. He stood up straight and forced himself to think with precision: his alarm clock – the one Martha had given him – his portable radio, passport, money: DM 8,400, leaving an even sixty thousand in the bank for Heidi. And the car keys on Heidi's bedside-table.

He looked at his watch: half past ten. Could he still risk writing a note? For the last time he sat down at his desk, custom-made, kidney-shaped, with a red leather top.

Envelope. 'Heidi' in big letters. Into the silver bowl in the hall. Hat, suitcase, umbrella. To the front door – and a quick turn to leave the front door key beside the note in the silver bowl – the clatter set his teeth on edge – and then out, closing the door softly behind him.

Downstairs, opening the front door, he felt sure he would run straight into Heidi. Or Frau Henning. But the faces hurrying past in the rain all belonged to strangers.

He walked down the street until he found a telephone booth occupied by a couple sheltering from the rain. He callously turned them out and laughed as they went off, cursing him for an 'old fart'. He hadn't felt so young for years.

He looked up the number and dialled, hoping she would be home. So far as he knew, she wasn't working at present and she liked to sleep late. What time was it? Quarter past eleven – high time he was on his way. She would be mad at him for waking her up and madder still when she heard what he had to say. Would he recognize her voice? He had only met her once, very briefly, the day after the wedding, and he'd spoken to her once more when she'd called up recently.

The phone only rang twice. 'Hello,' growled a sleepy, smoky voice.

'Frau Wennerstett? This is Kaspar.'

'Who?'

'Kaspar. Your son-in-law. Heidi's husband.'

'What? Oh, yes. Anything wrong?'

'No, but I have to tell you something.'

'Can't it wait till later?'

'Unfortunately not, or I wouldn't be calling you – '

She interrupted. 'Is Heidi okay?'

'Yes, but please listen to me for a few minutes.'

'Oh, my God! Don't tell me, I can guess.'

'I don't think you can.'

'No? Oh, well then, hold on while I get a cigarette. There we are. Okay, shoot.'

'Please go over to Heidi's as soon as you can. I've left her. She doesn't know yet, she wasn't at home this morning. I've written her a note, but it would be better if there's someone with her when she reads it.'

'What? You've what . . . ? You've left her, you say? Why? Have you had a row?'

'If that was all, I wouldn't be bothering you.'

'Wait a minute – Heidi's pregnant, isn't she? Or did I dream that up?'

'You didn't dream it up, but that's only the last straw, not the real reason.'

'Hm.' She stopped for a moment to cough. Smoker's cough. 'Do you want to tell me the real reason or not?'

'It would take too long. It's entirely my fault.'

'Now, wait a minute! Heidi's been having an affair with you for ages, hasn't she? Surely she should have found out before now . . .'

'I've only just found it out myself.'

'What do you mean, "it"? What have you just found out?'

'Frau Wennerstett, please go to Heidi right away. That's why I'm calling you; everything else is a waste of time. Goodbye.'

'Hey, Kaspar! Wait a minute, man! I promise I'll go over there right away, but I'd like to have a talk with you first.'

'It's a waste of time. Sorry, but I must go!'

'Okay, then, go, I'm not keeping you. I think I know what's been happening. You know how I feel about these things.'

'That's why I'm calling you.'

'Well, then, you ought to know that I'm on your side from the start, man.'

'That's not what I want at all.'

'Oh, come on now, don't be so hoity-toity, it's not all that important. Come over and have a drink with me this afternoon.

Heidi will never hear about it, I promise you, and I won't try to change your mind, either. As far as I'm concerned you can get the hell out. But I'm interested. From a purely clinical point of view. See you around six, then.'

'I'll be long gone by then, but I want to ask you once more, as urgently as I can: *please* hurry.'

'Wait, Kaspar. Wait!' she cried, although she had heard him hang up.

CHAPTER FIVE

HEIDI met her mother on the stairs. Up to now Elise Wenner-stett had never expressed a wish to see the flat, but Heidi was too excited to feel any surprise at seeing her there. That morning the gynaecologist had shown her a five-month foetus which happened to have been sent to him for tests.

'I was allowed to see it because I'm exactly that far along. Now I know what it looks like.'

She stroked the bulge in the front of her loose, brightly coloured summer dress. 'The one at the doctor's was a boy and it was sort of greenish because it was dead. But I'm sure mine's a girl. Now I know what's going on when it kicks me and prods me. Its little legs are properly formed already, you know.' She found her key and opened the door into the flat. 'I expect you'd like a cup of coffee, wouldn't you? Or a glass of sherry? Frau Henning!'

No answer. She went into the kitchen. Frau Henning wasn't there and – very strange – had left no Frau Henning note to explain why she had gone out.

She started the coffee. Elise remained standing in the hall, looking from afar at the letter in the silver bowl. Heidi called to her from the kitchen to take off her coat, the coffee was ready, she was going to make a sketch of that five-month unborn baby right away, Kaspar would certainly be fascinated.

She appeared, carrying a tray. 'Come into the living-room – oh, I forgot, you've never seen the flat, have you? Do you like it? Most of this is from his first marriage. It doesn't bother me. So long as he's comfortable, that's the main thing.'

Elise remained standing in the doorway and thought: I'll give her a few seconds longer, just a few seconds . . . Nonsense, how can she 'enjoy' them when she doesn't know they're the last?

'Heidi, there's a letter out here, in the bowl.'

'Must be for Kaspar.' She poured the coffee – lots of milk for herself, sugar for both of them.

'No, it's for you.'

'For me?' She took a few sips, then looked up. 'Why, you've still got your coat on. Do come and sit down.' She got up, helped Elise off with her coat and carried it back to the hall.

Elise looked frantically around the living-room. Where was the cabinet, or whatever it might be, where the liquor was kept? Nothing of the sort in this room. That door over there! She dashed into Kaspar's study, saw a glass-fronted cabinet and wrenched it open. Bottles, thank God. But she could only see vague shapes; her spectacles were in her handbag in the next room. Blindly choosing a squat bottle, she took a hasty sip – some kind of fruit brandy – found a glass and ran out of the room.

Heidi was standing in the hall by the window, reading. She was reading it for the second time.

Dear Heidi,
 I must go away. Far away, and I won't be coming back. I can offer no excuse, at best an explanation: I can't do it. I've tried, but I can't do it. I'm not a father and I'm not a husband. Anything else I could say would only hurt you more. *I must go away*, please believe me.

Kaspar

'Heidi . . .'
She looked up. Her mother was standing before her offering her a glass with some liquid in it. The letter fluttered to the floor. She reached for the glass with both hands, or she thought she was reaching for it, or was she trying to hold on to Elise? She heard the glass splinter on the floor as she fell.

When she came to herself, she was lying on her bed and saw the bandage on her arm. 'What happened . . .?' Then she saw her mother standing by the window, peering down at the street. Elise turned around.

'How do you feel?' She bent over her daughter and removed the cold compress from her forehead.

'What happened?' Heidi repeated, looking at her arm.

'It's nothing. You fell and cut yourself a bit on the broken glass.'

'What?' And for the third time: 'What happened?'

Then she remembered and screamed.

'Goddamned doctors!' muttered Elise, returning to the window. 'When I dial your doctor's number, I get nothing but a damn recording saying he's off somewhere, operating. But his associate, whoever that is, is on his way and he'll give you a shot and you'll go to sleep. . . .'

But Heidi didn't hear her; she was thrashing about on the bed and screaming. Frau Henning was standing at the open door, wringing her hands. The note lay on the table. Elise had read it; so had Frau Henning.

'There's a taxi now. That must be him, thank God!'

Frau Henning ran out into the hall and opened the front door. A youngish man was coming quickly upstairs. He gave the two women a curt nod. 'May I ask both of you to leave the room. You've already told me all I need to know.'

Heidi didn't take any notice of him. She screamed and threw herself about.

'Please go,' said the doctor, opening his black bag.

Frau Henning was already in the kitchen. Elise grabbed the brandy bottle and hastily pressed the note into the doctor's hand.

'Here, read this. And then for God's sake do something.'

She waited in the kitchen, with the bottle and Frau Henning to provide support. Frau Henning had accepted a drink 'just for once' and described to Elise in detail her last encounter with the Professor and her fruitless search for the pharmacy. No, she hadn't noticed any 'symptoms', the Professor was just as he always was, just as he'd been in the days of his late wife – in other words, a perfect gentleman. Elise wanted to know what she was like, the late wife. Oh, very nice really, was Frau Henning's cautious opinion, a perfect lady. Just like the present Frau Schulte.

Elise heard the bedroom door open and rushed out into the hall, still clutching her glass, to coax the doctor into the living-room. In vain: he had no time.

'She's asleep now. But she'll wake up in an hour or two – we can't keep her sedated indefinitely. I advise you to explain to her that it was a panic reaction on her husband's part and that he'll come back to her.'

'He won't come back.'

The doctor shrugged. 'I don't know him, but in my experience they always come back. This kind of thing happens all the time. In any case the only thing she can do is learn to wait, then the days and the nights will pass and the child will grow and keep her occupied until she delivers. And then we're out of the wood. After that, the presence of the husband isn't of primary importance any more. The child will take over. Better than any husband.' He glanced at the glass in Elise's hand. 'Does she drink too? No? Pity. It would do her no harm to take a drop now and again, especially during the next few weeks, until her husband comes back.'

'He won't come back.'

'In my experience . . .'

'Want to bet?'

It was getting dark when Heidi woke up. She kept her eyes shut and heard her mother and Frau Henning talking quietly. She forced herself to lie quite still, although she had a strong desire to thrash about on the bed and moan. And to reread the letter. Perhaps she had overlooked something.

No Kaspar. Never again. He wasn't dead, he wasn't a corpse, he was alive somewhere. He was there, yet not there. The baby! The impulse was too strong and she covered her stomach with her hands.

'Heidi?'

She opened her eyes and stared fixedly and with hatred at her mother, who sat down on the edge of the bed, then at Frau Henning, who had nervously withdrawn to the door. Nobody spoke. Breaking the long, heavy silence, Elise said: 'Is there anything you'd like? Anything at all?'

Heidi turned her head to the window. It was now quite dark outside. Slowly she turned round and looked at her mother. Elise nodded, fetched the letter, handed it to her daughter, and switched on the bedside lamp. Frau Henning fled.

'Dear Heidi, I must go away . . . and I won't be coming back . . .' She read very slowly, and one sentence twice: 'I've tried, but I can't do it . . .'

She laid the letter on the bedside table and closed her eyes. 'I'll have an abortion. I'll get rid of it. It's got to go.'

Elise nodded. 'Too bad you saw what it looks like this morning.'

A long pause.

'I hate it.'

'Naturally.'

For the first time Heidi looked her mother in the face as if she were really seeing her. 'What would you do in my place?'

'The same.'

'How would you do it? After all, it's . . . there.'

Elise shrugged. 'I'd find a way. The main thing is to get rid of the little brat.'

Out of the corner of her eye she watched Heidi's fingers moving slowly around and around her stomach – in disgust? Or could it – perhaps – be protective? She turned off the light, hoping Heidi would fall asleep again.

After a long time, a voice out of the darkness called: 'Bring me the telephone book.'

Elise asked no questions, looked around and found it in Kaspar's study. She set it down on the bedspread and switched the bedside light on again. Heidi tried to sit up and turn the pages but collapsed into the pillows.

'Who are you looking for?'

'Wegmann. Harold Wegmann. He has a nursery in Grünwald. Ask him to come here.'

An hour later he was there. Stefan came with him and Werner arrived soon afterwards.

CHAPTER SIX

HERR ALEXIS was amazed, pleased and puzzled to see Kaspar standing in front of him. 'Professor Schulte! How nice to see you again, did you make a reservation? I don't seem to remember . . .'

'Are you full up?'

'Not even a broom cupboard left. The height of the season, you know. Oh dear, I *am* sorry.'

'So am I, I don't like strange hotels. But if there's nothing for it, can you recommend one?'

Herr Alexis didn't know a hotel, expensive or cheap, that wouldn't also be booked solid. And he really couldn't recommend the little *pensions*, they were more for hippies, no running water, Frau Schulte would never . . .

'I'm alone.' Herr Alexis didn't say a word, not even: Oh? 'Do you think the porter would have any suggestions?'

'I'm the porter, Professor. That's a surprise, isn't it? This is his desk, remember? The old man really became impossible, and I still haven't found a suitable replacement.'

Kaspar thought for a moment. 'Did the old man live in the hotel?'

'Yes, of course, all our employees do. That is, they live in the annexe across the street.'

'Is his room occupied?'

'No, I'm keeping it in case someone should come along.'

'Couldn't I have his room?'

Herr Alexis stared. The Professor had seemed completely normal last time.

'I'm afraid not, that would be against the house rules. Only employees may live there. We couldn't do a thing like that here. I mean, I can't make exceptions, I'm sure you understand . . . Please excuse me for a moment.' He turned his attention to two American girls, who wanted to know where they could buy a rubber mattress for swimming.

'What, please, ladies?' The girls repeated their question, giggled, tried to demonstrate. Bewildered, Herr Alexis asked Kaspar in Croatian: 'What is it they want, Professor? An extra bed made of rubber?'

Kaspar explained and translated and the girls went off to the beach. 'Happens all the time,' sighed Alexis. 'I never can work out what they want. It's a wonder the hotel's still full.'

A kitchen boy in a white cap came rushing up. Would the manager please come at once. Two of the big ranges in the kitchen had conked out and the house electrician was not to be found. Alexis interrupted him impatiently. 'You know where he lives, Bruno. Run and tell him to come over right away.' As the boy darted off, Herr Alexis snatched the white cap off his head. Looking after him, he sighed and wiped his face with the cap.

'Go and straighten them out in the kitchen,' said Kaspar. 'I'll take care of things here.'

The manager lifted the hinged flap in the counter so that Kaspar could step behind the desk – stopped and reconsidered. 'I really can't accept, Professor, after all, you're . . .'

Kaspar assured him that, whatever he might be 'after all', he would enjoy it. Herr Alexis hurried off.

He stepped behind the desk, stowed away his suitcase and leaned on the counter that formed the barrier between the porter and the outside world. Beside him lay the tools of the trade: registration forms, calendar, street map of Bled, boating schedules, bus routes into the neighbourhood, postcards, pads and pencil. Under the counter, inside a half-hidden drawer, were the porter's secrets, his 'addresses' and discreet notes. Perhaps even photographs? Yes, photographs too. And on the floor, beside his suitcase, a metal button, probably a foot-operated emergency alarm. Interesting.

Too bad the lobby was empty, he would have enjoyed a chance to give out information. And too bad he couldn't stay at the hotel, he liked it here. He stepped back and inspected the cubicle. About six feet by nine, no window, just an air vent high up on the back wall, no chair, a low stool with a desk lamp on it and a folded deckchair propped against the wall. On one of the side walls a large calendar with a colour photo of the lake in the month of August. On the opposite wall a card had been pinned up. Under a heavy black cross was the name Draza Rukovina and a date: 10 May 1977.

He turned around and leaned on the counter again. Suddenly something shot through his mind, something that clicked, and it jolted him like an electric shock – although for a moment he couldn't pin it down. Then, almost immediately, it came to him: the date! 10 May 1977: the day of Martha's death.

He looked at the card again. Who was Draza Rukovina?

Herr Alexis raised the leaf, holding on to it while he caught his breath. 'Did anything come up, Professor? I can't thank you enough, it's a good thing I was there when our electrician came. Well now, let me relieve you.' He laughed and kept the leaf open for Kaspar, who was staring at the card.

'Who is Draza Rukovina?'

'What's that? Ah, yes, that was our night porter. He was with us for years. I hung that up there so that I wouldn't forget the date. He left money for five requiem masses. I've paid for two already.'

'And he died on 10 May 1977?'

'Yes. We found him here in the morning, lying quite peacefully in his deckchair: heart attack. He was about seventy. Why?'

'No particular reason; I just wondered,' said Kaspar, tearing his eyes away from the black cross.

'Coming, Professor?' Herr Alexis was still holding up the counter flap. Kaspar hesitated; he felt a strong desire not to leave, to stay on here in the dim quiet of the cubicle, screened off from the world.

A German couple stepped out of the lift and called: 'Where's the restaurant?'

Herr Alexis said with a little bow: 'Downstairs to the right, please.'

At the same time another voice behind him said, 'Downstairs to the right, please.'

Alexis turned around and laughed. 'You really enjoy it, don't you, Professor? Shall we give it a try?'

'Why not?' said Kaspar slowly. 'Then I could move into the room, couldn't I?'

Herr Alexis dropped the counter flap and stared at him.

Kaspar smiled. 'No. I'm not a fugitive from justice or a political refugee, no one's after me. But I owe you an explanation – anyway a partial one – before you hire me.'

Alexis cut him short: 'I couldn't hire you, Professor, even if I wanted to. We can't employ foreigners.'

'I think I told you already, I was born in Belgrade.'

'Oh. Yes, that makes a difference, of course. Still – a porter's job is a position of trust. He keeps all the keys to the rooms; the guests rely on him, sometimes in the most confidential matters – you know what I mean?'

Kaspar nodded. They looked at each other for a moment without speaking. In spite of the manager's poker face, Kaspar knew exactly what he was thinking: is the man a doubtful customer or is he my golden opportunity? He decided to lay his cards on the table.

'I've given up my professorship,' he said slowly. 'And I've left my wife. I want to start a new life. Head first.'

Herr Alexis said nothing and kept his face expressionless.

I'm a mind reader, thought Kaspar, a new achievement. Or maybe I could always do it and wasn't sufficiently interested. All Alexis is worried about now is my salary. He's afraid I'll ask for more than the going rate. But right now the thought strikes him that I have no notion of what I'm officially entitled to, so he's relieved and the idea of having me here as porter looks better and better. He's frowning just to make me think he's dubious. Any minute now he'll come up with a few objections.

An elderly couple passed by, dropping their key without a word of greeting.

'Have a good evening,' Herr Alexis called after them.

From now on I'll be the one to hope they have a good evening, thought Kaspar; not my main interest in life, exactly, but what the hell?

'If you'll forgive me, Professor, might this not be just a passing whim on your part? I'm sure Frau Schulte will soon . . .'

'My wife doesn't know where I am. But you're right to hesitate: I'm a bit hesitant myself. This may not turn out to be the place I'm looking for.' He ducked under the counter and emerged into the outside world.

Instead of handing him his suitcase, Herr Alexis held on to it.

'But then again it may be, Professor. I think . . . well, why don't we give it a try?'

A try . . . Kaspar heard Heidi's voice in Uncle Stilts's bedroom whispering: 'I'd like to give it a try.' Hers hadn't come off. He glanced over Herr Alexis's shoulder into the dark square of the cubicle.

'I don't sleep well,' he said. 'Why don't I start on the night shift? Night porter. And shall we say two weeks' notice on either side?'

'Agreed,' said Herr Alexis a shade too quickly, and waited for the counter-move, but Kaspar only nodded.

'You can drop the "Professor" now. The name's Schulte. As far as I'm concerned, you can call me Kaspar.'

Alexis made a mental note to drop the deferential tone, too.

'The porter is called by his last name.'

Kaspar nodded again and peered into the cubicle. What on earth was he looking at? Alexis searched his memory: had the man been so peculiar the last time he was here? Well, what did it matter? – he had a night porter. Now, at long last, he could go home to his own bed instead of sleeping in a deckchair in this stuffy hole.

'Would you like to take a look at your room now – er, Schulte?' Still not quite the right casual yet authoritative tone.

'Not necessary. I'd like to take a walk by the lake for a while. I can start tonight if you like. What are the hours?'

'Ten till six. Here's your contract: salary and deductions, insurance, old age pension . . .'

'Where do I sign?'

'My goodness, read it through first – Schulte.'

Kaspar folded the form and stuffed it in his coat pocket. He'll never read it, thought Alexis as he moved Kaspar's suitcase into the cubicle. Would such a scatter-brained man ever work out as night porter?

Kaspar wasn't scatter-brained; never in his life had he felt so alert and concentrated. It was all he could do to keep a tight hold on the turmoil of his thoughts until he was alone. Leaving the lobby, he tried to keep his pace unhurried, he knew Alexis would be watching him. On the road to the lake he had to push through crowds of people, and his hope of taking a quiet walk along the little path that ran beside the shore was dashed, too. Everywhere he looked children, parents, teenagers were lying, sitting, running around. He was lucky to get a boat and rowed as fast as he could past the hotel to the point where the path and the beach gave way to rocks and trees. He hadn't even taken the time to remove his shirt and shoes; now he let himself drift and stripped down to his underpants.

Draza Rukovina, night porter, died 10 May 1977. In his little porter's box. What do you say to that, Uncle Stilts? Is there such a thing as chance? Do you believe in coincidences? I've never paid any attention, never had any interest in such things, but now I suddenly believe in – what should one call it – connections? Tie-ups? I suppose when something of this sort does happen, it's bound to hit you like a stroke of lightning. Shall I be able to look quite calmly tonight at that card with the black cross – and then think about other things? What else, Inkworm, or do you think you're supposed to go down on your knees before it? An old man happened to die on the same day as Martha. Ten thousand other people did too, only you don't know them. Yes, but that's just it, Uncle Stilts. *I do know him now*, and the fact that I'm going to take over his job, sleep in the same deckchair . . . .

Oh, come off it, Inkworm, *you* set it all up. You took the job because you're determined to find some kind of meaning in it. Stop kidding yourself.

He looked around. His boat was almost motionless, drifting very slowly towards the bank, perhaps towards that nice shady place under the trees.

Heart failure, Alexis had said. Quite peacefully in the early hours of the morning. Draza Rukovina. Perhaps Luburic had known him. . . .

From one moment to the next he passed out of the light into the shade, out of white-hot, flickering sunshine that scorched his forehead, into dark, still coolness. What time was it? Four o'clock. He would lie here for a while: he hadn't had any sleep last night, sitting up in a crowded second-class coach of the Munich–Ljubljana night train. It hadn't bothered him at all; on the contrary, it had made him feel good. How very strange, he thought, and fell asleep.

Two hours later, his boat stuck in the shade under the trees, he woke up and decided to try and find Mariana Bogdan that very day. She wasn't listed in the telephone directory, but he found her address at the Registry Office.

On the other side of the lake, opposite the hotel, the little town of Bled clustered modestly beside the water, screened off by the huge, well-tended trees on the bank – backstage, as it were. Short streets medium-wide, an all-purpose medium-large central square, small, ugly cars, bicycles, mopeds, carts. Two-storey houses, painted light grey, no balconies, no window boxes, here and there a tree, medium-tall, medium-green. Small hotels, barely recognizable as such, small shops, medium-well paved streets. No steps, everything on the same level. Not many people about at six o'clock, but all dressed like townspeople, in neat skirts or trousers, in spite of the heat. No tourists.

He walked on, happy to find the flat grey gradually relieved by clumps of trees, small gardens and fences. An old peasant woman all muffled up in black directed him to Uliza Pavla, Paul Street, and she pointed along a dusty cart track. He strolled from one peasant cottage to the next, trying to guess which of them might belong to Mariana Bogdan, and finally came to the end of the long track: an odd-looking dwelling adjoining a field of wheat stubble. It might formerly have been a big stable; now it too was painted light grey. Each of its small white windows must once have framed a horse's head, brown or black, looking out and neighing.

He stood uncertainly by the gate in the wire fence and looked down the dozen or so overgrown stone steps into the courtyard below. Half of it was paved – perhaps that was where they used to groom the horses; the other half consisted of a garden of sorts, full of tall, rampant sunflowers. In between were rows of cabbages, cauliflower long gone to seed, and straggly runner beans.

At the far end of the courtyard a couple of steps led up to the open door of the building, and on the cool, shady stone stairs sat a woman in a bikini, plucking a goose. She was singing as she worked, lustily if not melodiously, plucking the goose to the rhythm of her song. Half of its feathers were already piled like snowflakes around her sun-tanned legs. She's too fat to wear a bikini, thought Kaspar. The dark flesh bulged out of the elasticized fabric in all directions. Revolting, although the flesh itself was firm and not unattractive. Still, skinny brown scarecrows were more to his taste.

'Excuse me . . .' She looked up and sang another couple of bars before he could continue. 'I'm looking for Frau Bogdan.'

'Yes?'

'You are Frau Bogdan? May I speak to you for a moment?'

She nodded, and he opened the gate and picked his way down the dilapidated steps into the courtyard. She looked at him without curiosity and went on plucking.

'Can you tell me where I might find Ante Luburic?'

'He's not here.'

'Have you any idea where I might find him?'

'Who sent you?'

Kaspar hesitated for a moment. 'Vlada Martinac.'

'Vlada!' She stopped plucking and grinned up at him. 'Vlada? Did she send me her best regards?'

'I don't remember,' said Kaspar, grinning back.

She pointed to a weathered old well and he sat down on the cool stones.

'Feels good in this heat, doesn't it?' she said, slapping her thigh against the steps. 'You've just arrived?'

'I haven't had time to change.'

'Is Vlada in such a hurry?'

'It has nothing to do with Vlada.'

'Oh?' Her light, slanting eyes smiled at him. 'Who are you then?'

'Oh, excuse me,' said Kaspar, and stood up, which made her laugh out aloud. He sat down again. 'My name's Schulte, Kaspar Schulte. From Munich.'

'Ustasha?'

'No.'

She studied him for a moment, shrugged and picked up her half-plucked goose. Its eyes and beak were wide open as if it was amazed at the dexterity with which the brown fingers stripped it.

'I don't believe you,' said Frau Bogdan. 'But at least you don't smell like the UDBA. Ante will be back tomorrow or the day after. You can drop in tomorrow after six if you like. Vlada wouldn't send anyone Ante doesn't want to see, that much I'm sure of. Or would you rather he got in touch with you? Where are you staying?'

'At the Hotel Godice.'

'At the Godice?' She laughed and shook her head in disbelief. 'You'd better come here tomorrow.'

He walked slowly back to the hotel. It was getting dark, and now the narrow path beside the lake was deserted. Someone had left a child's folding chair in the grass. He sat down on it and lit a cigarette. The water was smooth, with a whitish sheen. The faint sound of a bell chiming drifted across the lake; somebody was still on the little island, ringing the wishing-bell in the tower. Suppose it were he – what would he wish for? He couldn't think of anything. The bell trembled over the water like an old man's voice. Whoever was pulling the bell rope was trying to make sure. And what about him? He still couldn't think of anything to wish for.

The goose must be plucked by now, he thought. Will it go straight into the oven? The white feathers are probably still lying on the steps. Those chocolate-coloured thighs! And the knees, even darker, and the bare feet with red, broken toenails. A bit of a floozy, this Bogdan woman, and much too fat. Intimidating, too, with those broad shoulders and bulging grapefruit-breasts. He'd never had his hands on breasts like that; the mere thought made him uneasy. Obviously, Luburic and Martinac didn't have any inhibitions, though.

He tried to recall her face, the turned-up nose, a bit too broad, the light, inquisitive eyes, deep-set above the cheekbones, framed by long, dark, rather shaggy hair. What he remembered best was her teeth, short and pointed and white like a puppy's. But those thighs! Firm or flabby? How old could she be? Thirty? Forty? Come to think of it, she hadn't even shaken hands with him.

At ten o'clock that evening he was lying in the deckchair inside the night porter's cubicle, Uncle Stilts's folder on his lap, facing Draza Rukovina's black cross on the wall. He was still unable to break away from that cross; his eyes kept on spelling out the inscription: 10 May 1977, knitting a chain that linked him with Martha, a benign, healing chain. Dark silence. Occasionally a bird's timid chirping outside the shutters. Why did he still want to see Luburic? He'd already found a hide-out. Maybe he shouldn't go back to that woman at all. Just a minute: there was something he wanted to ask Luburic . . .

And now for Uncle Stilts. The folder was waiting for him. 'Moabit, 6 July 1914.' Cramped handwriting, obviously not used very much, childish, but with a lot of curious flourishes which no school would ever have tolerated.

At last they've given me writing materials. Courtesy of the chaplain, because of the chess lessons. All the extras, coffee, apples, books, are courtesy of the chaplain, but trying to teach him anything bores me to death. Brain like a sieve. He drops in for a game every evening, and when it's over, he starts in with his never-ending questions. Now I just lie, because if I tell him the truth, he says I'm lying.

There's no point in describing prison life because mine's completely different from everyone else's on account of the chaplain. That's how it's been all my life. Never like other people, always someone special. Well, I am *someone special. And I got assigned to a one-man cell right away. It doesn't save me from having to make paper bags like everybody else, though. At first they put me on net-making, but the cord made my fingers bleed and the chaplain got sick from just looking at them while we were playing chess, that's how sensitive he is. Makes you want to throw up.*

MOABIT, 15 JULY: *Now I see the kind of trouble I'm headed for. They want to use me as a girl because I'm so small. And pretty. Yesterday I only just managed to get away from Bathtub-Fred. He's a large fellow and I practically had to gouge one of his eyes out for trying to feel me up. He's called Bathtub-Fred because he held his girl up by the heels, with her head under water, until she croaked. Swore he'd do the same to me. I told on him to the chaplain. Bathtub-Fred got three days' solitary, but I don't feel very good about it.*

Everybody here is always whining and bellyaching about wanting to be 'free' instead of locked up in a cell. Now, that *doesn't bother me one bit. Maybe because I spent so much time in my box. Fear of confined spaces! Don't make me laugh. On the contrary, it gives me time to think, take a look at my life, go over it all again. For me that's a real treat, I never get enough of it. At first the guard thought I was crying and unlocked the door, but there I was, lying on my bunk, happy as a lark, chuckling. He's sure I'm crazy. When I think what kind of life everyone else here has led – and compare it with mine!*

· MOABIT, 20 JULY: *Bathtub-Fred gets out of solitary today. I'm scared shitless.*

The chaplain says there's a letter for me from Mother. Next week I'll have been here a month and I'll be allowed to read it. I like it here. Except for the chaplain. I'll lose my talent if I have to mess around with him much longer. He'll never catch on. Like Lisa. As I write that, I feel almost nothing. But I will say one thing for her: she certainly had a great pair of tits. I only mention it because that's all they talk about here.

MOABIT, 2 AUGUST: *Back. Infirmary. Bathtub-F. But I'm back.*

MOABIT, 8 AUGUST: *I can see out of my eyes again and eat a bit, but I've got a large hole in my skull and my head's shaved like a monk's. Everybody was expecting it, even the guards. They never took their eyes off Bathtub-Fred, but he was tricky, acting friendly as the devil. 'Come on, Stilts, I'm sorry. Let's shake on it, all right?' Handshake, eye to eye. And three days later, when everyone had forgotten all about it, he lay in wait for me in the toilet and held my head under the water in an iron grip. I was already*

217

unconscious, when someone happened to come in – you can't lock the doors – and saw Bathtub-Fred and two legs dangling like a puppet's, as he told me later. He screamed blue murder and tried to push Bathtub-Fred away from the basin, and that bastard quickly rammed my head against the tap to make sure I was dead. And then they came at the run. I was in the infirmary for ten days. Seven stitches in my head. It was a real deep hole, right down to the bone.

At least it gets me out of playing chess with the chaplain for a while. When he comes to visit me with his chessboard under his arm, I cross my eyes as if I'm having trouble focusing. Then he just says a prayer, but I can put up with that, it's soon over.

They've transferred Bathtub-Fred to another prison. It doesn't make any difference to him. He's in for life.

There was a sound of impatient knocking. Kaspar jumped up, blinking. Where was he? What was going on?

Two young Germans were hammering on the desk with their room keys. 'Well, at last, man! Are there any night spots in this god-forsaken dump?'

Night spots? Oh yes, of course. Alexis had shown him the file of 'addresses'. Rock music? On the spur of the moment he told them, in German, that he couldn't really recommend the Jazz Cellar. Leaning over the counter, they adopted a confidential tone. What about . . . you know . . . ? Oh yes, there were one or two places. He sorted through the brochures, apparently making a careful selection, enjoying the tension. Ah, here we are, the Strele Bar. First-class. Local talent, Italian girls, too. (The things he could suddenly invent!) Expensive? Well – yes. Of course, there were less expensive places but he wouldn't recommend them, not even – he dropped his voice – not even from the purely hygienic point of view. Oh, my God! The young men went into their personal problems, and before long Kaspar was bored and put on his classroom face. Even so, it was quite a while before they left. First lesson: be helpful but distant.

No chance to return to Uncle Stilts and Bathtub-Fred because between eleven and one o'clock guests were constantly coming and going, depositing keys, wanting a taxi, an all-night pharmacy, a flashlight, writing paper, condoms. Everybody wanted something from the night porter; nobody wanted anything from Kaspar personally. As a professor you had to put on a bit of a show, had to sell yourself; some of his colleagues were very good at that, even enjoyed it. He had always done as little as possible in that line, and this had sometimes been resented. Now he could be as anonymous as he pleased, like an actor hiding behind a false nose.

When he looked at the time again, it was half past one. His tiredness felled him like a punch on the jaw and he collapsed into the deckchair.

Next day he took the rowing-boat out again, swam, lay in the sun, and was pleased to see how quickly his skin was losing its greenish pallor. About seven o'clock he set off for Uliza Pavla.

The heat was still oppressive, but by now he was better equipped for it: jeans, sandals, open-necked shirt with the sleeves rolled up. He stopped outside a shop window – his room in the annexe had no mirror – and hardly recognized himself. He'd never even looked like this when he was young, so lanky and casual. And bareheaded. He had always been slim, sometimes even skinny and under-weight, but always neatly dressed, clothes pressed, shoes shined, and never ever without a hat. He stood for a long time looking at his reflection, unable to make up his mind whether he liked it or not. It didn't 'fit', but perhaps that was a good thing. Today Frau Bogdan too would be properly dressed, most likely peasant style; he pictured her as a raggle-taggle gipsy with a kerchief on her head and a long, colourful skirt.

The courtyard was empty. A dog barked close by as he descended the steps, slightly uneasy; invisible dogs scared him. But all was quiet. On the stone table by the door were mounds of purple plums, and from inside the house came the sound of a radio and someone singing along with it in a shrill voice.

'Frau Bogdan!'

He called again, twice – he didn't like just to walk in – and finally she appeared, carrying a huge basket, still wearing her bikini, her black hair dripping wet.

'Oh, Herr Schulte – I'd completely forgotten. Ante's not back yet.'

She indicated the rim of the well, sat herself down at the round table of rough-hewn stone and began to stone the plums with a short, sharp knife. The radio inside the house played rock music and made conversation unnecessary.

'Have you been swimming?' he asked during a pause in the music.

'No. Took a shower. It's too far to the lake.'

She sliced and stoned with machine-like precision and sang along with every number.

From up on the track came the loud, shrill sound of a bicycle bell. She looked up without stopping the business in hand. A young man of about twenty was sitting on his bicycle, leaning against the garden fence. He continued to ring the bell until she got up and went into the house to turn off the radio. She returned to the table, carrying it.

'What do you want, Milan?'

'Come up here.'

'You come down.'

She switched the radio back on. The young man stared up at the sky with a bored expression and began to ring his bell again. Frau Bogdan went on stoning plums and resumed her singing, louder than before. This was too much for the invisible dog – it began to howl, and Kaspar laughed. She looked at him in surprise and burst out laughing, too, pointing with her knife at the garden fence and tapping her forehead.

The young man gave up, chained his bicycle to the fence, swore violently in Croatian, and jumped down the steps into the courtyard. Taking no notice of Kaspar, he planted himself beside the table.

'Let me have thirty dinars.'

She shook her head and continued to stone and sing. The young man pounded the table with his fist. 'It's *my* money.'

'You owe me over a hundred.'

'I'll pay you back next Wednesday, when I get paid.'

'Wait till Wednesday then.'

Until now she had spoken only German with Kaspar, but with the young man she spoke Croatian.

'Damn you –'

'Get out of here.' She turned up the volume on the radio.

He stared at her with his light, slanting eyes, speechless with anger. She stared back, without interrupting her work, although it seemed to Kaspar that she was handling the short knife more slowly and carefully.

The young man thought for a minute, glanced quickly at Kaspar, the knife and the pile of plums. With a rapid gesture he swept the mound of dark blue fruit to the ground and ran back to the steps.

A few well-aimed plums hit him on the back of the head. He laughed, leapt up the stone steps two at a time, and an instant later his bicycle was out of sight.

She put down her knife and gazed after him. 'That's my son, Milan.'

Then she rose to pick up the plums. Kaspar helped her.

'He wanted to borrow some money.'

'Until next Wednesday,' said Kaspar in Croatian.

'How do you . . .?'

He explained about his childhood and Belgrade.

'And you're not in the Ustasha? Not even a supporter?'

'Perhaps you might say on the farthest side of the outer fringe.'

Most of the plums were now back on the table. Leaning over sideways, she broke off two large, scratchy sunflower leaves, handed one to Kaspar and with the other wiped the dirt and plum juice off her fingers. A church clock struck the hour.

'Eight o'clock. Ante won't be coming today.'

'I'll push off then. Maybe I'll try again tomorrow.'

She took the leaf from him, crumpled it and threw it away as though the courtyard were her rubbish heap.

'What do you want of Ante?' Her question was direct but not aggressive.

'It's a personal matter.'

'Concerning Vlada?'

'No, concerning me.'

She got up, picked a few seeds out of the face of a huge sunflower and began to chew them thoughtfully.

'I've got shishkebab on the grill. Can you smell it? You can have Ante's share.'

She didn't wait for an answer, turned her back on him, swept the rest of the plums into the basket, carried it into the house, and returned with glasses and a bottle. She wouldn't let Kaspar help; a pity, for he was curious to see what the inside of the house looked like. Not bothering with a tablecloth – 'I like this old stone, you can give it a good scrubbing' – she brought out a loaf of bread, goat cheese and tomatoes. On the rough whitish-grey slab everything looked more appetizing than on a tablecloth. Finally she appeared balancing four skewers of shish-kebab.

'Two leaves. Big ones.'

Kaspar obediently pulled off two sunflower leaves, and the skewers rested against the dark green background, like a model for still life. And the smell! He discovered – incredulously at first – that the expression 'to make the mouth water' could be taken literally.

Frau Bogdan withdrew one last time. Now she'll put on a dress and comb her hair, thought Kaspar, but she quickly reappeared in her bikini, the brown flesh overwhelming, her long black hair half dry now and straggly, carrying a three-branched silver candlestick. No need to light the candles yet, it was still dusk. He sat down beside her on the bench and traced the intricate design of the silver with his finger.

'Like it? A wedding present. From my first marriage. *Nazdravje!*'

The slivovitz was tossed back in one gulp while he hesitantly reached for the shishkebab, which was dripping grease on to the stone.

'Napkins?'

She tore off more leaves, wrapped one around the end of her skewer and bit into chunks of meat and bacon.

'Good?'

He nodded, watching her greedy, white puppy-dog's teeth. They ate in silence and he soon learned how to toss the slivovitz down his throat the way she did, without letting the glass touch his lips, and only becoming aware of the taste a second or two after the burning sensation in his mouth.

From time to time, below the rolled-up sleeve, her bare arm touched his. Everything she did seemed unintentional and at the same time deliberate.

Goat cheese, with crumbs all over the table; tomatoes, whose juice stained the stone red; more slivovitz. Never in his life, not even when he was a little boy poaching in next door's strawberry bed, had anything tasted so good.

A smell of coffee. He hadn't noticed that she had gone to fetch cups. Cigarettes. This was the only thing she would allow him to contribute. They leaned back against the wall of the house, smoking and drinking the thick, strong coffee. It was suddenly getting dark and she lit the candles. All at once the world around them vanished, except for the round stone table, luminous in the candlelight. The air was warm and still; the sunflowers began to release their scent.

222

They smoked the first cigarette in silence, as they had eaten and drunk. As she bent forward to light her second one at the candle, he thought nothing could prevent her breasts from popping out of the fabric like two brown rubber balls, but they rolled back again in good order.

'Well,' she said, crumbling up the remains of the bread and scattering it on the ground. 'Come on. Tell me. What are you doing here? What's it all about?'

Without a moment's hesitation, and perfectly at ease, he told her the whole story in proper order, starting with Martha's death on 10 May 1977. It seemed as natural as talking to himself. Not until the end, when he came to the porter's cubicle and the black cross commemorating the dead night clerk, did she interrupt.

'Draza?'

He looked at her in surprise. 'You knew him?'

She hesitated, staring for a moment into the darkness above the half-burned candles before she spoke: 'Better let Ante tell you about Draza. He knows all the details of how it happened.'

'How what happened?' He bent forward and stared at her.

She shook her head and said quietly: 'Ante will tell you. He'll be here tomorrow for certain.' She saw the disappointment in his eyes, smiled and put her hand on his arm. 'It can wait till tomorrow, can't it?'

He nodded, looking at the brown fingers resting on his arm. 'Where's your husband? Vlada said . . . .'

'My husband's a truck driver. Long distance. He goes to Germany, too, he's hardly ever here. Too bad, my children get along better with him than with me.' In answer to his unasked question, she went on. 'Politics. That's the cause of hatred in many families. Don't you know that in Germany? My son and my daughter don't want anything to do with the Ustasha. My daughter's a nurse in Ljubljana and the boy – well, you've seen for yourself. My husband, my present husband, he's anti-Ustasha, too. We've had some real knockdown fights about it.'

'Why did you marry him?'

She removed her hand from his arm, stubbed out her cigarette and threw it in a wide arc into the darkness. 'Bed,' she said flatly. 'And because he was nice to the children. And he was earning good money. And . . . I was scared at the time. Ljuba was only a few months old and I thought they might come back for me. I had quite a bit of inside information, naturally. Basically, though, I simply didn't care. When Karel disappeared, everything was finished for me. Time went by and I was slowly dying – inside, I mean. Outwardly everything went on, I ate, nursed the baby, but inside, I died a bit every day, every day that he didn't come back. No one knew where he was, whether he was alive or long dead, or whether day after day they were still . . .' She stopped for a moment and reached for another cigarette. 'That's the worst thing, not knowing. Dead is dead and there's nothing to do except try to make a fresh start. But to this day I don't know . . . that is, I do know that he's dead, of course, but I don't know when and how. You try living with that! And then Bogdan came along, an old Tito supporter, and I thought: they'll never touch *him*, we'll be safe with him.' After a moment's silence she murmured: 'That's why.'

The candles burned slowly down, the wax forming little peaks on the long-suffering stone underneath. One had already burned out; the others stood stiff and unflickering.

'Can I help you carry some of this back to the kitchen?'

'No. I don't want to go back indoors yet.'

'Neither do I,' said Kaspar, taking hold of a handful of her hair and drawing her towards him. And then he did what he had been wanting to do all evening: unfastened the bra of her bikini, freeing the brown rubber balls. They settled gratefully into his hands, overflowing them.

'Wait,' said Mariana, standing up and leading the way into the sunflower jungle. The dying candlelight flickered over her bare brown back, disappearing between the tall bushy plants and their yellow and black flower-plates. The last candle went out and she vanished.

'Here,' she called from somewhere in the darkness. 'This way.'

He groped his way forward, the huge, rough leaves scratching his face and the thick stems blocking his way.

'Here.' A hand groped for him and pulled him to the ground. It was quite soft. He felt around and recognized the outlines of a mattress.

'When do you have to be at work?'

'At ten.'

'That gives us an hour then.'

CHAPTER SEVEN

MOABIT, 15 SEPTEMBER 1914: *I haven't written anything for a long time; it's not worth the trouble. There's a war on out there, and I'm ashamed to mess up a sheet of paper with what goes on here. As a matter of fact nothing at all goes on here. You can't tell one day from another. I paste my paper bags together, give the chaplain chess lessons and he gives me the newspaper and I read it from start to finish. But I'm losing my talent, playing against that idiot, and that's no joke.*

Mother's been to see me twice. She brings Andros along so she won't cry afterwards when she goes home alone. I always tell her I'm fine. She can see it for herself, I've gained at least five pounds. No exercise! She says I'm pale. So what? These days people are dying like flies. She mentioned in passing that my brothers have come back and enlisted, Bernie in the infantry and that Leopold in the navy. Submarines.

Kaspar put down the folder. Submarines? His father had never breathed a word about that. The navy, yes. He remembered writing on his Hitler Youth application form: 'During the First World War my father was a lieutenant in the navy.'

And where have they been all these months? Mother was quite calm about it, but Andros got into a rage. 'They hid until the trial was over, and then they sent a letter, postmarked Danzig, saying they'd be back soon and they were doing fine.' Dirty bastards! Then they came to see Mother in Landshut, both of them in uniform. Nobody dared to say anything. I looked at Mother, but her face was quite calm. Well, what was she supposed to do? Turn in her own sons?

MOABIT, 3 OCTOBER 1914: *Today the chaplain told me I'm going to get a two-months remission on my sentence. He plays quite a decent game now. The other day I let him win because I wanted a bottle of brandy, and he pranced around the room in his long black nightshirt like a kid. I've taken to brandy and it helps. I read the newspaper every day. Our boys are doing pretty well against the French. I wonder if Lisa's husband is out there.*

MOABIT, 3 NOVEMBER 1914: *Mother came to see me yesterday. It's a* long journey from Landshut, but she insists on doing it. Andros didn't come with her, he's in the hospital in Stuttgart with pneumonia. It worries me. He's like a brother to me, a big brother. Ida came with Mother to carry the basket of eggs and butter and jam. It always makes me laugh to see her, and she laughs when she sees me. She gave me a kiss with her duck's beak across the table and the guard only grinned, didn't make a fuss. It's good for Mother to have Ida quacking about the house.

MOABIT, 10 NOVEMBER 1914: I knew it: Andros is dead. All the same, when I got Mother's letter, I cried and cried. She wrote that she laid a wreath on his 'graive' from me. Now, when I get out in January, I'll have no one left except Mother and Ida.

I can't stop thinking about that ribbon with all the medals around the machine, and about the shouting and the applause – have to pinch myself to be sure it was me inside there. And now I'm sitting here on my bunk, in my striped prison suit! Not that I miss that damn box. Good riddance to it. I'd rather stay here in my cell than crawl back in there. That's all water under the bridge. And though I take a little brandy before going to the chaplain's office every evening, it's all I can do not to get sick when I sit in front of that black and white chessboard. The chaplain knows it, too, he's not that stupid. Now I really have to put my mind to it and watch what I'm doing or the half-wit might beat me fair and square!

MOABIT, 12 DECEMBER 1914: Not long now till the first wartime Christmas. Everyone says it will be the first and the last. The big push will come in spring and then we'll really let them have it. When I think about Grandet, I can't wait. Okay, I'm small – not only in stature.

But the war aside – what am I going to do when I get out? Who'll provide me with paper bags to paste together?

MOABIT, 1 JANUARY 1915: I'm having more and more fun here. Last night we celebrated New Year with beer and doughnuts and lit the candles on the Christmas tree again. And then we sang! Someone was playing the piano and when he opened with the national anthem, I suddenly saw that parrot with its parasol and Paul, the old butler at the Yussupoff Palace, goggle-eyed with wonder . . . And I started to laugh and to cry, all at the same time, and they got quite alarmed and laid me flat on the floor. And then the guard poured some brandy down my throat and that brought me around.

MOABIT, 12 JANUARY 1915: I'm not telling anyone, but I'm scared stiff about getting out. Mother came yesterday, in spite of the cold. It takes her *twelve hours by train from Munich. On the 31st she'll be waiting at the main entrance with a car and a chauffeur. 'Bring Ida along,' I said. 'She's more important than a chauffeur. And no sobstuff or I'm staying here.'*

MOABIT, 25 JANUARY 1915: *What is there to write? I'm scared absolutely shitless, can't sleep. The chaplain has no idea, he's 'so happy for me'. Plays a damn good game of chess now, so good that he's entered a tournament. He asked me if I too would like to . . . I just shook my head. It was all I could do not to hit him, the poor fool.*

MOABIT, 30 JANUARY 1915: *It's driving me crazy. Everyone coming to congratulate me, shaking hands, picking me up, patting me. And the doctor and the warden with their good luck speeches and broad grins glued to their faces. I can never get a word out. Yes, yes, they say, brimming with sympathy, freedom calls.*

Freedom? For me it means loneliness.

That was the end of the Moabit diary, written in pencil on coarse grey paper, some of it barely legible. Next came some pages on different paper, white with a printed letterhead: 18 Gustav-Freytag-Strasse, Landshut, Lower Bavaria. That's right. That was the address young Kaspar, with the rucksack on his back, had been directed to – a house with a big garden. Herr Franz Schulte? No, he left years ago . . .

He closed the folder. Three a.m. Three hours to go until Alexis would come to relieve him. He checked the key rack. Empty – all his sheep safe in the barn. One last glance at Draza Rukovina's black cross – like a drowsy 'goodnight, sleep well' last thing at night, in the double bed – then he switched off the lamp on the stool and closed his eyes. He didn't want to sleep, just to sort things out a bit. Uncle Stilts on the right, Mariana in the sunflowers on the left. The dwarf was standing outside the main entrance to the prison. 'Mother', a small figure in black, and Ida-the-duck were getting into an old Daimler-Benz. A diminutive Uncle Stilts followed them. A chauffeur in a peaked cap closed the door and ran jerkily at top speed around the car to the driver's seat, like people in early newsreels, where everybody hurtled about, gesticulating wildly. Then the car rolled away down a long, long avenue. Rolled away. Uncle Stilts was rolling away . . . Mariana stayed, although he couldn't see her in the darkness. He could feel her, though, there on the mattress, between the tall sunflower plants, herself a soft mattress that you could burrow yourself into.

He had no illusions. Both those mattresses had spent a good deal of time out there. The harder one probably stayed out the whole summer long, until the sunflowers rotted and fell to pieces. The other one, the brown, sweet-smelling one, probably came and went. Often? Occasionally? Did it really matter? He heard himself heave a long, deep sigh in the darkness.

The next day he took himself in hand: he would not go to her house before the evening, he wouldn't even walk along the track and look down into the courtyard. Perhaps she was sitting there now on the steps, plucking a goose or stoning plums . . .

She had said tomorrow, after seven. After all, he'd come here specially to see Luburic. What had he wanted to ask him? It didn't really matter much any more.

Lying in the rowing-boat in the shade, he accepted the fact that nothing mattered except Mariana, accepted it with his eyes wide open. She's an old whore and I'm starved, and we just happen to fit, that's all. Strange, because all that fat really revolts me. Yes, it revolts me – but at the same time it attracts me, because it doesn't give a damn for me, all that fat, couldn't care less whether I like it or not. Martha and Heidi and all the others, the odd here-and-there ones, were what I chose for myself, 'my type', slim, clean, gentle. I knew exactly where I was with them. But where am I with Mariana? I'm cast up somewhere on an island, I don't speak the language, I'm without defence. But I've never felt so well in all my life.

He looked at the time: two hours and twenty minutes to go.

A fresh pile of plums. She kept on stoning them but nodded to him with a smile as he made his way down the steps. He wanted to put his arms around her, but she pointed with her knife towards the well. He sat down and lit a cigarette.

'What do you do with all those plums?'

'Slivovitz.'

'You make your own slivovitz? Here at home?'

'I'm famous for my slivovitz. You tasted it yesterday, remember?' She lifted her head, narrowing her eyes. 'Here comes Ante.'

Kaspar got up and scanned the cart track. 'Where? I can't see anyone, only a peasant woman in the distance.'

'That's him.' Kaspar looked so aghast that she laughed. 'How do you think he manages to come and go? The head of the Ustasha! With a price of two and a quarter million dinars on his head. All they know around here, the neighbours, is that my aunt from Ljubljana comes to visit me from time to time.'

The peasant woman approached slowly, carrying a large, obviously heavy plastic shopping bag in her left hand. Her right hand was out of sight, clutching her black shawl.

'Shall I help him carry it?'

'No.'

In the short time it took Luburic to reach the house, it struck Kaspar that the trips to the sunflower jungle were over. For him, not for Mariana. As he watched the cart track, she had never taken her light, slanting eyes off him. Now she smiled and said: 'Ante and I are friends. Just good friends now, nothing else.'

He turned towards her, searched her smile but remained unsure. The island, he thought; I don't know my way around here. The invisible dog began to bark furiously.

The peasant woman's long skirt made it difficult for her to negotiate the steep, wobbly steps down to the courtyard. When she got to the bottom, she was panting and set the plastic shopping bag on the ground for a moment, then picked it up again and walked slowly towards them. Halfway across the courtyard she stood still.

'Professor!'

'Professor?' Mariana stopped stoning the plums and stared at Kaspar. He had told her only that he taught Slavic languages. 'Shut up, Nero,' she shouted over her shoulder and the dog stopped at once.

Luburic came closer. Under the black shawl his face was fiery red from the heat and dark with embarrassment. 'I'm going inside,' he said curtly to Mariana, and added to Kaspar: 'You come with me.'

Kaspar glanced at Mariana, who was smiling and looking at him curiously. She nodded encouragement and he entered her house for the first time. The old stable had been partitioned off into rooms, which still retained a pleasant smell of horses, in spite of the whitewash. The room that opened on to the courtyard probably served as the living-room. A large peasant wardrobe, three rickety armchairs in loose chintz covers, a low table, and a lamp. On the floor in a corner Kaspar saw Martinac's typewriter.

Luburic propped the shopping bag carefully against the wardrobe, threw his spectacles on the table and tore off first his head scarf and then his wig, a pepper and salt one with a centre parting and a bun at the back. Kaspar picked it up and looked at it attentively in order to let Luburic get out of the long skirt unobserved.

'I wouldn't have recognized you even if I'd been sitting next to you in the bus.'

Taking a towel from the wardrobe, Luburic dried off his face, neck and arms, stood there in his trousers, his powerful chest bare, and roughly kicked the shabby woman's shoes under the sofa.

'We have a good wigmaker. Used to be with the Belgrade State Theatre. I've got some more of them here.' He lifted the frill of the loose-cover of one of the chairs and pulled out a cardboard box. 'This one's very becoming,' he said without a smile, holding up a short, curly red wig. 'This one . . .' – he picked up a straight, dark one – 'this is the way I used to look. Now I wear a beard with it. But the grey one's the safest when the going gets tough.'

'Is it tough now?'

Luburic nodded, sat down and motioned to Kaspar to do the same. 'It's going to stay that way, too. Watch out! That chair sometimes collapses.' He shut his eyes, his face still crimson, and took several deep breaths. 'Are you on vacation? Or did Vlada send you? Is anything wrong?'

'No, no. Everything's all right. She just told me where I could find you – *might* find you.'

'What can I do for you, Professor?'

'Herr Luburic, did you know Draza Rukovina?'

The man opened his eyes. For a second there was a baffled and then a threatening gleam in the black eyes – then the curtain fell again. 'You mean the night porter at the Godice? Yes, I knew him. Since my childhood. Everyone around here knew him.' Polite and impersonal.

With a smile Kaspar sprang his surprise: 'I'm the night porter at the Godice now.'

The effect was quite different from what he had expected. Luburic jumped up, stared at him, went over to the open door and glanced quickly at Mariana, singing over her plums. Then he closed and bolted the door and leaned against it, as though barring somebody's way. Kaspar, bewildered, waited for an explanation.

When none was forthcoming and Luburic just continued to stare at him in silence, he took a packet of cigarettes from his pocket, hesitated, then offered him one. Luburic ignored it; his head was lowered like a bull about to charge.

'Why are you the night porter at the Godice, Professor?' In a low, hostile voice. 'Who sent you?'

'No one sent me. I don't understand what you're talking about.' He saw Luburic quietly put his left hand in his trouser pocket. 'Herr Luburic, I don't *understand*. . . .'

'Why are you the night porter at the Godice? Come on, tell me. And be quick about it.' Curt and quiet and threatening, as the hand withdrew the gun from the pocket.

Behind him a knock on the door. 'Open up, Ante. It's getting dark, I want to come in.'

Without taking his eyes off Kaspar, Luburic opened the door and Mariana appeared, carrying the preserving pan of plums. She stopped in surprise midway between the two men, looking from one to the other.

'What's going on here, Ante?'

'Did you know? Did he tell you?'

'Idiot! Of course he told me. Put that thing away and open the kitchen door.'

Kaspar jumped and took the preserving pan from her and she allowed him to follow her into the little room that served as her kitchen. It was surprisingly clean and tidy. An old gas range, a sink, a cupboard for dishes, and a big wooden table. She set down the plums and returned at once to the living-room, where she dropped into the third chair and reached for one of Kaspar's cigarettes.

'Relax, Ante. Everything's all right. I'll explain it all when you have time. Pure chance, the whole thing.' As Kaspar bent down to give her a light, she patted his cheek, half tenderly, half mockingly. 'Don't worry, he won't hurt you as long as I'm around.' She inhaled, laughed and shook her head. 'Chance! There is such a thing, you know, Ante. Only we've forgotten about it, you and I and – our people. Tell me, is he really a professor?'

'He's Professor of Slavic Languages at the University of Munich.'

'I *was*,' interrupted Kaspar. 'Now I'm a night porter. And now I'd like to know what's so strange about that.'

'Explain it to him, Ante.'

'Did he ask you about Draza?'

'I promised you'd tell him. You seem to know him, after all.' She gave Kaspar an amused, searching glance and tapped the cigarette ash into her hand. 'If I'd known he was a real professor, I'd never have taken him into the sunflowers.'

Kaspar was horrified to feel his face burning, but Luburic only shrugged, sat down and muttered, 'I've got to leave again tonight. Until then, he stays here. In the sunflowers for all I care, but he's to stay here. You're the one who would pay for it. It's your decision.' They talked past him, as if he weren't around.

Mariana stopped laughing, looked straight ahead and remained silent for a moment. Then she said slowly: 'I don't think he knows anything. If I'm wrong, it'll serve me right, but I trust my nose. Have you had anything to eat? The goose must hang a little longer. There isn't much, a few eggs and cheese.'

'I brought some sausages.'

Luburic got up and slowly undid the shopping bag. The sausages were right on top. Mariana took them from him; then she peered intently into the plastic wrapper, inspecting the rest of the contents without touching them, nodded approval, and left the room. With great care Luburic picked up the bag – either hand grenades or ammunition, thought Kaspar – and hoisted it into the wardrobe. Then he went back to his chair, his head drooping between his broad shoulders as it used to do in Munich when he confronted German grammar.

A moment of reflection, then quite matter-of-factly: 'Did Alexis hire you? Did he mention Draza? What did he say?'

'He said he found him himself, in the early morning of 10 May 1977. A heart attack. Quite peaceful.'

'I see. Quite peaceful. Is that what he said?'

Kaspar stared at him. A long roll of ash fell from his cigarette on to the wooden floor.

'Watch out! We have to be careful about fire in summer,' said Luburic, bending down and neatly sweeping the little pile of ash into his gloved hand. 'Did he mention the empty bottle of wine on the stool? Though it's possible that it had disappeared by the time Alexis got there. All tidily cleared away, the bottle and the glass too, by a fellow called Petric, a waiter.'

'Petric? There's no waiter by that name at the Godice.'

'He gave notice soon afterwards. You must know Bruno, the kitchen-boy in the white cap. His father was shot by the UDBA.

Bruno saw the bottle, but he didn't dare to say anything, he was only fifteen at the time.'

'What was in the bottle, Herr Luburic?' A silly question, and Luburic ignored it.

'Draza was our man at the Godice. The UDBA liquidated him. Child's play for them.'

Kaspar smiled and put the cigarette to his lips. His hand was shaking.

'Do you find that amusing, Professor?'

Kaspar shook his head. 'You were right, Herr Luburic, somebody did send me to you. My uncle, the dwarf. Remember? He's dead. But – well, he helped you make your getaway, so to speak, didn't he? So I thought maybe *you* would help *me*. I've just been telling him about the bottle of red wine . . .' He stopped. Once again Luburic was staring at him, full of suspicion, this time no doubt because he was convinced – and not without reason – that he was out of his mind. That could be dangerous, too.

'Why did Alexis pick on you, Professor?'

'It was my idea, I needed a job. As porter I can make use of my languages. Is Alexis a UDBA man?'

'I don't know. Nobody does. The Godice's always been a hotbed of political activity even as far back as the early thirties, when we still had a king. He had his police agents in the hotel – his summer palace was right opposite it, on the other side of the lake; it's a hospital now. When the war began, the Nazis took over the Godice, and then came our Nazis – oh yes, we had our own Nazis, you know, they collaborated with Hitler under the leadership of a fellow called Ante Pavelic. Then Tito came along and threw them all out – except for Draza. All through the Pavelic regime Draza had been Tito's contact in the hotel. Passed him a lot of information – after all, he was sitting right at the source. Messages would be dropped through the ventilator into the porter's cubicle at night. No one ever suspected anything. Draza took care of everybody, or so it seemed, Nazis and Tito-Communists alike. It's an ideal position to work from, first for the night messages, and then in the daytime Draza could watch the guests coming and going, knew who was in his room when, who ordered a taxi and where to. Later, when Tito betrayed us and established the People's Republic of Yugoslavia, Draza quietly came over to us. *He* remained a Croat.'

Luburic's voice became almost inaudible, as it always did when something really stirred him. 'He wanted to leave, along with the rest of us émigrés, but we wouldn't let him. His position at the Godice was invaluable.' He remained silent for a while, brooding. 'He did a great job for us for years, promoted dozens of our – er, operations, without anyone ever suspecting him. But in April 1977, he went too far. The former director of the Zagreb power company was found in his room at the Godice, hanging from the ceiling by his necktie. He'd been head of the Zagreb UDBA for years, a man much hated. He'd just retired and planned to take things easy from now on, starting with a few weeks' quiet vacation in Bled. Draza couldn't resist it, although I was against it; I'm not in favour of revenge, what good does it do? But there were a few people who had permanent mementos to remember the bastard by, and messages came fluttering into Draza's cubicle. I have to admit, some of the mementos were unforgettable, and the people who sent the messages had been waiting for this chance for years . . . But Draza had to pay for it, he'd lost his head, quite irresponsible: he was the only person with a second key to every room. He was "asleep" when our people entered the lift one night and he didn't wake up when they left again a short time later. But, as I say, he had to pay for it. Two weeks later he was so fast asleep that he never woke up again.'

After a while Kaspar said: 'Now I know why Alexis says he can't find a replacement for him. He doesn't want one.'

'Perhaps. That would mean that he knows. Now he's hired you because he thinks you don't belong to either side.'

'He's quite right there,' said Kaspar.

'But where do your sympathies lie, Professor?'

'Does it matter?'

Luburic studied him in silence, thoughtfully flipping his black rubber fingers back and forth. 'Do you sleep in the deckchair, Professor? All night long?'

'Generally. I read my uncle's diary or I sleep.'

'While you're reading, have you ever heard the nightingale singing in the beech tree in front of the hotel?'

'I've never noticed it.'

'There's no nightingale and no beech tree either, just a large oleander bush.' The black fingers flipped rapidly back and forth, making a sound like somebody smacking his lips. It was getting on Kaspar's nerves.

'Herr Luburic, I'm not a child, I'm not interested in playing games. I'm sorry – it was a mistake to track you down.'

Luburic's face twisted into a wry, ironic smile. 'But you found a consolation prize in the sunflowers, didn't you?' And then quickly: 'I don't know why I said that. Please forget it. I have no right to interfere in your private affairs, and no intention of doing so.'

Kaspar didn't answer. Luburic brooded. When he looked at Kaspar again, his eyes were calm once more and concentrated.

'I have no time for games either. The oleander bush is important. Have you ever paid any attention to the chirping? Think back now, a high-pitched chirp every ten seconds or so?'

'Could be. Why?'

'That's our people. They know, of course, that there's a new night porter at the Godice – I got the message myself in Ljubljana.' He fished a note out of his pocket. ' "Tall, thin, reserved. Speaks fluent German. Suspicious." '

Kaspar had to laugh. 'And they chirp to see if the night porter will answer?'

'They'll leave you alone from now on. They'll be very surprised when I tell them who's behind the desk. They know all about you, of course, they know about our – disagreement in Munich, remember? But they also know that you didn't denounce us and that you rescued Miklos. He's still safe with the Danish girl at Kaiserplatz. So we're quits. But now! Night porter at the Godice – is that suspicious or is it promising?' The last word searching, almost beseeching.

'Neither. Pure chance.' Kaspar stood up and looked at the time. 'Herr Luburic, I go on duty at ten o'clock. Sorry, but I can't wait until you leave this house.' He calmly rolled down his shirt sleeves and buttoned them with care. Luburic never took his eyes off him, unable to make up his mind. 'If you really think I'm going to report your whereabouts to the UDBA or anybody else – you know what to do about it.'

Luburic got up and opened the kitchen door. 'Mariana, he's going back to the hotel.'

'Let him go,' she called back. 'He's going to miss some good sausages.'

The man closed the kitchen door, slowly crossed the room and took the key out of his pocket. 'I don't like it. I'll be safe, but she'll still be here.'

235

'Do you want me to give you my word of honour, or swear to it, or look you in the eye, or something?'

Luburic stepped right up to him, his black eyes naked and threatening. 'What did you want from me? Why did you come here?'

'It doesn't matter any more, but if it will reassure you, I'll tell you: I'm on the run, a deserter, absent without leave. I didn't know a soul outside Germany except you. You made a deep impression on my uncle in those few minutes, and he wasn't an easy man to impress. I didn't know that I would find a place to stay so quickly. I'm working – and I've found Mariana. Now I don't need help any more.'

Luburic stepped back and inserted the key in the lock. Then he turned around again. 'Professor, I'm not going to apologize. In our organization we can't make mistakes and we can't make exceptions either. We have no elbow-room, barely enough breathing space to keep going. You said just now that you're not a child any more. It seems to me you're still a child – in one respect, though, I repeat, it's no concern of mine.' Turning the key, he stepped out into the darkness. 'The sunflowers over there are drying out. When it begins to get cold, they'll fall to pieces. Most of them are so woody they're used for kindling. Think about that – firewood!'

He moved aside and Kaspar walked past him to the steps leading up to the cart track. Strange: when one *left* the house, the dog didn't bark.

CHAPTER EIGHT

LANDSHUT, 4 JUNE 1920: *It's a long time since I wrote anything. Why do I write at all? Nobody's going to read it, but perhaps it will amuse me later, in my old age. I've just turned thirty, not so young any more, but I look even older. Never any fresh air. The box, prison – I'm never out of doors. Not even nowadays. Don't want the people here gaping at me: they all still know me, of course. I just can't take it, can't take friendliness, company, playing chess with someone else. Chess is absolutely out . . . I knew it all along: pasting up paper bags, now –* that was the life!

LANDSHUT, 10 JULY 1920: *If I didn't have Ida to make me laugh, I believe I'd take to crime just to get sent back to prison.*

Mother's very quiet since she received the news about Bernie. At first they told her he'd get over it, but now they've admitted that that's not true. Mother visits him once a month in the military hospital in Munich, but he doesn't recognize her. You couldn't tell from looking at him, she says. His hair's grown back in and it hides the hole in his skull; still, it's a brain injury and there's nothing to be done about it. That Leopold came through all right, spent the whole war in Italy. Now he's in Trieste, studying engineering. Mother sends him money. He writes that he's engaged to a German girl, but he doesn't want to get married until he gets his diploma. His money's all gone. Inflation. Serves him right. It was my *money anyhow, he embezzled it.*

But Mother! Ehrenreich was right when he called her a genius. She got all her money out into Switzerland long before the war. Why? 'I don't rightly know,' she said. 'But I like the look of those people in Zurich. They're God-fearing and strict, and the money'll be in good hands there. I don't trust that Kaiser Wilhelm – he's too loud.' It's unbelievable. A genius!

LANDSHUT, 3 SEPTEMBER 1920: *I'm only writing this down because every story needs an ending: Lisa showed up. I said I was sorry but I was busy. So did Mother. Ida panted up and down while the 'lady in black' sat and waited downstairs. She refused to leave 'without having achieved her purpose' and in the end she took Ida into her confidence. She wanted to* make it absolutely clear that she'd known nothing about the knife. Ida's duck-eyes nearly popped out of her head. What knife? But Lisa wouldn't explain. She said she'd come only to make sure that I was aware of that. She had known nothing about it, her conscience was clear. So far as she knew, they were just going to give me 'some sort of lesson I wouldn't forget', a beating or something of the kind. Ida didn't know what to make of it. From upstairs I could hear her quacking excitedly: Beatings? Knives? A lesson? Then there was a long pause and Lisa said that her husband had been killed in the battle of the Somme – 'Oh dear, oh dear!' cried Ida, to be on the safe side – and that she now had a 'feeansay'. 'Whatever that may be,' said Ida, reporting the conversation.

Then she left. I watched her from the window. She's got fat.

LANDSHUT, APRIL 1921: A long time since I wrote anything. Don't think I'll go on keeping a diary. What's the use? There's not a thing about my life worth recording. What do I do all day? Nothing, believe it or not. Now and again I play chess by myself the way I did twenty years ago, only without the dialogue and the jumping around. I don't have to put myself on a pedestal any more, I've had it all, enough for a whole lifetime. The only thing I still hanker after is a woman. Sometimes I buy one. When I get home afterwards, Mother and Ida pretend not to notice. But I'd like to have something to love. Maybe a dog.

LANDSHUT, 21 NOVEMBER 1921: I feel an urge to write again because Mother's sick and I dread what may lie ahead. She insisted on digging up the last of her cabbages in spite of the snow, and now she's in bed with pneumonia. It's always pneumonia. I sit at one side of her bed and Ida at the other.

LANDSHUT, 23 NOVEMBER: Today she whispered: 'I've had a good life, laddie. Remember that. And the blessed Lord saw to it that you were the one to make it so. You've been my treasure all along. I'm content, you be content too. Don't go hanging around my grave, because I won't be there. I'll be here sitting right beside you, you'll see.'

LANDSHUT, 29 NOVEMBER: I didn't cry at the funeral. I thought about what she'd said: that she won't be there in the cemetery, she'll be waiting for me at home. Now I'm at home, waiting for her. She still hasn't come. The house is empty. Ida cries and cries. We have our meals together, she's a good cook.

That Leopold came to the cemetery. I recognized him right away. He was standing at the back, with a young woman beside him, tall, quite pretty, *with a pinched look on her face. Don't know why he should have come, it certainly wasn't to see me. Maybe on account of the inheritance?*

LANDSHUT, 25 DECEMBER 1921: *First Christmas without Mother. This year Ida baked the lebkuchen and trimmed the tree. She's a whole lot smarter than I thought, I like living with her, she never bothers me. In the evening I turn on the radio and get out my chessboard and she sits close by, knitting and watching me. When she's not talking, she doesn't look half bad; only when she speaks, she pushes her mouth out and squawks away. It still makes me laugh.*

The house belongs to me now. Mother left it to me as sole heir because that Leopold and Bernie had helped themselves to their share before. She also left a sealed letter, addressed to me, giving the number of the Swiss bank account and stating that upon her death it would automatically be transferred to my name. So I'm pretty well off. But she still hasn't come to sit beside me.

Kaspar rationed the last few pages of the diary and only read at night, around three a.m., when all the keys were gone from the board. He read them very slowly, sometimes putting the pages aside and switching off the lamp to get a better look at his father and mother standing by the grave, his mother 'quite pretty, but with a pinched look'.

He slept in his deckchair until Alexis arrived. During the day he rowed on the lake, lay under a tree in the shade – he had bought a bicycle – read, and slept for a few hours, waiting for six o'clock. Then he rode back to the hotel and walked along the shore, through the town, and down the cart track to her house, to be greeted by the invisible dog. When it was raining, he would find her stretched out on the narrow bed in her tiny bedroom – where did her husband sleep? – her arms folded behind her head, naked, eyes closed. The radio would be playing rock music, and he would stand in the doorway, watching her lying there and singing away. Until she noticed him and opened her arms.

End of October. Late autumn. The leaves were turning – they came dancing down on him as he lay under his tree. It was still warm and the mattress was still out of doors, but the sunflowers were starting to bend; some had already fallen over.

'They stink,' said Mariana. 'Tomorrow I'm going to pull them up.'

'Oh, leave them,' said Kaspar. 'Give them a few more days. I'm attached to them.'

It rained the whole of the next day, but then the sun came out and they sat outside again and ate supper by candlelight. A battlefield of slain sunflowers lay on the ground, their whitish-green stems splintered, their huge leaves torn and blackish. The round, once velvety faces looked like empty honeycombs, with a few late ants and flies scrabbling about over them.

'Are you going to use them for kindling, the sunflowers?'

'Too late, they're rotten now. Tomorrow I'll dig them up.'

Kaspar was pleased. Not firewood! Next year he'd be able to watch the new ones growing . . .

Only eight o'clock. It grew dark early now, he still had plenty of time. Mariana was sitting close beside him, wearing a long skirt and a woollen shawl, smoking one of his cigarettes and staring into the darkness. All day long she laughed and sang, but at night, whether here on the terrace or in his arms, she was silent. Was this a good moment? Probably not. Probably she saw Karel more plainly in the dark than in the daylight. But when would be a good moment?

'I want to tell you something, but it's not easy for me, I simply don't know how to put it. Maybe it's something that ought to be left unsaid.'

She turned her head and smiled at him, and this gave him courage.

'It would be much easier to confess to you that I'm unhappy. How do I describe how happy I am in a way that will make you believe me? I have no way of proving it. Only when I look at myself in the mirror, it seems to me that I look quite different now. Can you see it too? No? I know I'm being ridiculous – I'm perfectly aware of it – but this has been on my mind for so long that I've simply got to tell you about it. *It's* on my mind – and *you're* on my mind, every waking minute. I suppose because – and I realize that you won't believe it – because it never happened to me before, never ever. Everything revolves around how much longer I have to wait before I can come over here to you. Now maybe you'll understand why I'm sorry the sunflowers have to go. Suddenly everything has acquired a meaning. I want to hold on to even the most casual thing as long as it's in any way connected with you – I want to keep it alive – and preserve it . . .'

He stopped because she had got up and gone into the house. She quickly returned with a little glass dish, which she placed on the table. 'Here. I've picked out the sunflower seeds. They'll keep all winter. You take half and eat one every day, and I'll do the same with the rest.'

'Does that mean . . . ?'

She shook her head. 'It means that I want to share everything with you, except your feelings. That is, I want to share the feelings, too, but I can't, and you know why I can't. If Karel had died in the ordinary way, then – I imagine – then I could, and would, risk it one more time. I've tried before, of course, and I failed every time. I mustn't fail with *you*. I've known everything you've just told me for quite some time. You're a bit backward in these things and all of a sudden it's hit you and you think you're ridiculous.' She shook her head slowly and seriously, her voice low and tender. 'I don't even trust myself to say "I love you", although you mean so much to me that it's hard to draw the line. But the other thing – what *you* feel – it's just not in me any more. Or rather something inside me resists it, it simply says no, and I can't fight it. Can you understand that?'

'It's much more than I expected,' he said slowly.

The months went by, the season was long over, but the guests kept coming, and over the Christmas holidays the hotel was booked out again because of the ski resort nearby.

There was nothing about his duties that he disliked. His days were full of things he enjoyed, although – or because – they made no demands on his mind. He found his night porter's chores as amusing as his 'authority' over the guests, some of whom he came to know quite well, and they never stayed long enough to bore him. He kept the hinged flap down, and, although he occasionally leaned over the counter, he never emerged from his box. Now and again somebody – usually young people, girls too – would ask him what he was doing on his day off, but he was never free. On that day, at six o'clock in the morning, he was already en route to the cart track. Mariana would still be sleeping in her tiny bedroom and never stirred when he undressed and lay down beside her on the sunflower mattress.

He enjoyed the early morning walk after his night stint, particularly in the depths of winter, when it was still dark and the snow creaked under his boots. During the day he never ceased to wonder that no one made any demands on him, that he didn't have to worry about or impress or keep up with anybody. Could it last? Could one just *live*, without ambitions, without goals? Was it possible for a person's mental metabolism to change so radically?

One thing he was sure of: as long as he had Mariana he didn't need anyone else. During his many solitary hours he would talk to Uncle Stilts, often aloud, and he wasn't even surprised when one day, as he was sitting all alone on a bench by the lake, trying to imitate Ida with her duck's beak, a little boy in a yellow rain cape appeared out of nowhere and cautiously inquired whether he felt all right.

Munich and the Institute, Heidi and the boys never entered his head. Never once did he wonder whether the baby had arrived and whether it was a boy or a girl. Not that he suppressed it; his thoughts simply didn't run in that direction, nor was he aware that this in itself might be considered peculiar.

It was Mariana who reminded him. Leaning on her spade – she was digging trenches for her spring vegetables – she looked at Kaspar squatting on the stone steps with his eyes closed, enjoying the first warm sunshine.

'A letter came from Munich yesterday.' She reached into the pocket of her garden apron. 'There's a message for you.'

The letter, typewritten, without a single 's', was from Luburic. Half a page that was unintelligible to him and then a new paragraph:

'Tell K.S. I think I saw his wife yesterday in the park. I don't know her, but two young men were with her and one of them was his younger son. The woman was pushing a pram.' That was all. He handed the letter back to Mariana and squatted down on the stone steps again.

'Do you think it was your wife?'

'Could be. Luburic knows my son by sight. He and Martinac once tailed him when they wanted to force me to let them use my apartment.'

'Yes, I heard about that, Ante told me. You can be quite obstinate when people try to push you around.'

'Yes,' he said calmly.

'Are you glad your wife and your son are friends?'

'I'm surprised.'

'Why?'

'He used to hate her.'

Mariana stuck her spade in the ground, wiped her hands on her apron and sat down beside him on the steps.

'Tell me about it. Or is it hard for you to talk about it?'

'It's hard, but not because it's painful.'

She thought for a minute, her elbows propped on her knees and her face in her hands.

'You're lucky, you know, you can erase personal feelings altogether when you want to.'

'So can you,' he said, stroking her head, with the long, straggly black hair. 'You erase your children, for example, and probably your husband, too. But you can't do it with Karel, right? I couldn't erase *you*, however much I tried.'

She nodded, asked no more questions, reached for the radio, and began to sing. There seemed to be a station that played rock music day and night.

Kaspar took the radio from her and turned it down. 'What does the first paragraph of Luburic's letter mean? All that about the spring weather and the river level? Is it some sort of Ustasha code?'

'He's working on something. Something complicated. Tito's not going to last much longer.'

'And what does Ante hope for when he dies?'

'That'll be our chance. Perhaps not immediately, but we have to be ready.'

'What is it that you want so much? What's so intolerable for you under the Tito regime?'

She sat up straight and clasped her hands around her knees.

'Did you know that Napoleon once said: "Give me a hundred thousand Croats and I'll conquer the whole world"? We're the most important – no, the *only* important nation in the Balkans. We're not "Balkan people", we're Slavs, but we have nothing in common with our neighbours, neither religion, nor language, nor character. We belong to the West.'

She paused and thought hard. Why do they want to belong to the West, thought Kaspar, is that in itself so desirable?

'Hard to define,' she said slowly. 'We're a people made up of contradictions. I'm a Croat and that alone explains something to me – about myself. Did you know that we were the first Christians in eastern Europe? And that a Turkish sultan, our most powerful enemy, ended up by falling so much in love with us – as a nation – that he chose a Croat for his chief vizier?'

'No, I didn't know that,' said Kaspar, 'but I admire his taste.'

She didn't respond to his tone. 'We've got to have a country of our own, an autonomous country. Our children must be taught to write in the Roman alphabet, not the Cyrillic, like the Russians. They must read Croatian, not Serbian books. We don't belong to the East.' She punched her knee with her fist and closed her eyes for a moment. 'Just take a look at our history: we're worse off than the Poles. They've been torn to pieces by the Russians and the Germans, but we've been invaded over and over again by the Italians, the Austrians *and* the Balkan nations, as if we were fair game for the taking. And now they lump us together with the Serbs and the Slovenes and call us Yugoslavs! For Tito, this is the solution to our problem. And, do you know, he's a Croat himself? Or at least he was, he's long forgotten it. Now he has other plans, "more significant" ones. But I can tell you one thing: they'll have to *outlaw* us as a nation before we'll give in.'

Kaspar lit another cigarette, thinking to himself: why is it so important whether you use the Roman or the Cyrillic alphabet? Is it worth dying for? Or, worse still, letting your whole life be dominated by that one viewpoint?

Suddenly a picture flashed across his mind, one of those images that get stuck in your head and keep popping up, at odd moments. How old could he have been? Twenty, perhaps. He was a student in Munich and it was night-time. A history book, the sixteenth century, one of those countless and senseless small wars, but this one's 'cause' was so outrageous that for him it had come to stand for fanaticism itself. The 'cause' of the war – not the event which precipitated it, but the *cause* – was the date of the Last Judgement. Did it take place immediately after death or would one have to wait patiently in one's grave for the appointed day to arrive? Both sides 'knew' the definitive answer, and thousands of people allowed themselves to be torn to pieces for the sake of that 'knowledge'. The young student had been amazed and horrified and had never forgotten that 'holy war'. '. . . for whom the bell tolls.' Whether proclaiming sense or nonsense, when it tolled, people came running.

Although he had not spoken a word and was just staring into space, Mariana said: 'You *can't* understand it. It's a kind of explosion in your brain and in your . . . in your soul, if you don't like the word "heart". You might ask: what do you people get out of it? Nothing. But there's no choice once it gets you by the throat.'

She spoke in a low voice and without emphasis, as if she had said the words many times. *That's* the barrier between us, he thought, not Karel.

She looked at him sideways, smiled and suddenly nudged his knees with her elbow, humming along with the radio, and snapping her fingers. Lesson over, thought Kaspar, and watched her for a moment before he spoke: 'Tell me, did it have you by the throat before Karel disappeared?'

She stopped humming. 'No, not till afterwards. I simply took over his mission. Out of love. But that counts, too. People like Ante, people that had the calling when they were still young kids – they're in it for love, too. Passion – that's what it is. But you can't inject people with it. I know. I've tried. I deliberately brought up my children as good Croats, made them aware of their obligation, explained that it was their sacred duty to follow in their father's footsteps . . .'

'And to avenge their father?'

She hesitated. 'Yes, that too, when they got older.' A pause. 'What I achieved was the exact opposite: they don't want anything to do with the Ustasha and they don't want to hear about their father. Once, when Milan was sixteen, he said: "I forbid you to ruin my life."'

'He was right,' said Kaspar, well aware of the risk he was taking. Perhaps now she would throw him out. But this was too important for him to keep silent.

She stared at him resentfully. 'What do you know about it?' He didn't reply but he held her eyes. After a while she said, calmer, and in a very low voice: 'It's possible that I can't look at it objectively any more. Once I was sure that Milan was a good kid, and maybe he still is. Oh, he's wild and he's often pretty nasty to me. But some day he'll make a Yugoslavian girl . . .' – she pronounced the word 'Yugoslavian' as if it were a synonym for 'orang-utan' – 'a good Yugoslavian husband. That's the way he wants it. But I live the way *I* want. He's important to me, but I'm even more important to myself.'

245

Kaspar nodded. Armistice. At least she hadn't thrown him out.

Early in July Mariana said she was worried about Luburic. It had been a hot day, they were lying exhausted on the mattress, among the second-generation sunflowers. This year it seemed to Kaspar that the stems were less stiff and erect and the flower discs fringed with yellow reminded him of dark children's faces. They had nothing of last year's crop of pride and mystery. Mariana said she was going to plant a different variety next year.

'I have had no news of him for six weeks.'

I have news of him, thought Kaspar. Aloud he said: 'Does he usually write regularly?'

'At least once a month. Or someone writes for him, but I recognize the typewriter.'

'No Ss.'

'Martinac told you? Martinac and his big mouth!'

'Did you like him?'

'He was fun. I like to laugh.' After a while she went on: 'Sometimes the Ustasha makes such blunders. Martinac as Ante's bodyguard! It's sheer luck that Ante's still alive.'

'Does he tell you what he's doing?'

'Never. They might take it into their heads to question me again some time. They never forget you completely. But I haven't heard from them in twenty years, and anyhow we were still living in Zagreb then.'

'Do they know about me?'

'If they're still interested in me, of course they do. But I think they have other things on their minds these days: Tito and who's going to succeed him. My love life isn't very interesting compared to that – I hope. Though, there's one suspicious coincidence: you're the night porter at the Godice. They might follow you about a bit and remember me . . . *Our* people have given up on you, on instructions from Ante.'

After a long pause Kaspar said: 'Not completely.'

Mariana sat up abruptly and tried to see his face through the darkness. 'How do you know?'

'I heard a chirping sound a few nights ago.'

'Did you answer?'

'Even if I wanted to, I wouldn't know how. But I don't want to.'

He could feel her breath on his face. 'You'd better know the answer: that lamp on the stool, switch it off and immediately back on.' She lay down again, then, in a fast, excited voice he had never heard her use before: 'I wonder if it had anything to do with Ante's silence. If you hear the chirping again, please answer. Promise.'

'Don't ask that of me, Mariana. It's not fair.'

'Fair! It's a matter of life and death. Can't you understand that?'

Whose life and whose death? He thought of the conversation he'd had with Alexis yesterday morning, when he'd relieved him.

'Ah, Schulte, wait a moment, will you.'

Kaspar had already ducked under the counter; now he leaned across it from the opposite side.

'Anything wrong, Herr Alexis?'

Leaning over his side of the counter to get as close as he could to Kaspar, the manager whispered in his ear: 'Please, Professor, do be sensible. Don't get yourself involved with them.'

Kaspar felt silly whispering back, but it was not impossible that the cubicle really was bugged. 'Who do you mean, Herr Alexis?'

Alexis pointed to the ventilator. 'You wouldn't last long. The others know everything that goes on here.'

'What do you mean by "the others", Herr Alexis?'

With a tired smile Alexis shook his head; then, in a barely audible whisper: 'Both sides. For me they're both "the others". And as far as I'm concerned, they can both go to the devil. Right now I am talking about the UDBA. Be sensible, stay out of it. That's what I do and that's why I'm still alive. Of course they know by now about your – er, visits to Frau Bogdan, but apparently they're convinced that it's a purely personal attraction. I know her and I think highly of her, but I wish you'd never laid eyes on her.'

Out of the darkness came Mariana's voice, quiet and matter-of-fact but unmistakably determined: 'Promise, Kaspar, or else you can't come here any more.'

'Are you still in love with Luburic?'

'My God, won't you ever understand? I'm in love with Karel. Karel is the Ustasha. If they make contact with you again, that

247

means they need you. *Karel* needs you. How can you lie here beside me and refuse to help him?'

At night he lay in his deckchair waiting. There was no point opening Uncle Stilts's diary. For that he needed the peace of mind and the isolation he had enjoyed for so many months, but which was now gone. He lay there and listened, and dealt with the hotel guests as briefly as possible, lending only half an ear to their requests and complaints. Again and again he asked himself what he should do if he heard the chirping again. He still hadn't decided – he hoped for the right kind of instinctive reaction when the time came. They certainly fight with ruthless passion, he thought, one side as much as the other. It's like the war over the date of the Last Judgement. Insane.

That night all remained quiet. In the early morning he walked along the cart track and went to sleep as usual next to Mariana's bed. When he woke up, her first question was: 'Well? Did you hear anything?'

He spent the day helping her to take the rusty old distiller apart and clean it, a complicated, foul-smelling job. They sat side by side on the stone steps; it was a warm, late autumn day. Mariana in her old bikini, Kaspar shirtless, his long torso deeply tanned. Their hands touched from time to time, as one of them held the various parts and the other cleaned them. She hummed her rock songs as usual, but he knew that there would be no trip to the sunflowers that evening.

A few days later, as he was about to leave the hotel after his night duty, it was pouring with rain. He hadn't brought his umbrella, but he didn't turn back. By the time he reached the cart track he was soaked to the skin, right through his denim jacket. Suddenly a man stepped out from the shelter of a beech tree and opened an umbrella. Kaspar could hardly see him through the curtain of rain, but he was sure it was no one he knew. He stopped.

'Schulte?' Kaspar took a step backwards. Leaping over a puddle, the man grabbed him by the arm. 'I'm Mariana's husband, Mirko Bogdan. She was sure you wouldn't have an umbrella.' Hesitant and faintly suspicious, Kaspar looked up into the friendly, grinning face. A giant of a man, like a bear, with a reddish moustache dripping with rain.

'Come on, man. Breakfast! We're all waiting for you.'

'All?'

'I've brought my daughter along – my stepdaughter. She's come to take a course at the hospital over there on the lake.'

Hesitantly Kaspar followed him. He didn't believe the story of the umbrella, yet the man was not hostile. He would have liked to say something to him, but what? Thank you for being concerned about me – and please forgive me for sleeping with your wife?

They trudged through the pouring rain in silence. Just before they reached his house, Bogdan stopped and stared fixedly at Kaspar out of sharp narrowed eyes. Kaspar stared back blankly.

'Listen here, Schulte: last night while you were on duty, I went to see my old friend Alexis. Why you're doing this – and you seem to be making a good job of it – is your own business. I suppose you're on the run for some reason. But you're trapped, man, even if you don't know it yet, caught down there in Mariana's kitchen. Don't get me wrong now, I don't give a damn what she's up to, I got over all that years ago. But Alexis says you're a good man, and that's why I'm standing here in the rain, trying to talk you out of it. I promised him I'd do it. He says the night music's started up again . . . know what I mean? So get the hell out of here, man. And move fast.'

He gave Kaspar no chance to answer, turned around and pulled him towards the gate.

For the first time the dog didn't bark. Bogdan's dog! Where did the animal live? He had asked Mariana, but she had just made a vague circular gesture. They slithered down the crooked, wet steps into the courtyard and saw her standing in the doorway.

'Here he is,' called Bogdan. 'But he needs a hot bath.'

A young girl appeared behind Mariana and looked at Kaspar out of shy, dark eyes as he took off his dripping jacket.

'This is Ljuba. She'll keep the coffee hot for you. Come on, man, I'll run you a bath.'

Kaspar stood still and looked questioningly at Mariana. She nodded, smiled, and waved him on.

When he returned to the kitchen, wearing Bogdan's huge bath-robe, his jeans had been hung above the stove to dry while the others had finished breakfast. At Bogdan's insistence, Ljuba, the daughter, scrambled some eggs for him. She was as dark-haired as her mother, but unattractive, her face angular with a flat nose and her upper lip too long.

While Kaspar ate, Bogdan kept him company. He was on the way to Ankara with a load and had made a detour via Bled to have his truck serviced in the garage at the Godice; it would only take a few hours. He gave Kaspar a friendly grin from beneath his red moustache.

'Eggs all right?'

Then he asked him whether he had time to go swimming, whether he'd made a wish as he rang the bell on the island, how he liked Mariana's slivovitz – as if Kaspar had been a visiting brother-in-law.

From the living-room came the sound of rock music. Mariana was sitting in her armchair, smoking Kaspar's cigarettes and now and again throwing them a word through the open kitchen door. Ljuba cleared away and said she would have to be going, and her father got up: he'd go with her, his truck would be ready. Mariana hauled herself out of her chair and kissed them both on the cheek. Kaspar saw them to the door.

'I'd like to thank you for all the trouble you've gone to, Herr Bogdan.'

The giant shook his head, slapped him hard on the shoulder, opened the door – the rain was still pouring down – and held the umbrella over Ljuba. Mariana waved to them from her chair. The door closed.

'Well?' Receiving no immediate reply, she jumped up impatiently. 'What happened last night? All quiet?'

'No,' said Kaspar, watching the two figures through the window. The girl was resting her head on the man's shoulder and he had his arm tight around her, as if to comfort her. The raindrops sputtered around them on the paving stones like firecrackers. 'Last night I heard it again.'

She stepped close to him. 'And then what?'

'I answered.'

'And then?'

'That was all. No more chirping.'

'Good,' she said slowly. She returned to her chair, lay back, and shut her eyes. 'In a few days you'll probably get a message through the ventilator. It'll be for me, but you can read it.'

'I don't want to read it.'

'Idiot!' she said with a smile. 'You're still resisting, aren't you? Don't you realize that you've been in it for a long time already?'

She got up, stretched like a cat, yawned, and calmly left the room, watched by Kaspar, who thought, I'm welcome again.

The note that fluttered unannounced through the ventilator flap consisted of a long typed paragraph, with all the Ss missing: no address or signature, and its message unintelligible.

Mariana frowned and fetched a book from the wardrobe. The code book, thought Kaspar, incredible, just like a spy story. Laboriously she spelled out every word, constantly counting and comparing, copied it all out, read it through several times, reached for Kaspar's lighter and set fire to the note and the translation. Then she walked out onto the terrace and sat down at the empty stone table. It had taken her two hours. She looked exhausted, leaned back and closed her eyes.

'It's almost nine o'clock,' said Kaspar, who had been sitting close by, silently watching. He was hungry and would have liked something to eat. 'Can I – er, help you?'

Absently she shook her head, got up to fetch a bottle of slivovitz from the kitchen and took a good swallow.

'I'm on duty in an hour. May I get myself something to eat?'

She nodded, looked at him fixedly, but didn't say anything. He was by now used to these occasional brooding silences of hers, so he gave up and went into the kitchen. When he returned and set down a tray of bread, cheese and tomatoes in front of her, she paid no attention, but picked up the bottle again. She drinks too much, he thought.

Without a word she watched him eat and seemed purposely to wait until he stood up to get his jacket. Then at last she began to speak, rapidly and disjointedly, perhaps repeating the message: 'Ante has disappeared. Mission accomplished. International police alert. No one knows where he is or whether he's been caught. Not a word in the papers. May have to be replaced. Miklos might know where to find him; he knows UDBA hideouts.' She looked at him as if she had given him his cue, but he just stood there, waiting. 'Someone will have to go to Munich. *You'll* have to go to Munich.'

'Why? Your people can get in touch with Miklos on their own.'

'Miklos is in prison. A place called Stadelheim, near Munich. For questioning. They pulled him in a few weeks ago. Our people can't visit him there. But you can.'

Kaspar stared at her for a moment without answering; then he glanced at his watch. 'I've got to go,' he said, and left.

This time the dog barked as he climbed the steps. It barked insistently as if trying to prevent him from leaving. Kaspar looked around anxiously, but the cart track was deserted.

CHAPTER NINE

A WEEK later he was in the night-train on his way to Munich. He had already known it would come to this as he walked back to the hotel after leaving Mariana. Other messages would come through the air-flap – and they did – and those he would be able to resist, but he couldn't resist *her*. Better to go along as if of his own accord, whether she saw through it or not. Of course she *would* see through it. She had raised the stakes, an old rule of the game, and if he continued playing – well, that was his own choice.

There were still limits, though. A lot of people were in this game, in different roles. Mariana had roped him in from the 'outer fringe' and pulled him a little closer, but he was still a long way from becoming active. He would visit Miklos and perhaps find out something about Luburic's whereabouts. But that was as far as he'd go.

Alexis's unhappy face flashed across his mind when he had suddenly asked for 'leave'. 'Oh, my God, Professor, I knew it! What madness! Don't let them blackmail you.' His parting words had been: 'I'm giving you regular time off, Schulte, you have it coming. Four weeks' paid vacation.' As he put the dinar bills in his pocket, Kaspar had said: 'I'll be back, Herr Alexis, you can count on it.' The manager had sighed. 'I'm not sure that that's what I want – for your sake, I mean. In Munich you'll be safe – at least I hope so.'

Munich, of all places! Where on earth should he stay? His six thousand marks were still almost untouched; he had lived comfortably on his salary. But he needed to be careful; at all costs he must avoid running into anyone he knew. How weird – and disturbing – to be living in one's own town in hiding . . . A small hotel then, somewhere on the outskirts.

At the last minute, however, he gave the taxi driver a private address: 31 Kaiserplatz. It was barely seven o'clock, but perhaps Anya would be up already.

She opened the door in her old woollen nightgown and stared at him as if she were dreaming. He followed her into the kitchen and announced that he was hungry, the surest way into her good graces. As she put the water on to boil and set the kitchen table, he carefully probed to find out what she knew. Nothing. She didn't even know that he had left Heidi and been gone all this time. So much the better! He quickly asked after Miklos and she turned her back on him and sobbed, grinding the coffee. She'd come home one lunchtime, as usual, after her morning's driving . . .

'Driving?'

'You didn't see taxi outside? Beautiful black Mercedes? My taxi. I bought with money from Master. I'm taxi driver. I know Munich, every street. I earn plenty, plenty tips. And safety screen between me and passenger. I had good life with my Miklos.'

Tears ran down the angel face on to the coffee grinder. Miklos had been careless out of love for her. He had wanted to get her a Yugoslavian dirndl for her birthday. He still had old friends from Yugoslavia here in Munich.

'For heaven's sake!' cried Kaspar. 'Friends from his UDBA days?'

Well, yes. Those were the only friends Miklos had, though he hadn't seen them since the accident. This fellow had gone to school with him and he had thought he could trust him, and the man had indeed been very nice and given him one of his wife's dirndls.

'And then, instead of turning him in to the UDBA, his nice friend tipped off the German police, just to get in good with *them*. Right?'

'He won't tell me son of a bitch's name. He knows I wait in my taxi and run son of a bitch down.'

'When's his case coming up?'

She didn't know, but she told him visiting days were twice a month, the next one the following Monday. Kaspar nodded and said that this would suit him very well.

'What you mean, suit you? I not take you along.'

'Anya, I'm not going to take *you* along.'

She jumped to her feet, started to shout. Miklos *lived* for those visits, and so did she. What the hell did Kaspar have to come butting in for? Why? What did he want from Miklos?

He hadn't been prepared for this – stupid of him! – and hastily invented a couple of reasons, but she had suddenly become suspicious and sat down at the table, propped her face on her hands and faced him, eye to eye. What was he doing here so early in the morning anyway? Why wasn't he having breakfast with his wife? Why wasn't he on his way to the Institute? It was three months now since they'd taken Miklos away, why this sudden interest in him? Kaspar leaned back in his kitchen chair and thought. She waited, like a snow leopard ready to spring.

Finally he said calmly: 'I left my wife a year ago. I've been living in Yugoslavia. I came here specially to see Miklos.' She looked at him dumbfounded. 'Do you remember Ante Luburic? He's disappeared. They think Miklos may know where he is.'

'They? You Ustasha now, Professor?'

So she was in the know, Miklos had told her. All the better.

'No, I'm not the Ustasha, but I'd like to find Luburic, I was fond of him, he was a student of mine.'

Oh, well, in that case! She slowly nodded agreement. All right, he could visit Miklos next Monday in her place. But after she thought it over, the hard edge returned to her voice.

'Why you leave wife? She not good wife to you?'

'My fault, Anya. Entirely my fault.'

She gave him a swift, knowing look and her long eyelashes dropped like curtains. 'Where you stay, Professor? With your sons?'

'I don't know yet.'

Getting to her feet, she said firmly: 'With sons no good. You stay here. In Master's room.' Seeing him hesitate, she added: 'I not trouble you.'

She gave him no chance to answer but led the way to the dwarf's bedroom. The curtains were drawn. She turned on the night-light, and the great fourposter, piled high with pillows, emerged from the darkness.

'I sleep always in my room and Miklos in laundry room. This room belong to Master. Or you, if you want.'

He walked slowly over to the bed and stood by it uncertainly.

'Sit down,' she said in the tone of voice she used to her blackbird. 'Sleep. You look tired.'

It seemed to him that Monday would never come. He borrowed books from the public library, took long walks in the countryside. When it rained, he spent the afternoon at the cinema. At night he ate with Anya in the kitchen and listened to the tales of her life as a taxi driver, secretly marvelling at her handling of the never-ending game of cat and mouse with her male passengers. She wore plain-glass spectacles while she was driving, but that hadn't saved her from a lot of 'displeasantnesses'. He listened, laughed and wondered at himself. Such a magnificent specimen! What kept him out of her bedroom? In the old days he would have gone there on principle. And now? He realized with amazement that he didn't want to. Not because of Mariana – she would only have laughed. No, *he didn't want to.* The self-denial actually pleased him. The secret sensuality of the hairshirt? And besides, he wasn't at all sure that she would let him in.

After supper he always went straight to the bedroom. There were very few pages left in Uncle Stilts's folder, all brief entries. Come to think of it he hadn't yet got round to opening the folder for many months. Now he would read only one a day, slowly, with long pauses between sentences. The least he could do for the old man. Awful of him, to lose interest because of Mariana! And perhaps also because now there was only the endless grey vacuum of life in Landshut, the applause was past, and the medals, and nothing left but Ida-the-duck.

He had difficulty deciphering the writing because he wanted no other light than the red night-light, but it was worth the trouble to feel the little old man there beside him.

LANDSHUT, 4 MAY 1923: *I've just noticed that I haven't written anything for over a year. Nothing happened. I live a bit, read a lot, I've acquired a pretty fair education by now. Bought a car. And a chauffeur, because Ida just can't get the hang of driving. After all, I'm well to do, with no family. Nobody at all. Thank God.*

LANDSHUT, 10 JUNE 1923: *It's incredible. She's learning! I've taught her to play chess. Now she sits at the board all day long, quacking softly to herself, exactly like a duck at sunset, and breathing heavily, and in the evening we play regular games. How about that? I play badly because I don't pay attention and those excited button-hole eyes of hers just slay me.*

Once a week I go to the whorehouse. I like those girls. I take the car and the chauffeur waits for me. Ida stands at the window and watches me drive off. She's confessed to me that she's still a virgin. Had her share of heartbreak when she was young – like me. Now she has peace and quiet. Like me.

At two o'clock on Monday Kaspar was waiting at the Stadelheim jail. He had applied for special permission from the public prosecutor to speak Croatian with Miklos, had identified himself, by means of his passport, as Professor Schulte, wishing to visit his former student, and his request was immediately granted, provided that a witness was present.

From the outside Stadelheim looked to Kaspar like a hospital and from the inside like a modern hotel, though it was an old prison, built around the turn of the century. Now it was modernized – white paint, many glass walls, big windows. Here and there, a partition of iron bars extended from ceiling to floor, but even these looked decorative rather than threatening. As they walked the long distance to the visiting area, Kaspar heard music and bursts of loud laughter.

'That's the fellows in the workshops downstairs,' said the official accompanying him. Groups of men passed them. Visitors? No, prisoners. No uniforms? Well, uniforms were available, in fact rather popular, navy blue jeans and matching jacket, but it was optional. How long had this place been so progressive? The official shrugged, it had been this way for many years.

They walked past the huge cafeteria to a row of private rooms where the prisoners received their visitors. A small table, a few chairs – glass screens only for terrorists.

Kaspar waited. An elderly man in a turtleneck sweater appeared and introduced himself as a Yugoslav on the prison staff who was required to be present during the visit, sorry but . . . Quite all right, Kaspar assured him, he had nothing to hide.

And then Miklos charged through the door, 'Anya!' in his eyes – and stopped dead. Kaspar got up and smiled as cordially as he could.

'Professor!' exclaimed Miklos, opening his arms, and then turning pale. 'Anything happened to Anya?'

'She sends you her love and this package. She's got a bit of a cold – and I wanted to see how you're getting on.'

Miklos, dressed in prison clothing, looked almost elegant in his navy blue jacket. He sat down hesitantly and glanced inquiringly at the official, who was examining the package.

'A countryman of yours, Miklos,' said Kaspar carefully. 'A Yugoslav.'

Miklos stared straight ahead without a word. Something was wrong. When Anya came, no one had to sit with them. Kaspar

offered him a cigarette and gave him a meaningful smile.
'I've been away a long time, Miklos, and I only just heard of your
troubles. How are you doing?'
But all Miklos could say was: 'Anya?' bewildered and anxious.
'Anya's sent you these jam doughnuts – home made.'
Automatically the Yugoslav asked: 'Who is Anya?' and wrote
down her name and address in his notebook. 'I'll have to cut open
one of those doughnuts, if you don't mind.'
'Go ahead,' said Kaspar. 'Try them. They're good.'
At this the man declined the offer. He sat down by the window
and stared out with a bored expression.
Kaspar turned back towards Miklos.
'Anya would like to send some to Ante too.' He tried to penetrate
Miklos's puzzled stare. 'You know how he loves them. But she
doesn't know his address.' Here he paused to allow time for the
penny to drop.
Miklos opened his eyes wide: 'Doughnuts?'
'Yes. She thought you'd know where Ante's living now. He's
moved, you know. Or aren't you in touch with him any more?'
A faint spark of understanding flickered in Miklos's brown
dachshund eyes. He did his best to think, searching Kaspar's face
for a clue. There was a long pause. The Yugoslav by the window
turned his head and watched them. He had been informed about
Miklos: an ex-UDBA man. And the professor was his former
teacher. Was he UDBA too? Not likely.
Kaspar seized Miklos's hand and pressed it beseechingly.
'Don't worry. You'll soon be out and then we'll all have dinner at
that little restaurant where they had such good food – the
Yugoslavian place. What was the name of it, now? Ante took us
there once, don't you remember?'
The Yugoslav interrupted. 'Who is Ante?'
Kaspar turned his head and replied pleasantly: 'Another student
of mine, Ante Jelic, one of my best.'
The official wrote down the name. It would take some time to
discover that Ante Jelic didn't exist.
Miklos made a halting attempt: 'I don't know his new address,
Professor, but perhaps they'd know at Kovac's at the Harras.'
'Kovac's,' repeated the Yugoslav, writing it down.
This didn't worry Kaspar. Mariana had told him that both sides
kept track of each other's favourite hang-outs, but that it was

hardly ever worth trying to start anything there because they were always under heavy surveillance. And of course the German police had a list of all those places. Kovac's must be an Ustasha hang-out that Luburic had used. Might still use . . . A straw in the wind, but it was all he could get out of Miklos. He seemed to know nothing about Luburic's mission or his disappearance.

When Kaspar tried another opening, saying that he had heard that Ante was ill, Miklos said only: 'Is that so?' And added that himself, he was fine, it wasn't too bad here, good food, a cell to himself – except, of course, that he missed Anya, his angel. He started to sob, and the Yugoslav put away his notebook. Their half-hour was up.

Kovac's at the Harras. The next day Kaspar, wearing jeans and an old raincoat, stepped out of the subway train, walked up the steps and looked around. The wall of a cemetery extended the whole length of the street. On the other side, run-down houses, a few inconspicuous shops, but no tavern. He turned off at random into a narrow side street, and nearly missed Kovac's, because it looked like a store, with ham and cheese in the window. A small sign on the door caught his eye: Proprietor A. Kovac. Restaurant open 6-9 p.m. He would come back tonight, and in the meantime he'd look for a safe place where there would be a lot of people eating a good, inexpensive lunch. He couldn't let Anya give him board; she was saving her money 'for lawyer for Miklos'.

At a quarter past six he pushed open the door and a little bell rang. The shop was empty, but a girl was sitting behind the counter doing accounts. 'Can I help you, Sir?'

'I want something to eat,' said Kaspar curtly, and made for a door opposite the entrance that said Restaurant. He saw the girl press a button. A medium-size room without windows, a dozen tables, about half already occupied, red and white check table-cloths, ceiling lights. The door creaked and the faces turned to look at him. All men, most of them labourers in overalls, trousers tucked into work boots. He walked over to a table in the middle of the room and sat down. The faces turned away. Serbo-Croat was being spoken, at some tables German. He started in on his reconnaissance: behind the bar a sleepy man, sleepy-looking at any rate, behind him a closed door. *The* door?

The sleepy man, elderly, probably the proprietor, appeared

beside him and asked in German what he would like to eat. Frankfurters? Certainly, sir.

Kaspar looked around furtively. No one was paying any attention to him. A neighbourhood hang-out, where everyone knew everyone else and nationality didn't matter. Supposing Luburic was still alive, no chance of his showing up here: general police alert, the message had said. His only hope was to wait around until the place filled up and somebody sat down at his table. With luck a Croat, with luck an activist – though would such a man make himself known to a stranger? He'd have to play it by ear; patience, patience!

What other possibilities were there? Vlada? Out of the question. Her front door, her mail and her telephone would be under constant surveillance. Anything else? Yes: he must not identify himself as Professor Schulte any more, a 'well-meaning, non-partisan teacher'; someone was bound to call the Institute sooner or later.

Nothing for it, then, but blind chance, and chance plays a role in everybody's life. Without exception. Take his own honeymoon trip to Bled and Draza Rukovina's death. Except that people in danger couldn't afford to believe in chance, as Mariana had said to Luburic. On the other hand, chance was what they *lived* on, suddenly seeing 'someone' pass by or picking up a 'careless' word. Perhaps in this very room chance was just marking time. So he would sit here night after night, keeping watch, his ears to the ground.

CHAPTER TEN

IN HEIDI'S small apartment on Viktor-Scheffel-Strasse Elise closed the door to the baby's room and made at once for the kitchen. The top shelf of the cabinet was reserved for her and her bottles. It was a long day's work, babysitting.

I got hooked after all, she thought every time as she put the bottle to her lips in the early evening. That was permissible: first drink straight, subsequent ones in a glass with ice. She sat down by the window in the living-room, placed bottle and glass on the window sill and looked out into the darkness.

At this time of day, before Heidi got home and polluted the air with order and rectitude, Elise even felt quite reconciled to her role of devoted grandmother. Another two years and the child could be dropped off at nursery school in the morning and Heidi could pick it up in the afternoon. She'd miss it, of course, but still. Why the devil did the grandmother *have* to help out? And then to be told that she had a drinking problem! A granny with a drinking problem. Would Heidi give up *her* life to help her mother out? Like hell she would. Elise was only forty-seven. She was still full of plans.

The sound of a key in the entrance hall. Heidi.

'Must you switch on the light the moment you come in?' called Elise crossly. 'It was so cosy in here.'

Heidi took no notice, hung up her coat and cautiously opened the door to the baby's room. Silence. She closed it again, sighed and returned to the living-room, glanced at Elise and at the half-full glass in her hand and turned away. She'd been running up and down the stairs all day at the clinic; better to lie down for half an hour in her little bedroom.

At that moment the telephone rang.

'You take it,' said Elise. 'It must be Frau Henning. She's called twice already. She's all excited, says she absolutely must speak to you.'

Heidi picked up the telephone. 'Frau Henning? Well, how are

you?' She listened for a few seconds, then whispered: 'What? But that's impossible. . . .'

Elise turned her head. Her daughter was deathly pale, clutching the telephone with both hands for support.

'Heidi? What's happened?'

The young woman gulped, took a deep breath and spoke quietly into the telephone: 'You've made a mistake, Frau Henning, that's all, just a mistake.'

Then she listened again, staring wide-eyed at the wall. Elise was standing in front of her but didn't dare to repeat her question.

After a while Heidi said in a firm voice: 'Frau Henning, can I call you back later? Do you have a telephone?'

Elise rushed to the desk for a pencil and pad and Heidi repeated the number.

'Will you be home this evening, Frau Henning? I'll call you.'

She hung up and without a moment's hesitation dialled a number, waited, hung up, and dialled again. Elise finished her drink and sat down, never taking her eyes off her daughter.

'Hello? Stefan? Thank God. No one answers at Werner's. Frau Henning just called. She says your father's in town. He ate lunch at Mahler & Koch's, that new department store in Untersendling. She's the cashier at the lunch-room there . . . No, she says she can't possibly be mistaken. She recognized his voice immediately when he said: "How much is that?" But she couldn't leave her booth and go after him. That was yesterday, and he came back today . . . No, I believe her, after all she was with him for years. He was wearing a shaggy white wig, but she says she's absolutely certain . . .'

Werner, who lived close by, was the first to arrive, then came Stefan and Harold Wegmann. Heidi had thrown Elise out of the kitchen and insisted on preparing supper for all of them, alone, saying it was good for her to have something to do. Elise would also have liked something to do. She turned on the television, switched channels wildly, never giving any programme a chance, cursed and turned it off again. Then she drifted over to the window, counted cars and furiously emptied half the bottle.

Both women dashed to the door to let Werner in. He hugged them and immediately said he would put off his questions until the others arrived. Meanwhile he helped Heidi to set the table and at last Elise – muttering – was allowed to lend a hand. When the door bell rang again, everything was ready, including the bottle of wine that was always kept in the refrigerator for special occasions, to celebrate. But was there anything to celebrate? Heidi and the two brothers sat close together on the sofa, talking, arguing, gesticulating – Elise, feeling isolated in her armchair, mumbled and looked defiantly from one to another. Only Harold Wegmann sat quietly, staring at his hands. For months now the three young men had been coming over every Sunday morning. When the weather was good, they took Heidi and Elise to the mountains, taking turns at holding the baby. She was called Stefanie, and all three of them were her godfathers. They never missed a weekend. Werner felt like a father, Stefan like a brother, Heidi finally had a family, and Elise had an audience and someone to share a laugh with – and sometimes even a drink. Stefan especially didn't mind taking a drop with her. Harold Wegmann hoped, and waited. For the first few months after Kaspar's disappearance, they practically had to force Heidi into the station wagon, which sometimes smelled good, of earth, sometimes awful, of fertilizer. She would sit in the back, with Werner's arm around her, while the others kept up a slightly hectic conversation and enlightened Elise on the subject of frost and heating costs in greenhouses. They had at once started to look for another and smaller apartment for Heidi, found one and decorated it themselves. They picked up the furniture chosen by Elise in the station wagon and installed it: a bedroom for Heidi, a room for the baby and a living-room with a studio couch for Elise.

Here, at Viktor-Scheffel-Strasse, Heidi gradually came to herself, at least to the extent of participating in the conversation now and again. The last months of her pregnancy were difficult and Elise proved surprisingly patient. The labour pains started prematurely, in the middle of the night. The station wagon took them all to the hospital and the three young men carried Heidi in. No, they explained in the emergency room, while she was being taken quickly upstairs, none of them was the father. But they spent the rest of the night downstairs in the waiting-room, pacing the floor and besieging the doctor with questions. The child had three fathers.

After the christening Heidi went back to work at the lab. Werner had gone to see Dr Lamprecht, and shortly afterwards Heidi received a letter saying that she was very much missed and would she consider . . .? No one there asked about Kaspar, no one expressed surprise that she was so thin. Stefanie, on the other hand, was fat and jolly and crowed all day long. Heidi functioned again, and behaved quite normally, although she looked older than she was. She did her work well, enjoyed the baby, tolerated Elise, and felt grateful to her. On Sundays she stood at the window, watching for the station wagon.

Sitting in Heidi's living-room that November evening in 1980, all five of them had done some secret calculating: it was now a year and four months since Kaspar had disappeared.

The room was just big enough to seat five people. They were all on their best behaviour; no one paced the floor.

'Werner,' said Heidi, 'call Frau Henning and let her tell you about it.'

She gave him the number and he dialled. The others sat still, watching him. Heidi folded her hands in her lap.

'Frau Henning? This is Werner . . . Fine, thank you. Please tell me the whole thing again. Yes, from the beginning.'

He listened for a long time without raising his eyes from the telephone. Finally he said: 'All right, we'll be over on Monday. Thank you very much. Goodbye,' and quickly hung up.

'What makes you so sure we'll be over?' exclaimed Stefan. 'I don't want to see him, damn him.' He stopped and glanced at Heidi. 'You're the one to decide whether we should go or not. What do we want of him anyway? Do you want to see him again?'

Werner was looking for the address of Mahler & Koch in the telephone book.

'It's only just opened,' Elise said. 'An enormous place.'

Stefan was grumbling to himself. 'The man's mad. What's he doing here and why is he wearing a white wig?'

'Because he doesn't want to be recognized, that's obvious,' Heidi said in a low voice.

'Well, to hell with him then. We don't need him. It'll just cause a lot of stinking fuss.'

'You don't have to come along,' Werner said. 'I'd like to see him – but of course only if Heidi doesn't object.'

'I have no right to object.'

'But would you rather forget the whole thing?'

She thought it over and remained silent.

After a while Harold Wegmann spoke up for the first time: 'You can't just forget a thing like this.'

'That's right,' said Werner. 'After all, we know he's here.'

'To hell with him!' Stefan shouted. 'He's bound to be somewhere. What the devil does it matter to us whether he's in Honolulu or Untersendling?'

'Listen, man,' Elise said, leaning forward so far that she almost fell out of her chair. 'He told me when he left he was going a long way off. Now he's here. Maybe he wants to come back. Are you going to tell him he can't?'

'Yes,' roared Stefan, pounding the table with his fist. Looking at Heidi, he said, almost beseechingly: 'You don't want him back, do you, Heidi?'

'I don't know. Please believe me – I really don't know.'

'I'm going over there on Monday. There are a few things I want to find out from him,' said Werner. He reached for Heidi's icy hand and kissed it, looking anxiously into her eyes. 'Would you like to come along? No? I didn't think so.'

'I would, though,' exclaimed Elise, looking defiantly into the three faces, turned towards her.

'What about the baby?' asked Werner.

'I'll take her along.'

'No, you won't,' said Heidi quietly but in a way that made Elise drop the subject and only scowl sullenly to herself.

'Okay, I'll come with you then and see what happens,' said Stefan.

Elise stood up. 'High time I got something to eat,' she said, holding on to the table.

On the way home to Grünwald in the station wagon Stefan brooded. Harold Wegmann sat at the wheel and stared out at the dark streets, his face impassive. He was driving too slowly for Stefan's state of mind.

'Say something, man! You're always the first to fret about Heidi – why didn't you open your mouth all evening. Why? Didn't you see the way she was looking at you? She didn't give a damn what *we* said, she wanted to hear from *you*.'

'I don't agree with you and Werner, but I don't have the same right to say what I think.'

'That's a lot of crap. Say it.'

'I'm glad your father's here. Perhaps he wants to come back to her.'

'And you're glad about that? Man, are you mad? I thought you were in love with her.'

Wegmann didn't answer but drove a little faster. Stefan leaned across and tried to see his face through the darkness.

'Don't act the saint, man, it gets on my nerves. I can't stand martyrs.'

Wegmann smiled, and without taking his eyes off the road replied: 'I'm not a saint, you can be sure of that.'

At noon on Monday Werner and Stefan were standing outside the enormous stone and glass structure of Mahler & Koch. The department store was still a novelty in the neighbourhood; crowds streamed in and out and blocked the pavements in front of the huge display windows.

The two young men were caught up in the stream and carried towards the escalators. Slowly they glided upwards, changing three times and winding up in front of the restaurant, which took up the entire fourth floor. Right at the entrance was the cashier's booth, a glass box with a turntable for the money.

Werner knocked on the glass. Frau Henning waved excitedly and slid back a little panel above the turntable. He hadn't come yet, she'd been watching carefully; how were they all getting along at home?

'Fine, everyone's fine,' said Werner, waved to her and sat down at the table Stefan had chosen, one with a good view of the people crowding in.

They sat in silence, never taking their eyes off the entrance. People poured in by the hundreds, but no one with shaggy white hair, no one who looked anything like Kaspar. Everybody immediately lined up in the queue, which extended the whole length of the room, took a tray and shuffled slowly forwards, one step at a time.

For the first half-hour Frau Henning sent them alternating signals of surprise and resignation, shrugging her shoulders and raising her hands; later on she was too busy attending to the lengthening line of customers waiting to pay.

'He's not coming,' said Werner at half past one.

'The whole thing's a wild goose chase, the old cow was just trying to be important,' growled Stefan. 'I knew it all along. Come on, let's go. Or should we have something to eat?'

They took trays and went quickly down the serving-line. The restaurant was almost empty now; Frau Henning had time to go through her whole repertoire for expressing disappointment. Half an hour later, when they were standing in front of her booth, she slid back the panel and desperately insisted that she hadn't been mistaken. No, no, she'd swear to it . . .

'Do you think he might have recognized you?' asked Werner.

She didn't think so, he hadn't looked up once, he had concentrated on the bill and his money.

'I'll be back tomorrow.'

'I won't,' said Stefan grimly.

The next day, a Tuesday, Werner, riding his motorcycle, got into a traffic jam and arrived late at Mahler & Koch's car park. He ran to the main entrance, pushed his way through the crowd and finally stood on the escalator, panting. He looked at his watch: a quarter to one. Perhaps his father was already there. How would he ever find him? There were over a hundred tables. He changed escalators for the third and last time. Oh well, Frau Henning would know whether he was there or not and point him in the right direction . . .

At that moment he caught sight of Kaspar standing opposite him on the down escalator. For a second he froze. His father was staring calmly ahead and didn't see him. Werner furiously tried to push his way up to the next landing, but found himself blocked by a fat woman holding a child, with another one next to her. The few seconds to the top seemed endless. As soon as he reached it, he darted like a weasel to the down escalator and ploughed so roughly into the crowd of diners, contentedly digesting their lunch as they glided downwards, that there were angry shouts of: 'Hey, you! Kindly take your turn! Son of a bitch!'

'Sorry – excuse me – beg your pardon –' he muttered, racing towards the next down escalator. This one was blocked, too, no way of gaining a step this time. He caught a glimpse of the white wig far below him; then it disappeared in the crowd.

By the time he had reached the ground floor and fought his way out into the street, his father was gone. He ran up and down the street, searched the car park, and finally gave up. But at least there was no longer any doubt.

He got on his motorcycle and sat quietly for a while to catch his breath and think. Then he got off again, went to the public telephone and called Elise, who was cooking her lunch. She was abrupt with him – she had a spinach soufflé in the oven.

'Jesus! Hold on a minute.' She went and turned the oven down. 'So he's really here, is he?'

'Maybe he never left – never left Munich, I mean.'

She thought for a moment, watching her soufflé sink, and then said slowly: 'One thing's certain: he doesn't want anything to do with us.'

'That's right.'

'So what's the use of waiting around for him?'

'I want to hear what he has to say for himself. I'm going back tomorrow – earlier.'

'Oh, well, you may find out what's up. But for the present I won't tell Heidi anything. I'll say you didn't see him today either, old Henning must have been mistaken.'

A short time later, while Elise was cleaning the oven, the telephone rang again and Frau Henning informed her excitedly that 'he' had been there today – but where were the boys?

'Okay, okay,' grumbled Elise. 'Tomorrow, Frau Henning. Tomorrow for sure.'

The next day Stefan told his partner that he wanted to take one more long lunch hour. His father was indeed in town and he simply must . . .

'Take as long as you like.'

From the window Harold watched Stefan tear off on his motorcycle. Then he hung a sign on the door of the nursery saying CLOSED UNTIL 4 P.M. Taking a different route, he drove as fast as he dared in his station wagon to Mahler & Koch's and sat down at the little fruit-juice bar beside the escalator, where exhausted shoppers revived themselves. On the dot of twelve he watched the two brothers glide up. And not long afterwards – Kaspar.

This time the two boys didn't sit down but remained standing against the wall in the restaurant, where they could keep an eye on the door.

'There he is,' said Werner.

Stefan stood motionless, staring at a man in a strange white wig, who, unlike the rest of the hurrying customers, was sauntering slowly towards the queue.

'Quick,' whispered Werner, pulling his brother after him. Out of one eye he could see Frau Henning, almost choking with excitement in her glass booth. He waved to her, signalling: yes, yes, relax, we've seen him all right.

It was a difficult manoeuvre. They wanted to remain close to him yet on no account overtake him, so they let themselves be carried along by the crowd into the single-file queue between the buffet and the railing, where they managed to take their place directly behind him.

Kaspar took a tray, Werner took the next one, Stefan the next. The line advanced an inch at a time. Werner was so close to Kaspar that he could smell the camphor from his wig. He couldn't remember ever having stood so close to his father and it upset him to an extraordinary degree. Turning his head, he whispered: 'Don't push, for God's sake.'

'I'm not pushing,' Stefan hissed in his ear.

Kaspar took a tray, a plate, a glass and cutlery; the young men behind him did the same. A few more steps forward. Stefan was jostled against Werner, who managed to absorb the shock. Whatever happened, he mustn't touch his father. Kaspar eyed the food critically and took a helping of hot sausage and potato salad. Werner and Stefan followed suit. The line moved more slowly and finally stopped altogether.

Stefan exploded: 'Speak to him, man. I can't stand it any longer.'

'Wait a minute – what should I say?'

'Say hello, or anything you like, but say something or I shall.'

The line began to move again. Kaspar reached the dessert section, helped himself to a caramel pudding, then held his glass under the apple-juice dispenser.

'Father . . .'

Kaspar turned his head and saw Werner and Stefan behind him. Silently Werner cursed his brother's impatience; he couldn't have chosen a worse moment because Kaspar had to turn away again to stop the apple juice overflowing on to his hand. Setting his tray down, he grabbed a handful of paper napkins. Then he turned back to look at Werner, who was staring at him anxiously, and at Stefan, gaping at him over Werner's shoulder.

Behind them someone muttered: 'Come on, come on,' but Kaspar just stood wiping his hand on the napkins. From farther back in the line came other voices: 'What's the hold-up? Get going. We haven't got all day.'

'Come on,' said Werner. 'Let's get out of here.'

Gently he nudged his father's tray with his own. Kaspar woke up, saw that there was no one ahead of him, got hold of his tray and stepped out of the narrow passage. Werner and Stefan followed quickly, and there they were, face to face. Since all three were holding trays, there could be no question of shaking hands; they just looked at each other without speaking. Werner was the first to pull himself together.

'Shouldn't we sit down? There's a table back there.'

They fell in line behind him and sat down, Kaspar, naturally, in the middle. Way back, within Werner's field of vision, Frau Henning pressed her nose against the glass panel. What were they saying to each other? She was dying to know – and almost at once a consolation prize came her way, for Kaspar's first words were: 'How did you know . . .?' and Werner pointed to the cashier's booth. Kaspar turned his head and peered.

'Frau Henning?'

He nodded a greeting to her. She waved excitedly – and he turned back to his sons, smiling to himself. Chance. How right Mariana had been! 'There *is* such a thing, you know, Ante, only we've forgotten . . .'

'Well?' he said and looked calmly from one to the other.

Stefan burst out: 'Why are you wearing that funny wig?'

'Does it look funny?' He patted it affectionately. 'It reminds me of Uncle Stilts.'

'But why a wig at all? If you want to hide, why do you come to Munich?'

Werner kicked his brother under the table. Why make bad blood right at the start?

'It's not by my own choice, believe me.'

'And – can't you tell us why?' ventured Werner.

'No.' So final that even Stefan was momentarily at a loss.

Kaspar began to skin his sausage. 'May I ask what you want of me?' His tone was not hostile, simply objectively curious.

'Father,' said Werner resolutely, 'we have no right to question you about what you do or don't do . . .' Kaspar gave him a faint smile, then returned to his sausage. 'But Heidi! You can't just . . .'

He stopped. This was proving much more difficult than he had expected. His father was quite different, not nearly so – so passive and get-at-able as he used to be. How could he ever have thought of 'confronting' him and making him give an account of himself?

Kaspar stole a look at his son and thought: he has Martha's good, searching eyes and my way of endlessly mulling things over, poor kid.

'So you've made friends with Heidi? I'm glad of that. How is she? And the baby? What is it? A girl? That's good. I'm glad of that.'

Stefan exploded. 'What do you mean, you're glad? You don't give a shit and you might as well admit it.'

'That's true,' said Kaspar, without reacting to Stefan's tone. 'But I'm glad just the same.' After a moment he added: 'I knew she'd come through all right and I hoped the baby would help her. But I wasn't expecting *you* to make friends with her. I'm glad about it. Yes, I'm glad about that, too.'

'We're a family,' said Stefan rather too loudly.

'Good,' said Kaspar. 'That's good news. Is that why you came?'

Werner was struggling to say something. 'I . . . I really wanted to know why you left.'

'Don't you know what I said in my letter to Heidi?'

'But there must be another reason too.'

Martha's son, thought Kaspar again; I really like him. But what good does that do him? He shook his head slowly and seriously. 'That was it.'

Werner thought he felt the beginnings of a thaw. 'Wouldn't you like to see your daughter?' he ventured. 'Her name's Stefanie. She looks a lot like you.'

'Would it be good for Heidi? Has she got over it?'

Stefan grabbed his knife and angrily sliced his sausage in half lengthwise. 'Not yet. But she soon will. Give her time.'

'Exactly,' said Kaspar.

'So you have no intention of coming back?'

Kaspar looked so astonished that Werner felt his own face flush. Stefan put down his knife and stared at his denuded sausage.

After a lengthy pause Kaspar said: 'Tell me about yourselves. How did you do in your exam, Werner? And you, Stefan? Are you still at the nursery?'

Werner answered for his brother, who maintained an obstinate silence. The exam was behind him, and yes, Stefan was still
at the nursery and he liked the work very much.

'That's good. That's very good,' said Kaspar, finishing his
caramel pudding. He glanced for a second at the boys' untouched plates and at the pale, distorted face of his younger son.
'I still don't quite understand why you wanted to track me down
like this, but since you've gone to so much trouble, I'll explain a
few things. Of my own free will – I don't owe you any explanation, you know.'

'You're wrong there,' said Stefan in a quiet, hostile voice. 'You
owe us far more than an explanation. We're the ones who've
had to pick up the pieces.'

'Had to?' asked Kaspar sharply.

'Yes. Had to.'

'No,' Werner interrupted. 'Of course we didn't have to, no
one forced us. We wanted to.'

Stefan was not to be overruled. 'You simply dumped Heidi.
We've put her on her feet again.'

Kaspar looked at him reflectively. 'Then I really am indebted
to you, but it's thanks, not information, I owe you. I would
never have asked it of you. I hoped that Heidi's mother, and
especially the baby, would help her. And time, too, of course.
Time always helps, provided you're young enough. At my age
it's harder. Your mother's been dead for two years and six
months now, and I still haven't been able to come to terms with
it.'

They stared at him, Werner astonished, Stefan sceptical.

'And yet I don't even know whether I loved her. One isn't
always aware of it, you know. I don't think I did, but she meant
much more to me than I knew. Heidi often reminded me of her;
that may be why I married her. Do you see the resemblance?'

Neither of them spoke. For the first time Stefan looked help-
less.

'I didn't make your mother happy and I soon realized that it
was going to be exactly the same with Heidi, only worse because
I was so much older. I'm not one of those people who are en-
chanted by youth for its own sake. Associating with young
people makes me feel older, not younger. I'm afraid I'm not a
very lovable person; I mean that. I often wondered why your

mother didn't leave me years ago. I'm best off alone. That's how I
function best, without harming anyone.'
   He stopped. Stefan said in a low voice: 'Where are you living
now?'
   'A long way from here. Alone. I'm working. A completely
undemanding job that I enjoy.'
   'What are you doing here then? Holiday?'
   Kaspar considered. 'Yes, let's put it that way. I won't be staying
long. By the way, does Heidi know I'm here?'
   They nodded, and Werner gestured with his head at the
cashier's desk.
   'Oh, yes, of course, Frau Henning. I'm sorry about that, very
sorry indeed.' He thought for a while, looking calmly at them both.
'I have to go now and I must ask you not to follow me.'
   They nodded. Tears suddenly came to Stefan's eyes and he
stammered: 'Why does it have to be – like this?'
   Kaspar didn't answer but put his hand on his arm and squeezed
it. Then he got up, said goodbye and went over to the cashier. They
watched him exchange a few friendly words with Frau Henning
and put down a bill.
   When they followed a little while later – luckily the line of
customers prevented Frau Henning from asking any questions –
they found that their father had paid for all of them. Force of habit.

Kaspar looked around several times as he rode down on the
escalator, and again when he stepped out into the street. Then he
walked calmly to the subway station. Nobody's following me, he
thought with satisfaction. But he was wrong.

Heidi got home early. 'Have they called?'
   'No,' lied Elise, who was feeding Stefanie.
   Actually, the brothers had telephoned hours ago and discussed
everything with her. The upshot had been unanimous: Kaspar
'hadn't shown up'. Even Frau Henning had been warned in case
Heidi tried to pump her.
   Elise took a furtive look at her daughter, who had taken off her
coat and settled down beside the high chair to watch.
   'Taa,' said the baby happily. Heidi smiled, grasped one of the
tiny hands and kissed it.
   'What do you think it means?'

'It means, he wasn't there.'

Heidi nodded. She looked pale and had hardly eaten anything for the last few days. Elise plunged right in.

'Would you have wanted him back? Don't just say: "I don't know." What's upsetting you so much? The uncertainty – or the possibility?'

Heidi, who had been about to answer 'I don't know,' chewed her fingernails.

'Stop that,' said Elise, 'or the baby is going to copy you.'

Heidi looked at her ragged, bitten nails and murmured: 'If he came back, you'd be free, Mother. You wouldn't have to play grandma any more.'

'Taa,' said the baby, pushing the spoon away.

'That would be nice,' said Elise, wiping baby food off her sleeve. 'But then again, it might not be. You get on my nerves, the whole lot of you, and I'd miss that. But that's not the issue. I'd really like to know whether you've ever seriously thought it out how it would be if he suddenly showed up again. How you'd fidget and fuss over him, wondering the whole time: is he happy? Does he like my cooking? Does the baby make too much noise? Am I nice enough to him? Am I *too* nice? Should I act as if he'd never been away? Am I handling this right? Will he – should I – will I – should he?'

She glanced at her daughter's face, at her eyes gazing longingly through the window, and asked no more questions.

CHAPTER ELEVEN

PUNCTUALLY at six o'clock that evening, Kaspar was back at Kovac's. Every day he sat out his time, from six to nine, but so far he wasn't a step nearer his goal, although he had left no stone unturned, sometimes at considerable risk. Unfortunately no one had taken up the cue.

He had made friends with the proprietor, and occasionally a Croat would share his table and he would strike up a conversation in Croatian, but the result was always the same: no reaction to the name Luburic. And even the lack of reaction told him nothing, because it was genuine.

Yet he didn't give up. Mariana had said she wouldn't expect him before February: he would need to give it at least two months. Patience. Three more weeks. The worst thing was that he couldn't write to her. Mail from Germany would be risky.

He was one of the regular crowd by now and was often invited to join other tables: they all thought he was a bachelor who worked in an office. Today, however, he declined all invitations, sat by himself, and ordered only a coffee. His lunch-time meeting with the boys had upset him deeply. They were still sitting opposite him, staring at him, and he tried to recall every word. Boys? Two young men, grown-up and child-like, single-minded and vulnerable – Martha's children. She would have been proud of them. What about himself? Yes, he had felt pride in them, though only too conscious all along that they were as they were without any guidance or help from him. As usual, I'm quick to recognize my failure, he thought, and I'm even ashamed – but that alone just isn't good enough any more. I wish I could do something to my credit, some conscious effort for somebody else *at my expense.*

Why on earth did he suddenly feel the need of moral substance? Because of the boys? Because of their unvarnished, stubborn, decent Martha-faces? Yes. But also because of Mariana and her lonely, dedicated life. He disliked the object of her dedication as much as ever, yet he acknowledged its power. She was out of anybody's reach.

He suddenly felt very low. Should he order a slivovitz? No point. Alcohol lulled him, but never gave him a lift. Well then, he'd go home now and lie in Uncle Stilts's fourposter and read the last entries in the diary.

He paid and left. At Kaiserplatz he stuck his head round the kitchen door and waved goodnight to Anya, who was watching television. In the bedroom he took the folder out of the suitcase and laid it beside the bedside lamp. But just as he started to undress, the doorbell rang and Anya came knocking at his door, asking indignantly whether he was expecting a visitor. It was almost ten o'clock, who could it be? He accompanied her into the hall.

'Who is it?' she called.

'Harold Wegmann. Please ask Professor Schulte if I may speak to him for a few minutes. Only a few minutes. It's important.'

She looked questioningly at Kaspar. 'Is okay?'

He frowned, thought it over, nodded, and returned to the bedroom. How the devil did the fellow find out where he was staying? But he could hardly refuse, could he? A moment later the young man came in, peering around in the dim red light.

'Please sit down,' Kaspar said, indicating the only chair, beside the bed.

Hesitantly the young man sat down and looked up at Kaspar leaning against the bedpost with his hands in his trouser pockets. It was too dark to make out the expression on his face.

'Excuse me, Professor . . .' Kaspar didn't move. 'I may as well tell you right away that your sons don't know I'm here. I've been following you since lunch-time. They don't know that, either. I called Stefan while you were at that place with the strange name and he told me about the lunch and about your . . . your decision. Then I knew I had to talk to you.'

'Why?'

'Because of Heidi. And because of myself. Because of Heidi and myself. Of course she has no idea I'm here, either. She's been told that Frau Henning must have been mistaken.'

'That's the best way.'

'Yes, but it could be better still. It could be really good if . . .' He stopped. But Kaspar refused to ask the obvious: if what? 'If you could bring yourself to come back to her.'

'I thought Stefan told you . . .'

'Oh, yes, he told me, and it was just what I expected. Just what I had hoped for.'

He paused again, and after a while Kaspar said: 'Please be kind enough to express yourself more clearly. As you know, I don't particularly like you, and, besides, it's late.'

'Do you mind if I stand up?' He couldn't keep on staring up into that dark face. 'I'll be as brief as possible – and I apologize if I sound clumsy. The thing is – when your wife died in my lap, I thought I could never bear to part from her. I know this sounds crazy because she was dead, and I had to accept that. Then I met Heidi. For me, Heidi is Martha, as if Martha had come to life again. I love Heidi. I know you'll understand that, I'm quite sure you realize how much alike they are. Werner and Stefan don't see it, but you do, don't you?' Bending forward, he peered into Kaspar's face.

'Go on.'

'The trouble is that Heidi can't get over your leaving her. She can't understand it, it's something she still struggles with every day. It's thrown her completely off her bearings: she doesn't trust her feelings or her instincts any more. She does her job at the lab, she loves the baby – but she doesn't wish for anything or hope for anything to happen, she refuses to give herself a chance.'

He stopped and stepped back so that Kaspar wouldn't feel harassed.

Kaspar turned and sat down on the bed, his hands limp between his knees.

'Does she talk to you about this?'

'She doesn't need to. I know it, anyhow.'

'And what do you think I can do for her? I suppose that's why you're here.'

'You must go back to her.'

Kaspar raised his head and looked into the helplessly exposed, hungry eyes, filled with tears. They overflowed and the young man wiped them away roughly with the back of his hand and whispered: 'I'm sorry. I can't help it. For me everything depends on this.'

'And how is it to be managed? My return, I mean. No doubt you have a plan.'

Harold nodded vigorously and struggled to keep his voice steady.

'It's not a plan, it's . . . I think you should act as if you really
wanted to come back. I would imagine you'd phone her up,
wouldn't you? Simply ask if you could come over. Or if that seems
too – well, direct, perhaps you could write her a letter.'

Kaspar shook his head firmly. All that manoeuvring would take
up far too much time. For God's sake, how much longer was he
supposed to go on playing good Samaritan to other people, first
Luburic and now Heidi – though Heidi did have some claim to his
help. When could he finally start living his own life again and go
back to Mariana?

The young man watched Kaspar's grim face anxiously, clenching his teeth so hard that the angle of his jaw stood out under his
cheekbones.

'I know it's – asking a lot,' he stammered. 'I know you don't like
me, but I think you'll do it – for Martha's sake.'

What an extraordinary young man. For Martha's sake. Actually,
he wasn't extraordinary so much as wise. And in love.

'Go on.'

'The main thing is that Heidi must believe that you've come of
your own accord. She must never find out that you've already seen
your sons.'

'I understand. And then?'

'Then you come to the apartment to see the baby – and her. And
then – what happens next is up to you.'

'You want me to move in and act as if I'd come back for good?'

'Yes.'

'And how long am I supposed to keep up this act?'

'Until she realizes that it doesn't work, that it could never, never
work. That might be quite soon, she's learned a lot, she doesn't just
hope blindly any more. But she's immobilized by your inexplicable
disappearance. If you can make her understand it, she'll be able to
get over it.' He hesitated, then added: 'If you don't mind my saying
so, your letter was too short, Professor. You made it easy for
yourself, you explained nothing.'

'Should I have told her that she gets on my nerves and that I
found the idea of a baby intolerable?'

'Yes,' cried the young man, his head high. 'Yes, yes, yes! It
would have knocked her out, but at least it wouldn't have left such
a hole. It's this awful hole that you've got to fill. Look . . .' He
raised both hands imploringly and his tone became almost

fatherly. 'You carried on an affair with Heidi for six years while you were living with Martha. So you were lucky enough to have a sort of double Martha – or a double Heidi, if you like – and you were content with your life. Then Martha died and you lost half of your daily ration. Single Martha hadn't satisfied you, so you'd added Heidi. How could single Heidi ever satisfy you?'

Kaspar was startled; he suddenly found himself under attack, but openly and without malice. The boy deserved a fair answer.

'You think I'm irresponsible and insatiable. I admit that I function badly when responsibility is thrust upon me. I never wanted to get married, I pronounced the fateful words twice against my better judgement. I never wanted children, but neither Martha nor Heidi ever asked me. For them it was a matter of course that a normal man should be a father. I'm not insatiable, either. For the last year I've been in love with a woman who gives me less than half of herself and I'm content with that.'

The young man stared at him with glowing eyes.

'Then there is hope,' he whispered hoarsely. 'If you're in love with someone yourself – then you'll do it, won't you?'

Later, as Kaspar lay in the fourposter, with Uncle Stilts's folder in front of him on the bedspread, he went over his encounter with Harold Wegmann once again. Well, here was a chance to improve his moral standing, wasn't it? Strange that this fellow should have shown up tonight with his weird plan, his dreadful plan. Yet he had got him to agree that he would try it, he would phone Heidi and see her and the baby every day, but he would remain here and sleep in the fourposter. That had precipitated another extraordinary, passionate battle.

'Then it's pointless,' Wegmann had exclaimed in despair. 'Then it's not worth your calling her at all. Can't you see that you've got to go the whole hog?'

'What do you mean: the whole hog?' Kaspar had shouted. 'Are you trying to tell me I've got to sleep with Heidi to prove to her that it won't work? And you say you're in love with her!'

'Yes,' the young man had whispered, and he had pounded his forehead with his fist. 'That's it. That's the only way. It's terrible – but it's the only way.'

After that there was no more to be said. He would call Heidi the following afternoon . . .

'Inkworm!' said Uncle Stilts, right next to him. 'Have you lost your mind?'

'Go away, will you, I want to finish your diary tonight.'

LANDSHUT, 28 NOVEMBER 1925: *I've just reread something I wrote recently. 'Nothing else is going to happen to me for the rest of my life.' And now just look what's happened! Except that this time the people involved are little people, quite unimportant, in keeping with my present life. But it's shaken me as much in its way as hobnobbing with those society swells – even more, I'd say, because in those days I lived in clover all the time, but now I'm used to making do with a thimbleful.*

Well, anyway, last winter Ida began hobbling around as if everything hurt everywhere, but nothing would make her go to the doctor because it was – embarrassing. Then in February she had a fall, so I simply sent for the doctor. He's a real old fogey, but he's no fool. He joked around with Ida and examined her without her even noticing. Later he told me she had cancer, terminal; two or three months to live. I spent all my time sitting by her bed, and late one afternoon, when it was nice and warm outside, I opened the window and propped her up on her pillows. The sun was just setting and it turned her face an orange-pink. She watched the sunset without a word, and then she suddenly sighed: 'I wish I had got married.' 'Whatever for?' I cried, aghast. 'So I could have got rid of my name.' And for the first time it hit me that I didn't know what her name was. 'What does it matter anyway?' I said quickly. No, no, she insisted obstinately, it was especially embarrassing to her now because they'd have to put her name on her death certificate. And, worse still, on her gravestone. Everybody would stop and look at it and giggle. 'For heaven's sake!' I exclaimed. 'What ever is your name, then? You'd better tell me so I'll be prepared.' She took a deep breath and said: 'Ida Betworthy,' and she couldn't begin to tell me what she'd had to put up with at school on account of her name and that mug of hers.

I thought fast, and then I said: 'Ida, I'm grateful to that mug of yours. It's often given me a laugh when I really didn't feel like one. And as for your name, we can change that easily: we'll get married. I'll see about the banns tomorrow. And the pastor can marry us right here in the parlour.'

She lasted a few more months. Yesterday I had her gravestone set up, a marble one, with the inscription IDA SCHULTE *in gold.*

MUNICH, KAISERPLATZ: *I'm not going to put the date any more. Don't want to see the years fly by. I sold the house in Landshut after Ida's death and moved to Munich. I like it here; no one knows me. I indulge myself. I've bought an enormous fourposter bed – just for the hell of it. In winter I sometimes bring a girl home with me to warm it up. I get into my pyjamas and wait around and when she says: 'It's warm now,' I make her get out and I get in. In my fourposter there's only room for one.*

MUNICH, KAISERPLATZ, 10 SEPTEMBER 1962: *I've had to put the date after all because this is important, it's absolutely beyond belief. Suddenly someone comes in the door and says: 'Good morning, Uncle Stilts.' I was so flabbergasted I couldn't get a word out. That Leopold's son! Can you beat that? That Leopold's dead, and his wife too. This one – Kaspar's his name – is a professor at the Institute for Slavic Languages, would you believe it! He's tall and skinny and I think I like him. Quiet, a bit reserved, but no bundle of virtue, so far as I can tell. Has it easy with the girls, I dare say, but he's married, the poor fool.*

I still can't believe it. A grandson of Mother's! So there is somebody in my life after all!

MUNICH, KAISERPLATZ: *Yes, there is – but not quite. I don't like his wife. Her name's Martha and she's a good woman, no doubt, but she's not exactly perceptive and she looks at me sort of suspiciously. For good reason. If I had my way, he'd be a free man. He's got the itch, only he doesn't know it. He's stuck in his box – Institute, wife, children. But his life's no bed of roses, I'd take my oath on that.*

That entry, the last but one, was again undated. The little dwarf must have added it some time during the last ten years, having seen the whole picture quite clearly.

The last one was written in shaky writing on a different sheet of paper, and Kaspar knew at once that the old man had added those lines specially for him.

MUNICH, KAISERPLATZ: *From time to time I play around with a crazy idea: I'd like to adopt someone. Not a child but an adult, someone who knows something about my life. He'd have to know all about the box – and how tricky it is. How you think it protects you forever, and then all of a sudden you're out in the open – and on your back like a beetle, clawing the air.*

Yes, I'd like a descendant, somebody to lie here in my big bed and think about me, so that everything I've managed to scrape together in my lifetime won't just be snuffed out. Amen.

Kaspar carefully replaced the loose sheets of paper in the folder and put it aside. He switched off the light and stretched out, his hands clasped under his head, staring into the darkness. What a disappointment it must have been to the old man when he'd presented Heidi to him, right here in this room. The story of Stilts, the lesson of the box – all for nothing. No descendant.

But at least he was lying in the 'big bed' and thinking about him.

CHAPTER TWELVE

HEIDI got home at five o'clock, as usual. She found Elise and the baby still in the bathroom; Stefanie had taken a long nap in the afternoon and they were a bit behind.

Soon after she arrived, the telephone rang. Elise wrapped the little bundle in a bath towel, deposited it in Heidi's lap and left the bathroom. When she returned, her eyes were wide with amazement.

'It's Kaspar! He wants to talk to you.'

'Oh, my God!' whispered Heidi. 'What am I to do? I thought he wasn't . . . I don't understand. . . .'

Elise, too, was puzzled. What had made Kaspar change his mind all of a sudden? She pulled herself together.

'Well, it's quite simple: Frau Henning was not mistaken. He is here and he wants to come over. Go on, talk to him. You can always say you don't want to see him, right?'

Heidi went to the telephone. A faint 'Yes?' was all she could manage.

'Heidi? Frau Henning told you that I'm in Munich, didn't she – er, would it be all right if I came over or are you too tired from work?'

'No, no – I mean, I'm not tired.'

'I'll be there in half an hour, then. Will the baby still be awake?'

'Oh, yes.'

'Fine. See you soon.'

Heidi collapsed into the chair beside the desk. Elise came in and placed the naked baby in her mother's lap. Stefanie was always in high spirits after her bath, crowing and pulling at her hair.

'Hold on to her,' said Elise, trying to wriggle the little legs into a red sleeping suit. 'There's no need to pull that face. He's back. That's what you wanted, isn't it?'

'Yes, but not – not like this.'

'How else? With a registration form in his hand? He hasn't just dropped out of the clear blue sky, you know. You've been waiting for this for days and now it's happened.'

Half an hour later the bell rang. Elise opened the door and was startled to see that Kaspar was carrying a suitcase. Really! Wasn't he taking things a bit too much for granted? They looked at each other for a moment without speaking. She rallied and said in a loud voice: 'Well, hello, Kaspar,' took the suitcase, shoved it hastily into a corner, and called out: 'Heidi!' Kaspar stepped into the living-room and she closed the door behind him.

Heidi had jumped up when the door bell rang. Then she remembered that a woman doesn't get up when a man enters, and sat down again. But when Kaspar came in, she was standing again. He walked over to her and kissed her lightly on the cheek. My God, he thought to himself, she looks quite different.

'Come and sit down,' she said in a hoarse voice, and noisily cleared her throat.

He looked around and caught sight of the baby in its high chair. 'Taa,' it said, stretching out a little hand towards him. Kaspar waved and smiled but made no move to touch it. Not yet.

'She's not shy with strangers, is she?' he said, and realized instantly that this hadn't been exactly tactful. What could he say that would be neutral?

'No, she's not shy,' said Heidi, thinking, if only Elise would come back. 'Would you like a drink?'

'That would be nice.'

Heidi was already at the door, calling: 'Mother, Kaspar would like a whisky and soda.'

Elise materialized with a bottle and a glass, avoided looking at them, and disappeared again so quickly that Heidi had no time to find an acceptable way of spelling out an SOS: for God's sake, stay!

Kaspar leant back in his chair, apparently at ease, and asked whether she was back at the lab. Yes, she said, she needed the money . . . and checked herself. Wasn't it tactless to mention that? But Kaspar only nodded and asked whether it was enough to live on. Oh yes, plenty really, because Elise had rented out her apartment for a good price, and so she, Heidi, had started part-time at the lab, but now she was back to full-time. She talked animatedly – too animatedly? She wasn't even sure whether he was actually listening or actually seeing the baby he was looking at.

But hadn't it always been like that? The idea struck her forcibly – how strange that it had never occurred to her before – now suddenly it disturbed her and wouldn't go away. Hadn't she always reacted for him, on his behalf? Hadn't she always, by proxy, been happy or sad or surprised or indignant or delighted? What had made him come back? Why couldn't he just open his arms and say: I missed you. Very simple: because he hadn't missed her – or was she jumping to conclusions? On no account ought she to watch out for – let alone trust – her inner voice. It's all too sudden, she thought in despair. All I want is to sit here and look at him. I've got to get used to the fact that he's really and truly back – and after that I only want to hear what he's got to say.

'I'm afraid I've taken you by surprise,' said Kaspar slowly. 'I didn't give you time to decide whether you do want to see me . . .' He checked himself: he had been about to call her Martha.

'Why did you come?' asked Heidi quietly.

The first of the obligatory questions. From now on he'd have to lie. And lie really well because her large grey eyes were not flickering imploringly, as they used to, but meeting his own with a challenge.

'I wanted to see you again. And I have some business here in Munich.' Why ever had he mentioned that? 'That wasn't the reason, though. I wanted to see you again.'

Quietly and persistently she said: 'Did you want to see me or the baby?'

'You. I wanted to see you again. The baby's still a stranger to me – for the present.' They had to fumble and feel their way towards each other, like two blind people. 'You know how hard it is for me to talk about my feelings, they're always so tightly stacked on top of each other. When I left you, they seemed clear enough to me: I felt I had to go away – and stay away. And now here I sit, looking at you. I'm afraid I'll never make you understand – I can't really make head or tail of it myself.' Pretty lame, he thought, it will never satisfy her. But perhaps that's all to the good: it shouldn't satisfy her. She had to be confronted – right from the start – with the stark fact that their relationship didn't work. Could never work. And in the end *she* must be the one to tell him it was over, not because of a cheap desire to turn the tables, but because she had come to realize that he was a stranger. Or rather an intruder. And then she would begin to defend herself and counter-attack.

She was looking at him in silence, searchingly.

'It wouldn't surprise me if you asked me to leave. I was just – trying.'

'Trying – or wishing?' What a stupid question. I'm cueing him, she thought.

'Wishing, of course.' Then he added in a low voice: 'It's hard – it's hard for both of us.' Unfair, he thought. Now I'm covertly appealing for her sympathy because I know that will do the trick.

She said nothing, and suddenly had to struggle to keep back the tears. Finally she managed to whisper: 'I'll do all I can to make it easy for us.'

Thank God, he thought. After supper he would unobtrusively move his suitcase into the living-room.

CHAPTER THIRTEEN

FOR THE first few days he did surprisingly well. All roles had been definitely assigned and they had started acting as an ensemble. Elise served as stage manager, gave the instructions and raised and lowered the curtain.

On the very first evening she set the course. Heidi had brought out the emergency bottle from the refrigerator and lifted her wine glass. 'You really ought to say "du" to each other, don't you think so?'

Kaspar automatically raised his own glass. 'Of course.'

But Elise didn't touch hers. 'First we'd better get to know each other a bit.'

Kaspar at once agreed with her and took a sip. Heidi followed suit, looking unhappy. When would she ever learn to let matters take their course and not feel compelled to wag her tail to make everyone feel good?

'I suppose you'll be sleeping on the sofa in the living-room.' Elise looked from one to the other, and, when no one contradicted her, went on resolutely: 'I'll pack my things later and spend the night with a friend of mine.' She turned to Kaspar. 'Lives just around the corner, very handy.'

Heidi thought: funny, she's completely sober. And immediately afterwards: Oh, Lord, she's too sober. You don't go about making decisions of this sort as casually as that.

'The apartment's too small,' Elise continued in the same breezy tone. 'It's either you or me. If you want to get to know the baby, you'll have to take over my role.'

'And what is your role?'

'Baby-sitter. Or do you have work to do here in Munich? Why don't you start telling us something about yourself? We're all in the dark, you know.'

Oh, God, thought Heidi.

'Yes. I do have something to do here.'

'Every day?'

'Except on Sundays.'

'What hours?'

'From six until nine in the evening.'

'Couldn't be better. Heidi will be home by then. I'll come over tomorrow morning and show you the ropes. Do you know anything about babies?'

'Nothing at all.'

'You're lucky, you won't have much trouble with Stefanie. She's not one of those babies that squawk all day long. But she's not dry yet.'

Oh, God, thought Heidi, and decided to intervene, but Elise didn't give her a chance.

'Most fathers have to lend a hand these days, however old they are, and some of them do a better job than the mothers. Well, cheers, anyhow! Chin-chin.'

Heidi raised her glass along with them. Cheers! In those few minutes her mother had certainly cut through a lot of knots. She felt doubly relieved, both for herself and for Kaspar. How extraordinary that he had agreed to take care of Stefanie during the day. Kaspar! She didn't know what was what any more. Admittedly, it was a practical solution, at least for the time being, until – until what? Would he go back to the Institute? Was there an alternative? He had 'something to do' here. What in the world could that be? Why didn't he say what it was? Where had he been all these months? What had he been doing during this time? Three questions that would have to be answered – but not tonight. She didn't feel up to any revelations.

Kaspar, too, hoped that no one would ask any more questions.

Even Elise had had enough. Right after supper she began to pack, making a good deal of commotion. The commotion was deliberate because, although Heidi and Kaspar sat watching her with smiles on their faces, they looked more like silkworms wrapped up tight in their cocoons.

There's something fishy about all this, she thought, as she was finally getting into her taxi. Why has he come back? When the boys asked him to, he refused point blank. And then, out of the blue, the very next day, he rang up. He hadn't given any explanation, just asked what she thought of his coming back to Heidi. 'Why not? What can happen?' she had said – just to say something, because she had been so flabbergasted. A pretty stupid thing to say, now that she came to think of it; a whole lot of things could happen. 'Fine. I'll come over tonight', he'd said. 'Wait a minute!' she had cried. 'Talk to Heidi first!' 'All right,' he had murmured. All very mysterious. And yet the atmosphere up there in the flat wasn't bad – no rancour, just paralysing embarrassment. That would fade away with time – perhaps.

Heidi lay in her narrow bed, her hands pressed to her chest to keep it from exploding. Next door, just a few steps along the hall, lay Kaspar! He had stroked her hair before he wished her goodnight, looking as if he was about to say something. She thought she knew what he had in mind. How right he was, it was all very difficult, Her mother had left a sleeping pill and a glass of brandy on her bedside table, and she had swallowed both of them. Now she felt dizzy.

The living-room sofa was too short for Kaspar's long legs; he thought longingly of Uncle Stilts's fourposter. Though, all in all, it hadn't been too bad so far. No tears, no probing, above all no demand for affection, however tactfully hinted at. There was nothing primitive about Heidi, thank God. Although, the primitive element which he had always thought repellent, was apparently precisely what he craved! He heard Mariana singing, saw her sitting on the steps, firm flesh bulging unashamedly from every angle, her brown thighs against the rough stone. . . He pressed his face into the pillow and smothered his breathing until he could hold out no longer.

Elise was back at seven in the morning. He heard her moving around the kitchen and talking to the baby. The kitchen table was laid for three, with Stefanie's high chair drawn up to it. There was a good smell of coffee and rolls.

At the last minute Heidi came stumbling through the door as if she were drunk. Kaspar gave her a shocked look but thought it better not to ask any questions.

'Doesn't take much to knock you out, does it?' muttered Elise remorsefully, filling Heidi's cup to the brim with black coffee.

'Sorry – I overslept. I must dash.' With an attempt at a smile for Kaspar, she fled the kitchen.

'Taa,' called Stefanie after her.

'Well now,' Elise said vigorously, 'let's get started. This is what she gets for breakfast, see? Two tablespoonsful and then some milk – thinned out a bit. And make sure that she always has a rusk to gnaw on, she's teething.'

Kaspar acquitted himself quite well. He wasted no time on cuddling, bundled Stefanie into her clothes and buttoned her up speedily and without fumbling. Elise watched him in amazement, smoking one cigarette after another, and the baby, after a short period of token resistance, crowed at him with her toothless smile.

'Have you really never done this before?'

'Martha, my first wife, always wanted to do this kind of thing on her own.'

'Big mistake. You mark my words, in a few days you'll be really proud of yourself. Er . . . I was going to say . . .' She hesitated for a fraction of a second. 'It's raining today, but when the weather's nice, you must put her in her carriage and take her out for some fresh air. In the park. Think you can manage that?'

'I've had worse things happen to me.'

Like sitting on a bench across the river, at the foot of the Angel of Peace, unable to move, afraid I'd lost my mind, he thought.

Kaspar saw his sons – apparently 'for the first time' – two days later, on Sunday. Heidi had been nervous. She wasn't worried about Werner, but what about Stefan? Would he suddenly explode? And how would Kaspar react to Harold? When the time came, everybody's self-control amazed her. Coached by Harold, the boys played their roles of genuine embarrassment without any difficulty. Kaspar remained pokerfaced throughout.

Harold Wegmann didn't come along. A pity, but he had some 'important business' to attend to.

Under a cloudy sky they set out in the direction of Salzburg. White mountains and salt and pepper fields glided past, a strong wind blew the early snow off the trees and rattled at the windows of the station wagon, getting on everybody's nerves.

It's not the wind, thought Heidi, it's Kaspar, although Kaspar was sitting quite quietly, holding Stefanie on his lap. If only she'd had the courage to ask him those three questions right away, maybe she could have relaxed now, and he too. And the boys would have sensed it and stopped sitting there like statues. They would start laughing the way they usually did and telling each other off and kidding her and kissing Stefanie.

Was it something to do with Harold's absence? She was so used to having him at the wheel. His presence always made her feel confident, even important. To him a word from her was worth its weight in gold; she never had to think before she spoke. Yes, that's the way it was with Harold. Would he and Kaspar ever get along? Never.

Elise wasn't very talkative either; she chain-smoked and stared out of the window. Stefanie was the only one who enjoyed the outing, crowing, laughing and flirting with Kaspar. Surely he must be enjoying it, Heidi thought, but she managed not to say so aloud. It was a long, silent trip. She was not the only one to weigh every word carefully.

She waited two more days, then she made up her mind.

It was half past nine and Kaspar had just come in. Usually he sat and watched television with her for half an hour, although she wasn't sure if he really saw or heard anything. Sometimes he would hold her hand, stroking it in a tender, absent-minded way, as if he were stroking a dog's head. Nothing had changed since he had reappeared; they hadn't come a step closer. What was he thinking, what was going on inside? Nothing? Was that possible? Something ought to be happening. A man can't just show up again after all those months and say: well, here I am! without any explanation and, above all, without any attempt to bridge the gap. Lord knows, she wasn't asking for a *mea culpa*, but when would he bring himself to the point of doing or saying something to patch up their marriage? Or did he think they could go on like this indefinitely?

Kaspar sensed that she was gradually becoming hostile, but acted as if he hadn't noticed it. It was the right kind of reaction. Give it time.

That night, when he walked into the living-room and saw that the television wasn't on, he sat down facing her in an armchair. There was tension in the air; perhaps the time had already come.

'Where have you been for the last year?' Without preliminaries. And rigid, cross-examining.

'In Bled.'

'In Bled!' she repeated, dumbfounded and thus thrown off balance at the very outset.

'I liked it very much when we were there before.'

'The whole time? In Bled?' He nodded. 'But what were you doing there?'

'I was night porter at the Hotel Godice.' She stared at him, uncomprehending. He went on calmly: 'Remember the old man who always got the keys mixed up? I took his job. I never got them mixed up.'

'But why? Why night porter?'

'I needed a job. Make a living.'

'And you've – you've been a night porter all this time?'

'I enjoyed it.'

He was obviously telling the truth. Night porter at the Godice – no one could invent that. And yet, there was – there had to be something more to it.

'Was there a woman?'

'No.' Surely Wegmann would have had sense enough to keep his mouth shut.

She said in a low voice: 'I still don't know why you've come back.' But when he didn't answer, she suddenly screamed: 'Where do you go every day at six o'clock? What is it that you "have to do"?'

He had never known her to behave like this, or suspected how painful it would be for him to witness it.

'I sit in a little Yugoslavian restaurant, waiting. A former student of mine has disappeared. His family in Bled is worried and I've promised to find him for them. The restaurant used to be his favourite hang-out.'

'Why are they worried? Is he in trouble?'

'Possibly.'

'What's it got to do with you? Are you his keeper? Can you spare the time – and the money – just to sit around for weeks?'

'It's worth it, believe me.'

She screamed again: 'And I'm also supposed to believe that you wanted to come back to *me*?'

'Heidi, you can't force – I mean you can't rush this kind of thing.' Not too calm. A slightly beseeching tone. Let her feel that it touched him too, and it did, deeply. 'Yes, I do want to come back to you, but that isn't enough. *Your* good will isn't enough either. I've been here almost a week now and I haven't been able to make friends with anyone but Stefanie. She's easy because she doesn't know anything, above all she doesn't know I'm her father. She likes me and that's that, and that makes it easy for me. But the record of my previous behaviour, of my sins, stands all the time between me and the rest of you. Perhaps it's not possible to change things; perhaps everyone's become even more suspicious *because* I've come back.'

No trick; it came from the heart. Heidi felt it, and chewed her fingernails helplessly.

'I understand,' she said at last. 'I understand what you mean – but that doesn't help me. It's a terrible thing to have to say, but all of a sudden you're a complete stranger to me. And – I feel you don't *want* me to get to know you again, you don't give me a chance. You never tell me anything but the bare facts, as if you're afraid of giving something away.'

Touché, he thought, hating himself and Harold Wegmann. How was he to blather on after those devastating truths that had just come out in the open? He forced himself to think of her future: she would rid herself completely of him, Kaspar, and turn to Wegmann. He couldn't stand the fellow, but he was most probably the right man for Heidi. No fool, not by any means. A strange bird, not uninteresting.

He'd been silent for so long that she exclaimed bitterly: 'You admit it, don't you? You don't want to talk to me.'

'Isn't that what we're doing now?'

'No! You're giving me reason after reason why we can't talk, not now, not tomorrow, maybe never. I'm full of questions: why did you marry me, why did you leave me, why have you come back?'

Brusquely he interrupted: 'You know the answer, but you want to go on lying to yourself. You refuse to recognize the kind of man I am. You won't admit to yourself that in all those years you never got anything except a rotten deal from me. I'm still the same man I was, and you're just the same, too – blind! Blind with rage from your own pig-headedness, and deaf, too. You complain about my silence – doesn't it scream at you?'

Now she would throw him out.

She did get up, but she didn't look at him. She held on to the back of the chair, shaking her head violently as if there was a ringing in her ears. Then she ran out of the room.

Not quite, he thought, and closed his eyes. Almost, but not quite.

Early next morning he heard Elise in the kitchen. For the last few days she hadn't shown up, she'd let him look after the baby by himself. Ah well, Heidi had probably told her about last night. Yet when he entered the kitchen a little while later, Elise gave him a friendly nod. Heidi was nowhere to be seen; she had obviously left early for the lab.

'Taa. Taa,' Stefanie cried jealously. He took her on his knee and kissed the little head. Elise watched closely as he fed the baby.

'I miss the little brat.'

'Me too,' he murmured.

'What did you say?'

'I mean, I'd miss her too.'

But Elise had caught on. 'How long are you going to keep this up?' she asked nonchalantly, lighting a cigarette.

'As long as it takes.'

'Did you think this up yourself?'

He shook his head and put the baby back in her chair.

'Who did, then?'

And suddenly it dawned on her. 'Harold? Of course! How could I be so dense? Harold, who else?'

She seized Kaspar's hand and squeezed it hard.

'Well, well – isn't that something! Hats off to you!'

He got up to reheat the coffee, but she beat him to it, threw her arms around his neck and kissed him.

'Good Lord,' she said over and over again, kissing him each time. 'Now I finally get the hang of the whole business.' She slapped her forehead. 'But the boys don't know about it, do they? That wouldn't do at all, it would mean Heidi is the only dumb cluck. No, no. Nobody must know about it. Come on, man, we've got to celebrate this. And now that you're leaving, you can say "du" to me. Look, there's still a bottle of mine up there.'

Kaspar accepted the drink. Now that Elise knew about it, the situation seemed grotesque to him and his own role in it absurd.

'And now you're waiting for her to throw you out, is that it? Well, judging by the state she was in on the telephone last night, she won't be long about it. Get on with it, man, on to the bitter end, full speed ahead! Although I must admit I'll be terribly sorry to lose you.'

Stefanie started to wail and wouldn't quieten down until he took her on his knee again while Elise looked on.

'She's forgotten all about me, the little rascal – but you know what?' She stopped, reflected and suddenly turned serious. 'The baby's your best accomplice. Understand what I mean?'

He looked at her doubtfully and shook his head.

'Oh well, never mind, I can't spell it out for you. Don't worry, you'll find out for yourself, you won't have to lift a finger, just let things take their course.'

There were grim days ahead, no getting around it. Elise had promised to spend as much time as possible at Heidi's on the pretext that she missed Stefanie. She dropped in each evening, kept Heidi company while she ate supper, drank too much, and talked about Kaspar. What a wonderful father he was. Quite extraordinary.

Heidi stared at her plate, pale and tight-lipped. She was quietly seething, and, for the first time in her life, she despised herself. Before Kaspar left, she had often wished she could transform herself and turn into a totally different woman, one with a thicker skin, sharper elbows, a goodly amount of healthy self-love. She had no love for herself, that was bad enough. But self-contempt – that was something new, something she couldn't live with, and the realization that she would have to break away from her cherished principles of decency and tolerance put her into a state of turmoil. Cherished principles? She felt like savagely hitting out and kicking someone. Not someone – Kaspar. High time she stopped being considerate and 'fair'. Time to act. Challenge him and to hell with his eloquent silence and mealy-mouthed excuses.

The most painful thing of all – more painful even than the final loss of Kaspar – was the loss of the Heidi she had known all her life. She was crumbling away, bit by bit; she didn't exist any more.

For the next two days she avoided Kaspar, left the house early without eating breakfast and shut herself in her bedroom when he came back from Kovac's at night.

At half past five on the third day, however, she stormed up the stairs, hoping to find him still at home and ready to have her say

straight to his face. In the course of the day she had made her
mind up; the right words were bound to come to her when she
confronted him.

But instead of Kaspar, there was only Elise, carrying the baby
into the bathroom.

'Go away, Mother, for God's sake, go away! Leave me alone
for today.'

'Stop shouting. I'll do nothing of the sort. How can I leave the
baby with you in the state you're in? She'll start crying any
minute. And she was in such a good mood – until Kaspar left.'

Heidi turned on her heels, ran to her bedroom and locked the
door. She lay on the bed, motionless, until she felt calmer, then
she called the nursery in Grünwald.

'Harold? Where were you last Sunday? I – we missed you.
Listen, can you by any chance spare half an hour? I'd like to
talk to you.'

She wasn't really sure if she ought to tell him, or to ask his
advice. Above all she just wanted to have him there and hear his
voice.

The young man at the other end of the telephone cleared his
throat before answering. He was sorry, terribly sorry, but he
couldn't come unfortunately. Stefan was out in the station
wagon and – er – his own motorcycle was in the garage for
servicing.

'Can't you borrow Stefan's?'

He wished he could, but Stefan always took the key with him.

Heidi hung up.

The young man slowly replaced the receiver and wiped his
hand across his forehead. Oh God – could he afford so recklessly
to jeopardize whatever feelings she had for him?

Stefan, who was sitting at the desk beside him, making out
bills, stared at him.

'What on earth is the matter with you? Why do you lie to her?
She wanted to talk to you, didn't she? Why don't you drive
over?'

'Not yet,' said the young man, crestfallen and quiet.

'On account of my father?'

'Yes. And on account of your mother, too.'

Stefan looked at the clenched jaws, the desperate eyes, and
left the office without a word. He was used to this crazy idea of

his friend's that Heidi and his mother were synonymous. But that his father's return should have ruined everything . . .

Elise prepared supper for herself and Heidi as usual. Of late she had been eating with her and had always left the apartment at half past nine, before Kaspar returned. But her daughter stayed in her room, refusing to answer Elise's knocks or her coaxing. Oh well, Elise really wasn't hungry either. She cleared everything away and listened again at Heidi's door, but heard no sounds of crying. Then she left.

When Kaspar entered the hall, the apartment was dark. Perhaps Heidi had gone out. He hoped so. At Kovac's two Croats had sat down at his table and even begun to speculate about Tito's death. He had dutifully tried to turn the conversation towards underground activity, but once again it hadn't led anywhere. When the two Croats had left, he had sat on, putting off his return to the apartment as long as possible.

He switched on the lamp in the living-room so that the light would shine out into the hall, went to the baby's room, opened the door noiselessly, and went in. Never before had he felt an urge to look at the sleeping child, but tonight he was alone in the apartment, which was a relief. Yet he was miserable, and, for the first time since he had left Munich eighteen months ago, utterly discouraged.

Footsteps. He looked up. Heidi was standing at the opposite side of the crib. Her face was in shadow, but he could hear her rapid breathing.

For a moment they stood motionless, silent because of the sleeping child, and then a furiously hissed: 'What are you doing here?' reached him.

'I wanted to make sure she was asleep.'

'Why?'

'I thought no one was home.'

'You think I'd leave the baby alone in the apartment?'

'No, of course not.'

How stupid of him. Naturally the baby would never be left on its own. It was just that he wasn't used to thinking along those lines, but there was no point in explaining. Her breathing became still more agitated, and now he could see her eyes glowing in the darkness.

'You have no right to – to just walk in here – I don't want to find you here ever again. You think all you have to do is stretch out your hand and we'll all fall on your neck – my mother and me and the baby –'

'Come,' he said quietly, 'or she'll wake up.' And he left the room.

She didn't even give him time to sit down in the living-room but confronted him, her fists clenched and held high, and her lips trembling.

'How dare you say that to me: "or she'll wake up"? To me – to her mother!'

'She was about to.'

'So what? What if she does? She wakes up – and sees her mother.' She was shaking so violently he could hardly make out the words.

'I would have been sorry if she'd woken up.'

'Oh, you'd have been sorry, would you? Does she mean anything to you then?' Fists relaxed, voice almost normal again, but her eyes were smouldering.

I mustn't retreat, I mustn't pacify her, he thought, I've got to stick it out.

'Yes, she does.'

'Do you love her?'

He hesitated. What was she getting at? Why did it suddenly matter to her that he loved the baby? All at once he heard Elise's words: 'The baby is your best accomplice . . .' So that's what she had meant! He calmly met Heidi's eyes: 'Yes, I do.'

'More than Werner and Stefan?'

Lay it on thick! Go on! 'No comparison. I can't imagine life without her any more.'

'You don't say! Well, well. Now just you listen to me: I'm sorry – no, I'm not sorry at all, pack your suitcase and get out. This minute. And when she wakes up, you won't be there any more. She won't see you again. You won't see her again, understand? I have no more questions to ask you, I've found my own answers . . .' She swayed, stumbled backwards to the wall and closed her eyes.

He took a step towards her and reached out with both hands.

'But Martha, listen to me . . .'

Aghast, he dropped his hands and stood still.

Heidi opened her eyes and stared at him. Gradually she stopped swaying and trembling, though she was still leaning against the wall, pressing herself against it as if she needed support, from her head right down to her feet.

Slowly her face relaxed and her lips parted, no longer distorted, almost smiling. She nodded once or twice – as if to say: of course! How come I didn't realize it before! – lowered her head and left the room.

CHAPTER FOURTEEN

THAT VERY night he returned to Anya's, on foot, carrying his suitcase through the dark streets, walking slowly; no hurry.

It was snowing lightly, yet he didn't feel the cold, even without a coat. The suitcase dated back to Martha's time, good quality. The snowflakes wouldn't hurt it, and for Kaspar they were positively beneficial. They settled carefully on his hair and shoulders, even on his nose, as if they meant to make him laugh. He met them halfway, standing still from time to time and raising his head, to give them a chance. They perched on his face, one after another, soundlessly, tenderly, and so lightly that it hardly got wet.

He couldn't remember ever having lifted his head at night to let snowflakes fall on his face. He'd never been without a hat and he'd never wandered about the streets alone, carrying all his worldly goods in a single suitcase, his mind set on a peaceful, solitary destination.

When he had first fled from Munich, he had left everything open: all personal ties were *meant* to remain severed so that there could be no turning back. Now, in the few remaining days before his second departure, everything had taken on a different complexion. The break remained; the difference was that while everyone else had taken up his or her assigned place, he himself was free.

He still had to make one telephone call and write one letter and then he would at last be able to return to his own life. One bit of business remained: Luburic. So far, a complete flop. Never mind, he thought, as he stopped outside the house in Kaiserplatz, offering his face up to the snowflakes one last time. Why must a mission necessarily be successful at all costs? Mariana ought to be used to setbacks; in Luburic's 'missions' failures were probably more common than triumphs. He wouldn't be in disgrace; she wouldn't punish him. 'I don't even trust myself to say "I love you", although you mean so much to me that it's hard to draw the distinction. I hate to send you away.' She hadn't said that lightly. He knew that in blackmailing him she was punishing herself too.

Anya, wearing her woollen nightgown, opened the door – and threw her arms around his neck.

'Professor! I am happy.' She quickly released him, blushing, and added: 'I thought you had left. I must tell you good news.'

She picked up his suitcase and accompanied him into the bedroom. When the night-light was turned on and Uncle Stilts's big bed emerged, he stood still and closed his eyes. Soon it would be gone for ever.

'You coming back here?'

'Just for a short time, Anya, a few days at the most.'

'Perhaps better you stay not long. I have spoke with lawyer.'

She ran out of the room and came right back.

'Look: German passport.' She drew herself up, until she was almost as tall as Kaspar. 'I am now constant German Frau. I can marry Miklos in prison. The lawyer say: next month trial, then verdict, then prison. But not long, maybe only one year. What you say?'

'I say: splendid, Anya, and the best of luck to you.' He embraced her, took her by the shoulders, holding her away from him and smilingly studied the glowing angel-face. 'And Miklos has hit the jackpot. Tell him so from me.'

'Better not tell. Is very jealous, my Miklos. He better not know you were here or he has thoughts . . .'

She stopped, confused, and began to rebraid a corn-yellow pigtail. Then she turned and ran from the room.

Almost midnight. But late as it was, he must call Elise and ask her to take care of the baby for him from tomorrow onwards.

'Elise?'

'I know, I know. Heidi's told me. I'm packing now.'

'Are you going over there tonight?'

'Yes. I'd better get there as soon as possible. So you're off. Congratulations. I don't even want to know how you handled it. You did it, that's all that matters. Well, *bon voyage*, then. And by the way, if the wolf's ever at your door, you can always come back.'

'Come back?' Kaspar repeated, horrified.

'Not to Heidi, you idiot – to me!' She hung up.

He felt wide awake. No point going to bed. He took his writing pad out of his suitcase.

Dear Werner, dear Stefan,

This time I'm not sneaking off. I'm making what you might call an official departure. Heidi approves and I'm sure you will, too. That doesn't mean I feel my presence here was a burden to you. On the contrary, I think we are closer than we've ever been before. You know the full story now, and I've stopped being your father. I think you no longer feel cheated out of something I've always owed you. We've got rid of the bitterness, and that's important to me. I'm not worried about you, and there's no need to worry about me. From now on I'll be living the way I want to, and there are not many people who can say that.

I'm grateful for all you're doing for Heidi and Stefanie. I'm grateful – and ashamed, too, because you're making it easy for me. I think I know the road Heidi will take and I feel sure it's the right one. Keep well.

P.S. I spend my nights in a small cubicle, looking at a black cross with the date 10 May 1977. I know it's mere chance that my predecessor died on that day, nevertheless it makes a bridge between me and your mother, and that does me good.

Every evening he went to Kovac's. Where was 'chance' now – chance that had been lying in wait for him in Frau Henning's cashier's booth? Did chance strike only if you didn't run after it? He'd given it one more week.

And then one evening the owner sat down at his table. 'I hear you're looking for someone. Who is it?'

Kaspar liked the man. He seemed intelligent and discreet and had joined him several times before.

'Why? Who told you that?'

The owner made a vague gesture with his head towards the other tables. The first risky moment. Should he chance it – now, at the last minute? The man didn't look like an UDBA informer, but then what did an UDBA informer look like?

Slowly the man twisted his mouth into a grin. Everything he did was done at a leisurely pace, in slow motion.

'You've got nothing to worry about – as far as I'm concerned.'

'I'm looking for a man by the name of Luburic. Do you know him?'

'He hasn't been in here for a long time.'

So he did know Luburic!

'Do you by any chance know where he might be? He's a former student of mine.'

The man shook his head and played with the breadcrumbs on the table. Kaspar sensed that there was more to come. After reflecting for quite a long time, the proprietor got up.

'Why don't you stay on a bit tonight?'

He shuffled back behind the bar and disappeared through the mysterious door.

Suddenly Kaspar panicked. Whom was the fellow alerting? Or was someone always at the ready behind the door, waiting? And he was supposed to remain here until everybody else had left? A sitting-duck? He jumped up – and sat down again.

No. This was too simple-minded to be a trap, you don't give warning of an ambush. He looked around; nobody was paying any attention to him. All right, then, he'd take a chance. After all, this was what he'd been waiting for these last two months. Could they possibly kill him outright just for asking about Luburic? Nonsense. Perhaps they'd question him – that was a risk he'd have to take. Or was that plain silly? If only he knew the ropes!

For the next half hour, until nine o'clock, he was torn between a compelling desire to get up and leave and the urge to find out who would show up. One person? Several? Perhaps even Luburic himself?

Around him, the tables began to empty. The owner had long ago gone back to his seat behind the bar and was taking no notice of Kaspar. At nine o'clock he lumbered over to the entrance as usual, shook hands with the last departing guests, locked the door after them, and leaned against the wall as if he expected to unlock it again very soon.

Kaspar's eyes travelled back and forth between the entrance and the door behind the bar. Silence. The owner had his eyes shut and seemed to be asleep. Five minutes ticked by, then ten. Was the man really asleep? On his feet? Or was he trying to give Kaspar the feeling that all was well? Should he call out: Hey you, I'm sitting here, waiting, remember? He didn't dare to. There was something spooky about that man. Now he was actually snoring.

Almost half an hour had passed. The silence was gradually becoming unbearable – it throbbed in his head. Trapped! How could he have put himself –

A knock at the door. Did the UDBA knock? And so brazenly at the front door, right next to the proprietor? The man blinked, shook himself awake and took the key out of his pocket again.

Hesitantly and cautiously Vlada Martinac stepped inside.

She looked around as if in search of someone. The place was empty except for one table. Kaspar had been too frantic, and then too surprised, to get up. For a moment she didn't recognize him and peered at him suspiciously, although he never wore his wig at Kovac's. Then she ran towards him. 'Professor!'

He stood up and kissed her hand. The owner watched, grinned at Kaspar, winked and waited, and then, not having been invited to join them, withdrew behind the bar.

'He telephoned,' said Vlada in Croatian. 'He said there was someone here who wanted to ask me something. We often used to come here.'

We? Kaspar wondered. Did she mean Ivan and Luburic and herself or only herself and Luburic? Not that it mattered.

Vlada tried not to stare at him. The Professor in an old turtleneck sweater, his face still scrubbed shiny and sun-tanned from his daily walks and bicycle rides! What happened to that pale, correct, cautious gentleman who had once sat in her parlour as if on stinging nettles?

Kaspar, for his part, found Vlada unrecognizable too. She was no longer dressed in black but in something rather too colourful, and her hair was cut short. She looked like a young girl. The tragic pallor had disappeared, and the veiled black eyes looked him over without embarrassment. She appeared to be strong and healthy and not nearly as attractive as the last time he'd seen her.

'What is it, Professor? We can talk here, it's not bugged. My place still is, but by now they may have given up listening.'

Kaspar hesitated. The Vlada–Mariana situation was dynamite.

'Luburic has disappeared.'

'Yes. But – how do *you* know?' Hesitant and suspicious.

'Frau Bogdan told me.' At once her eyes narrowed. 'I'm supposed to help find him.'

'I knew it,' she whispered.

'You're wrong. Mariana and Luburic are just friends, comrades in arms, that's all.'

'Mariana? You too? I might have known.'

The owner came and placed a cup of tea on the table in front of Vlada. He glanced at them and quickly returned to the bar.

'Do you know where he could be?' Kaspar asked and, when she didn't answer, added coldly: 'Is he still alive?'

He immediately regretted it because at once the tears streamed from her eyes. Last time, too, they had cascaded down like a waterfall, fast as lightning. Slow crying wasn't her style. She groped blindly for her purse and blew her nose hard, then drank the tea.

'I don't know,' she said at last. She had taken a piece of paper out of her purse along with the handkerchief and handed it to him. 'This is all I have. An old friend of Ivan's brought it. He got it from another – friend. I don't know where it comes from. No envelope.'

The Croatian text had been written on Martinac's typewriter with the 's's' missing. 'Ivan's old friend sends greetings to his godson Ivan.'

'His godson Ivan? Oh, yes, Luburic is your eldest boy's godfather, isn't he? How long have you had this note?'

'Three months.'

'And that's the last you heard? Can I talk to him, to Ivan's friend?'

'He's gone back to Zagreb. He wouldn't tell me the other one's name. Too dangerous.'

'What was Ante's mission? Did he tell you?'

'He never tells anything.' She raised her head, her wet eyes shining again. 'But I know that a bomb exploded in the Munich –Belgrade express three months ago. Tito's Consul was badly hurt.' She added more quietly: 'And a conductor was killed.'

'A German conductor?'

She nodded. Her eyes travelled around the room as though in search of something, then reluctantly turned back to him. He said nothing, but kept looking at her. She shrugged.

'In a revolution non-participants get killed too.'

'I hope that's a consolation to his widow.'

She lifted the long-empty cup to her lips, and pretended to drink. Here's a woman, thought Kaspar, who's a widow herself. She knows what it means and yet she can speak of another widow

– and one whose husband had nothing to do with the Croat 'mission' – like an abstraction. And she's not hard either, she's just making it easy for herself, with the help of one of those easy, criminally dissembling phrases.

'Can I keep the note?'

'For that Bogdan woman?' she cried, so loudly that the proprietor behind the bar looked across at them.

'No. For Mariana's people. Ante's people. Your people, Vlada.'

He put the little piece of paper in his pocket. It probably wasn't of any value, anyway. Three months ago.

'You and Mariana should make friends. You're very much alike in many ways, it seems to me.'

'I'm not a whore.'

'Neither is she. She's not out for profit. And she's in love with someone – same as you.'

'With whom? You?'

'Unfortunately not. With her first husband.'

She stared at him for a long time. Finally something like regret crept into those black, jealous eyes, and she nodded and looked down at the tablecloth.

He got up. 'I think our host would like to be rid of us.'

She wished the man behind the bar 'goot day' and followed Kaspar to the door.

'Professor, my mail isn't opened any more. If you hear anything – will you let me know?'

CHAPTER FIFTEEN

FROM the station in Bled, Kaspar went at once to the Godice.
A strange face at the desk. But it recognized him and gave
a welcoming grin. It took him a few seconds to realize that this was
Bruno, the kitchen-boy, minus his white cap and sporting a
moustache.

'Ah, Herr Schulte! Alexis *will* be pleased. Are you back – I mean,
back here with us?'

'As long as you haven't hired a new night porter in the
meantime.'

'Oh, we'd never do that.' Bruno gave him a significant look.
'Herr Alexis has been working the night shift himself . . .' He
stopped and his smile froze.

'What's the matter, Bruno? Has anything happened?'

Kaspar raised the counter flap and pushed his suitcase into the
cubicle. It was noon and the hotel lobby was empty.

'No, no,' the boy said hastily, but his eyes darted around the
hall, as if he needed support.

'Herr Alexis will return about – about four. Would you like to
wait for him here or in your room?'

Kaspar leaned across the counter. 'What's wrong, Bruno? Don't
you feel well?'

'Oh yes, I'm quite all right, Herr Schulte, really I am. I'll let Herr
Alexis know you're here and he'll probably come in early.'

'Never mind, let him sleep. I'm going for a walk by the lake.'

'By the lake,' Bruno repeated. 'Very good. I'll give him the
message. Er – Herr Schulte, you probably haven't eaten, wouldn't
you like . . . the dining-room's still empty.'

'Maybe later. I'm not hungry now.'

'You'll be back then? You're just going down to the lake?'

'Yes, of course I'll be back, Bruno, and I won't be going away
again.'

Outside the hotel he hesitated for a moment. Straight ahead to the cart track? Or should he stand on the shore, just for a few minutes, consciously enjoying the anticipation?

He strolled down to the lake. Not a soul in sight. It was a grey day, lake, sky and mountains all the same foggy colour, the water smooth as glass, barely moving up and down the shallow beach, only an occasional wave slapping ill-temperedly against the lonely rowing-boat tied to the dock.

He stopped and took a deep breath of damp air. I love the lake at this time of year, he thought. Nobody else loves it now, nobody strolls along the path by the water's edge or sits on the dock, fishing. The mist and the half-light and the still water – that's what I like. In summer, when everything's electric blue and brassy, I'd just as soon look at it through the window.

Dampness began to penetrate the soles of his shoes.

'Okay, okay, I'm on my way,' he said aloud.

Slowly he walked beneath the tall, bare trees towards the little town. Its houses, though still grey on grey, seemed to him, in contrast to the lake, no longer sleepy but smartly drawn up in neat ranks, and bustling, the streets full of people: housewives with shopping bags, office workers, children on bicycles. Winter was manifestly *their* season. He knew every shop, and was glad to see every street corner again. Several people turned to look at him; he must have smiled or said something aloud.

There, beyond the last house, stood the great beech tree where Bogdan had waited for him with his umbrella. And now at last, after more than two long months, he could finally walk down the cart track again.

Here the air was clearer and drier than by the lake. At the far end of the road he could already see the fence surrounding Mariana's house. Nothing stirred around him, except for a dark patch on the muddy path right next to the fence. It moved and then became still again. A few more steps and he could see what it was: a dog. Bogdan's invisible dog.

Kaspar slowed his pace; dogs didn't like strangers to approach too fast. But was he still a stranger to this dog? Surely it must recognize his step, perhaps even his voice? 'Hey, dog,' he called in a loud voice. He could see it plainly now, sitting in the middle of the path, not moving, but it didn't bark as it always used to when he approached the house. A large black creature with short, pricked ears and an unusually big, shaggy head.

He slowed down even more, advancing one step at a time, and reached the corner of the fence. He looked down into the courtyard. Empty. The paving stones carefully swept, the bushes in the garden neatly cut back and the ground turned over. Perhaps in his honour. Mariana must be in the kitchen or, if he was out of luck, in town doing her shopping.

He stopped. Surely she couldn't have gone away? No, the house looked lived in, the shutters were open and the front door leading into the courtyard was ajar. He looked back at the dog, which was still sitting there, watching him.

'Here, dog!' he called again, hesitantly stretching out his hand. The animal didn't stir, but he was relieved to see it wag its tail once or twice.

A few more steps and he stood at the gate. Just beyond it he suddenly noticed a bicycle propped against the fence. Milan's bicycle. He glared at it, disappointed and resentful. Should he go away and come back in the evening? He hesitated, thinking of the long, depressing walk back . . . He simply had to see her.

When he opened the gate, the dog suddenly began to whine. Perhaps it wanted to accompany him.

'Here, dog!' It didn't move, but watched him descend the steps, whining more loudly.

Down below, through the open door, a man's voice called: 'Shut up, Nero. Quiet!'

Bogdan! *And* Milan. Another family get-together. Turn around and get out – fast! But before he could reach the road, he heard Bogdan's voice: 'Schulte! For God's sake, man – come on in, we're all waiting for you.'

'We're all waiting for you' – exactly what he'd said the last time. Why were they 'all' waiting for him? He didn't want anybody but Mariana, damn it. But he stopped because the giant had come racing across the courtyard and up the steps. He grabbed Kaspar by the shoulders, peered into his face, panting, then hugged him so violently that they swayed back and forth on the shaky steps. Releasing him just as suddenly, he muttered: 'Come on. Come on,' and to the dog, with unexpected ferocity: 'Shut up, I say.'

Kaspar had no choice but to follow him down. As he arrived at the foot of the steps, he glimpsed Milan and Ljuba, the daughter, in the doorway at the far end of the courtyard – but they immediately vanished inside.

Bogdan, Milan and Ljuba . . . nobody else?

Bogdan crossed the courtyard in large, hurried steps, calling to him over his shoulder: 'Come on, man, come on . . .' and entered the house, leaving the door wide open.

Kaspar was still standing at the foot of the steps, a single thought in his head: I don't want to go in.

Yet he propelled himself forward, one foot in front of the other – and suddenly found himself standing by the stone table, holding firmly on to it.

Bogdan reappeared in the doorway, grabbed him by the shoulder and pulled him into the house. In the semi-darkness of the living-room he pushed him into a chair and growled at his stepson, who was leaning against the wall: 'Stop gawking. Fetch the bottle.'

Kaspar still hadn't said a word. He stared up at the huge man pacing back and forth across the room, carefully avoiding his eye. When Milan returned, with Ljuba behind him carrying a tray and glasses, Bogdan snatched the slivovitz bottle from his hands.

'Clear out now, both of you.'

He tossed his head back and drank, then bent down, held the bottle to Kaspar's lips and barked: 'Drink, man! You *must*, believe me. Come on, now.'

Kaspar drank.

'One more, Schulte, you need it. You won't make it without.'

He grabbed an armchair and pulled it over to face Kaspar's. Below the frill of the loose-cover, a box slid into view. Bogdan's violent shove had knocked the lid off and half a dozen wigs tumbled out on to the floor.

'What the hell is that?'

'Luburic,' Kaspar barely moved his lips.

'Disguises, eh? Goddamn shit!' said the giant, kicking out at the tangled black, red and grey heap. 'Shit. Shit. Shit.'

He sat down so close to Kaspar that their knees touched, took the bottle from him, drank, choked, wiped his moustache roughly, seized Kaspar's hand, and pressed the bottle into it once again.

'Medicine! Drink up, Schulte, it helps.'

Instead Kaspar set the bottle down heavily on the floor and laid his clenched fist on Bogdan's knee.

'Go ahead,' he whispered.

'She's gone. Three weeks ago a car came during the night. The neighbours back there on the cart road saw it. It was quite late and the dog was barking like mad. Later the car left, but they heard the dog bark all night, and in the morning he came limping up to the house with a bullet in his backside. That's why he's sitting up there . . .' He stopped and rubbed his forehead violently with the back of his hand. 'These neighbours – quite sensible young people – came over immediately. The whole house had been ransacked, everything upside down – no sign of her. The bedroom was the worst; she must have put up a fight. They got hold of me through my company, I was in Milan. The police came once – *once*! – and that's it.'

For the first time he looked Kaspar in the face and answered the question in his eyes.

'Not a thing. Not one word since then. No one knows where she is or who was in that car, but you can probably guess. Alexis thinks it's something to do with that bastard . . .' He gave the tangled pile of wigs another kick. 'They say he was responsible for a bomb that exploded in a train some months ago. They knew of course that he and Mariana at one time had . . . maybe they thought he was here.' He laughed furiously and shook his head. 'Maybe they sat right in this chair. But they never found all that shit here.'

Kaspar asked no more questions.

Bogdan sat facing him, motionless, except for the lifting of the bottle to his mouth from time to time. Once the door opened soundlessly and Ljuba looked anxiously into the room. Her father just shook his head slowly and she withdrew.

Outside, dusk was gradually creeping into the courtyard. It was so dark in the room that Kaspar could no longer see Bogdan, only the heavy breathing was proof of his presence.

Later, when night had fallen outside, the big man suddenly sat up with a jerk and asked in a quiet, sober voice: 'Is that why Mariana sent you to Munich? On account of Luburic?'

'I was supposed to find him.'

'Christ! And did you? Are you working for the Ustasha now, Schulte? It's your business, after all, your life.' Kaspar stared straight ahead. 'I'm only asking because, if you are, you'll hear from them. When you're back on duty, the night music will start up again, know what I mean?'

Kaspar moved, tried to stand up, but fell back into the chair.

'For the time being you're going to stay right here with us. We're about to have dinner.'

The kitchen table was set for four. Milan and his sister were already sitting there, the young man holding his head in his hands. When Bogdan entered with Kaspar, they both jumped up and Ljuba went quickly over to the stove. Leg of lamb with mashed potatoes. They ate in silence. Kaspar ate, too.

Later Bogdan said: 'I'll see you back to the hotel.'

Nine o'clock. His shift began in an hour. The young man accompanied them up the steps. Nero was still sitting in the same place, wagging his tail and whining.

'Yes, yes, Nero, you can come along, but only as far as the beech tree, understand? Milan, your bicycle is still out here. And carry the dog into the house later, it's cold tonight.'

'Goodnight, Herr Schulte,' said the young man. 'I . . . I wanted to say . . .'

'Don't,' Bogdan muttered. 'There's nothing to say.'

He took out his flashlight, grabbed Kaspar's arm and led him along the cart track. In the beam of the light Nero limped ahead of them.

Alexis was waiting behind the porter's desk. His face showed no surprise when Bogdan entered the lobby with Kaspar.

'Good evening, Schulte. Your suitcase is in your room. Bruno unpacked for you and put everything away.'

Bruno . . . oh yes, of course, Kaspar thought, now I know why he looked so anxious. He wanted Alexis to prepare me.

A group of Americans came up the staircase from the restaurant. Alexis raised the counter flap and left the desk.

'You can start right away, Schulte. Good evening, gentlemen. How are you? May I introduce our night clerk? Yes – very good English. Please ask him everything, yes? He is very good. Have a good time.' And to Bogdan: 'Mirko, how about a drink? See you in the morning then, Schulte.'

He headed towards the bar. Bogdan laid his heavy hand on Kaspar's shoulder and murmured: 'We'll be expecting you tomorrow. Don't forget.'

In the meantime the Americans had been selecting postcards. Kaspar raised the flap and entered his domain. A quick glance: the black cross was still there . . .

'Say, porter, can you let me have some stamps?'
He turned around. 'Here you are, sir. One of these and one of these.'

Later, when the lobby was empty, he switched on the night lamp on the stool and collapsed into the deckchair. His cubicle and the black cross on the wall were still exactly as he remembered them. Everything else was gone. Mariana had disappeared. Like Karel. That's the worst thing in the world, she had said.

The paralysis that had come over him in Bogdan's living-room returned and he thought of the days of mild anaesthesia after Martha's death. How good that had felt. No gentle, protective atmosphere cradled him now; all the paralysis could do was to stop him from screaming.

He lay there for a long time without moving and never noticed that Alexis had slipped into the dark cubicle and stood for a moment watching him lying there in the light of the little lamp, with his eyes fixed on a certain spot in the wall that Alexis recognized.

Then, about four o'clock in the morning, he heard it. Quite distinctly. A regular chirping sound outside. He listened for a while, then switched his lamp off and on again. The chirping stopped.

He got up and opened the air flap next to the ceiling. A little while later a rolled up scrap of paper fell to the floor. A typed message in Croatian, with the 's's' missing: 'Patience. We are searching. Don't lose heart. You'll be hearing from us.'

He spent the few days before Bogdan's departure at the house on the cart track. Milan and Ljuba came to supper every evening. They never spoke of their mother. Companionship with Kaspar was all they could offer her, in place of a funeral wreath.

Bogdan had read the note and shrugged. The missing 's's' did not necessarily mean that it came from Luburic, you could do that on any typewriter, it only indicated which side had sent it.

On the eve of his departure – a six-week trip to Holland – he said to Kaspar: 'Move in here, man. Milan has his own place and Ljuba sleeps at the hospital. You'd be doing me a favour: I can leave Nero here. The house shouldn't be left empty – that is, unless you're afraid they may come back.'

'Let them come.'

He moved out of Draza Rukovina's old room and from then on slept in Mariana's bed. When he woke up in the afternoon, he cleaned the house, cooked, and swept the courtyard. Then he went to the lake and rowed over to the island, climbed the long flight of steps up to the church and pulled the rope of the wishing bell. In the early evening mist above the lake its tinkling had a ghostly sound.

Sometimes, if it had been a beautiful day, he would sit for a while on a bench in front of the church. He was nearly always alone on the island. At this time of year there were very few tourists, though occasionally someone in urgent need of the wishing bell would hurry by.

'See that, Uncle Stilts?' Kaspar said. On this bench he always had a particularly close rapport with the dwarf. 'See how he sneaks past me as if he were up to no good? And yet I'm giving him an extra friendly smile, because I've come here to ask for something too. But he sees me as a rival, he thinks I'll divert the bell's attention.'

The little old man giggled. 'Do you remember my doctor, that fat old chap who used to play gin rummy with me? He told me he once went to see an old bedridden peasant, sat him up and stuck a thermometer under his arm. When he came back in the evening, there he was, bolt upright, just as he'd left him, with the thing still under his arm. "For goodness sake!" the doctor exclaimed. "Have you been sitting here all day like this?" And the old man said: "I don't mind, Doctor, as long as it does some good . . ."'

'Yes, I remember, Uncle Stilts. You've told me that story several times.'

'Damn it, where do you expect me to find new ones?'

'That's all right, I like the old ones. This one fits me nicely; I ring that damned bell every day, thinking: as long as it does me some good . . .'

He could never stay long on the island because 'the family' was waiting for him. One day the strangeness of it all struck him: Heidi had a new 'family' – and now he also had been adopted. Though that was where the parallel ended. Heidi's new family was permanent; his own would go its separate ways sooner or later – and that was as it should be. Perhaps he could stay on in the house, alone, he would pay rent. Just himself and Nero, who now slept beside his bed. He needed the house, the garden and the courtyard; he needed her kitchen, her bedroom, her radio, still tuned to the same rock music station. Soon he would plant sunflowers; he was already carrying a packet of seeds around in the pocket of his jacket.

One night last year, in the month of August, they had been lying side by side in the sunflowers, counting shooting stars. 'Make a wish,' she had said, as the thirteenth star fell. 'I wish that everything will stay as it is – except that you'll love me,' he had replied. 'And you? What do you wish for?' 'That everything will stay as it is – and that you won't love me.' One of the rare moments she had shown her feelings for him. She knew that things might turn out as they had, and she knew what it would mean for him. She knew.

He always rowed back very slowly. When you have no firm ground under your feet, it's hard to be with people who are aware of it. Every evening he spent an uncomfortable hour with Milan and Ljuba over supper. The air was full of good intentions and good deeds; only good words were in short supply. Fortunately, they ate in deep silence.

It was easier at the hotel. When he had to deal with guests and *their* troubles, his blood pressure rose as though he'd been skipping for half an hour.

And then, late at night, when everything was still, came the moment he had been waiting for all day: the feeling that the sleep of all the people in all the rooms had merged into a dense cloud drifting down over his desk, muffling everything and sealing it off so that he too could sleep.

Once or twice during the week he would be awakened by the chirping sound outside and a note would sail through the ventilator: wait . . . Hope . . . They were searching . . . Never say die . . . More news soon.

They had done the same for Mariana after Karel disappeared.

CHAPTER SIXTEEN

O NE DAY in mid-March, while Kaspar was digging in the garden, getting ready to plant his sunflowers, Nero suddenly limped over to the steps, looked up at the road, whined, and wagged his tail vigorously.

Kaspar looked up and searched the cart track. Right at the end he made out the figure of a woman, an old peasant woman . . .

'For God's sake!' he whispered. 'For God's sake . . .'

He clutched the handle of the spade with both hands and held on to it for support, feeling the sweat breaking out. He straightened up and wiped his face on his jacket sleeve. He's back, he thought, he's actually back, he's been living somewhere all this time and now he's back, that's all – and *she's* gone.

Nero tried to climb the steps but couldn't keep his footing and finally sat down on the bottom stair, howling softly. The peasant woman, in her dragging long skirt, picked her way slowly down the rickety steps. This time she wasn't carrying anything, both hands were encased in black leather gloves.

Kaspar leaned on his spade and watched her stroke the dog's head, then look around searchingly. Slowly she crossed the courtyard and stopped in front of him. She wore her babushka so low that it covered her entire forehead and almost touched her glasses.

'Professor . . .'

'I wouldn't have recognized you – again,' Kaspar said without offering his hand. He was about to add: and I don't want to recognize you either.

He had been convinced that Luburic was dead, and his disappearance seemed so logical that he had spent little time analysing his feelings about it. But now that the man was standing before him, and in this grotesque get-up, he realized how essential it was for his own precarious, straw-clutching daily existence that Luburic should not be alive. He was the instigator, the wire-puller, the killer. He had planted that bomb, one among many. It was because of him that Martinac had been shot and God knows how many other people. After all, he, Kaspar, only knew about a tiny fraction of his 'missions'.

And he had spent months looking for this man in Munich, when he might have been here in the house with Mariana, the night the car came. Who knows, perhaps he could have done something. At any rate, she wouldn't have been alone, wouldn't have had to fight them alone. They would have taken him away, too, with her or killed him outright. Anything would have been better than standing here, confronting the old peasant woman again.

'What do you want of me, Herr Luburic?'

'I've only just arrived, I haven't talked to anyone yet. Part of my uniform . . .' – he pointed to his skirt – 'is still missing. The most important part.'

He attempted a smile, pushed back the black woollen head scarf, revealing for a second the shiny crown of his huge, almost bald head, and quickly lowered it again.

'Are those things still there, the wigs, or – did they find them?'

'They're still there.'

Luburic studied him attentively. The professor looked very pale, his eyes exhausted and twitching; his hands clutched the spade handle so tensely that the knuckles stood out white.

'Professor – I know all about it. They sent word to us in Boston.'

'In Boston? Have you been in America all these months?'

'We have a large group there, an entire Croatian colony. Most of the time it's not active, but they raise money for us or find us a place to stay.'

Kaspar's face twisted into a grim smile. 'I'd have had a hard time finding you there.'

'I know. I'm sorry, but it had to be kept secret. I'm sure you understand.' Kaspar didn't answer. 'I don't know any details yet, Professor. I've just arrived, I've still not been in direct contact with any of my men. From here I'll go to Ljubljana, and I'll find out right away what's being done, I promise you.'

'Is anything being done?'

'Yes.'

'Why? It was you they were concerned about, and you're back.'

'We never give up on a comrade in our organization so long as there's any hope. And there is hope, Professor.'

317

'How do you know? I thought you hadn't been in contact with them yet.'

'If she were dead, they'd have sent word to Boston. We have people inside the UDBA.'

That's the sort of stuff they must have told Mariana after Karel's disappearance, month after month after month.

'Shouldn't we go inside, Professor?'

Kaspar was still standing there, leaning on his spade, staring at him. That bomb in the train had gone off, the German conductor was dead. Too bad. 'In a revolution non-participants get killed, too.' And participants? They, too, got killed, sooner or later. Some comfort . . .

Luburic came a step closer and laid his black-gloved left hand on Kaspar's arm.

'I didn't come just for the wigs, Professor. I wanted to see you, too. They told me in Boston that you're living here. Now that I've seen you, I think the time has come. May I tell my people they can count on you?'

'Yes,' Kaspar said, without hesitating.

'I knew it. It was only a matter of time. You've come to understand the meaning of our revolution, haven't you? You're with us now.'

'Not in the least.'

Luburic took off his glasses. 'What do you mean by that?' he asked quietly.

Kaspar stared over Luburic's head into the distance. 'Did you know Karel?'

'Yes.'

'Was he worth it?'

'How do you mean?'

'She told me that it was only after his death that she joined your movement, that it was for his sake. Was he worth risking her life for?'

'Yes.'

'Well, she's worth it, too.'

'I understand.'

'You understand, do you?' Kaspar said between his teeth. 'You don't give a damn why you can count on me. I'm the night porter at the Godice and I have no choice. My only way out would be to go back to Munich – and that way is barred. For good. If I hold out much longer, your people will liquidate me. I think – in fact I know now – that Mariana has been protecting me.' His voice was almost inaudible. 'She probably kept telling them: don't worry, I'll get around him, just give me time.'

He came a step closer and fixed Luburic with burning eyes.

'I'm pretty certain you know all about that, too, don't you? Did she say that to you, too?'

'Yes,' Luburic said calmly. 'She promised, that time I came back and found you here. I almost wiped you out then and there, remember? I didn't trust you. But after you left, Mariana said: "Don't worry, he'll work for us, I promise you."' He stopped, and continued a moment later in a dry, matter-of-fact voice: 'I'm sorry that it was you the Godice picked for night porter. Ever since Draza died, we've been waiting to replace him. Alexis knows, of course, that the job represents a key position in our organization, that's why he'd rather do it himself than give it to a Yugoslav. You were a godsend to him; he thought he could count on your not having any – ties.'

'Why is the night porter so important? What else does he do, besides picking up notes?'

'In a little while Bruno will put you in touch with certain people. That's the first step, and then . . .'

'Thanks. I think I have a pretty good idea. And then, when I'm finally active, the UDBA will come along and present the bill, the way they did with Draza, except that these days the whole process has been speeded up. Right?'

'We'll provide protection, of course.'

'You mean Bruno? Will Bruno be a kind of bodyguard for me – like Martinac was for you? Bruno's not even eighteen, Herr Luburic.'

'Age doesn't make any difference. His father . . .'

'I know. His father was shot by the UDBA.'

Luburic did not answer.

Kaspar nodded slowly. He felt as if his mind was suddenly wide open, as though everything was understandable and even logical. There was nothing now that he didn't know. Or almost nothing.

'One more question, Herr Luburic: why is Alexis allowed to stay out of it? Why didn't he disappear long ago?'

'Because if he did, they'd close the hotel.'

'Who would?'

'Tito. He is Alexis's godfather.'

Kaspar nodded again. Everything was falling beautifully into place, it all made perfect sense.

Luburic looked at his watch. 'Let me get my wig. It's very hot and uncomfortable, but it'll be safer, later, in the bus.'

Kaspar followed him into the living-room. The Croat looked at the chairs and at once picked the right one and pulled out the box. Kaspar had carefully disentangled and combed the wigs. Luburic sorted through them and held up a shaggy white one.

'This one's new. Where did it come from?'

'I wore it in Munich so no one would recognize me.'

'But why a white one? And that strange cut?'

Kaspar came closer and looked at the wig in Luburic's hand.

'Do you remember my Uncle Stilts, the dwarf? That night you came to his place, with Miklos?'

'I remember a blonde woman who gave us something to eat . . .'

'He was in bed, in a big fourposter. Don't you remember?'

'A fourposter?'

Kaspar stepped right up to him and stared into his face as if trying to hypnotize him.

'Now think back: don't you remember who was lying in that bed? An old man, a tiny little man, with hair like this.'

'An old man?' Luburic shook his head. 'And he was a dwarf?' He shrugged. 'Sorry, he didn't make any impression on me.' He looked at the white wig again. 'I'll take this one along, too, for one of my people, if you don't mind.'

'I do mind,' Kaspar said, taking it from him and replacing it in the box.

The Croat pulled out his old wig, the grey one with the bun in the back, pulled it in a single skilful movement over his head, put his glasses on again, and tied the scarf under his chin.

'I'd better go now or it will be dangerous for you.'

He doesn't remember Uncle Stilts, Kaspar thought. He sees nothing, hears nothing, feels nothing; he's planning his next 'mission'. Someone gave him something to eat, though, and that he remembers.

Luburic opened the door and stepped out into the courtyard. Kaspar followed him, went past him to his vegetable patch and picked up his spade again. Nero was lying across the path and wagged his tail, but didn't get up. His hind legs were getting stiffer all the time.

'What's wrong with the dog? Is he sick?'

'He's got a bullet in his backside. He was trying to protect Mariana.'

'Oh,' Luburic said, turned to go – and looked back once more. 'You'll be hearing from me, Professor.'

'I don't need to hear any more from you,' Kaspar called across the courtyard and started to dig.

Luburic walked over to him. 'I thought you'd want to know for sure.'

'I know for sure now,' Kaspar said, and went on digging. 'She's dead. I'd like to know how it happened, but you're not going to tell me that. You'll keep me going with little notes through the ventilator so that I'll die a slow, lingering death, working for the Ustasha all the while. I accept that.'

The Croat hesitated, trying to make up his mind.

'Professor –' He waited for Kaspar to stick his spade in the ground and look up at him. 'You're right. She is dead.'

Kaspar stared at him; nothing moved in his face.

'She was shot that same night. One of our people was there when they buried her. In the early morning.'

Kaspar remained silent, just went on staring.

'I'm telling you this because I trust you. Even now that you know, you'll fight with us. It's worth it for Mariana's sake.'

'That's right,' Kaspar said.

Luburic turned away.

Kaspar raised his spade. A furious, overwhelming passion burst inside him. The spade whistled through the air and came crashing down on the back of the old peasant woman's head.

She fell forward without a sound.

CHAPTER SEVENTEEN

LATER, after midnight, when the silence in the hotel was drifting down over his cubicle, when he had set up his deckchair and turned on his lamp, he stretched out, closed his eyes, and told Uncle Stilts what he had done.

The dwarf sat up straight in his 'big bed' and stared at him, speechless, for a long time.

'Hats off to you, Inkworm!' And then, at once practical: 'How did you get rid of him? Dig a big hole?'

Kaspar smiled, and shook his head.

'Well, how then? Did you have a wheelbarrow handy? Cart him off at dead of night? Are there woods around somewhere?'

'No, just fields. But the wheelbarrow, Uncle Stilts – you're on the right track there.'

'Come on, come on! Don't keep me dangling. Tell!'

'Well, there he was, your Roman emperor. He'd fallen right across the ditch I'd been digging. If he'd fallen on the paving stones, that would have been a nice mess. The dog came limping up and sniffed around at his head scarf. Then it looked up at me, wanted to know what was going on and wagged its tail. I knelt down and investigated: the thick woollen scarf had soaked up some of the blood and the rest was slowly seeping into the ground.'

'And he was really . . .?'

'Dead as a doornail, Uncle Stilts. Strange, my anger was gone and the passion as well; I really didn't feel anything. Nothing whatever. One single thought drifted into my mind: "In a revolution even participants get killed." A variation of something Vlada had said . . . My only worry was where to bury him. The garden was too small, and anyway I didn't want him under my sunflowers. So what was I going to do with him? The children would be coming over in the evening, I had to get rid of him by then, with the help of my wheelbarrow. I looked around. There it was, my wheelbarrow, standing by the well . . .

'That well, Uncle Stilts! It was much older than the house – Mariana had told me that. Quite ancient, and twenty-five feet deep. In summer it was dry and it stank, but in winter you could hear a rushing sound at the very bottom of it: water from an underground spring. It never surfaced, the well never filled up; the water just flowed on and on until it finally reached the lake somewhere. It was no good for drinking, but in springtime she would haul up a few bucketsful to water the garden. It was quite sinister, that well, so very deep and black, you couldn't see the bottom. When the children were small, she always kept it covered.

'I sat down on the stone ridge around it – Nero stayed beside me – and dropped a pebble down. We heard it plop into the water far, far below.'

'Inkworm! You lucky devil.'

Kaspar laughed, his eyes tightly closed.

'Half an hour later it was all over and done with, the courtyard cleaned up, and the earth in the garden turned over and over until Nero couldn't find anything to sniff at any more.'

'But listen, Kaspar – won't they do you in now?'

'Who's "they"' Uncle Stilts?'

'Well, you know – one side or the other.'

'Sure they will, you can count on that. And you know what? I can hardly wait.'

There was a chirping sound outside. Kaspar reluctantly opened his eyes.

'Hear that, Uncle Stilts? That's the Hotel Godice's night music.'

'I've no ear for music, Inkworm, I don't like it.'

'Neither do I. Wait a second, Uncle Stilts, I'll be right back.'

He switched the lamp off and then on again.

Shortly afterwards a note fell on the floor beside him. He picked it up and looked at it for a moment. When would they decide to take the 'first step'? And then the next one . . . What if they knew Luburic had gone to Mariana's house today? There weren't going to be many more nights to lie quietly in his deckchair listening to the night music, that much was certain.

He unfolded the note. 'We've found a lead. Patience. It may take a few days more. There is hope.'

Kaspar put the scrap of paper in his pocket and closed his eyes.

'How do you like that, Uncle Stilts? "There is hope," they say.'

He heard the dwarf laugh. Then he fell peacefully asleep.

323